LESSON PLANNER

WORD BY WORD
Second Edition

Steven J. Molinsky • Bill Bliss

Contributing Authors
Sarah Lynn
Diane Terry
Valerie Ashenfelter

Contents

Illustrator: Richard E. Hill
WordSongs: Peter S. Bliss

Pearson Education, 10 Bank Street, White Plains, NY 10606

ISBN 0-13-193972-6
Longman on the Web
Longman.com offers online resources for teachers and students. Access our Companion Websites, our online catalog, and our local offices around the world.

Visit us at longman.com.

Printed in the United States of America
3 4 5 6 7 8 9 10—ML—09 08

To the Teacher

Welcome to the *Word by Word* Lesson Planner! This volume provides a wealth of reproducible resources to accompany the activity suggestions contained in the *Word by Word* Teacher's Guide. These materials are also included on the *Word by Word* Lesson Planner CD-ROM. They may be reproduced for classroom use only.

The following resources are provided in this volume and on the CD-ROM:

Needs Assessment forms are designed to gather input from students about their needs and interests in order to guide the selection of *Word by Word* vocabulary lessons. A Pictorial Version provides a simple format for low-beginning-level students who can check pictures representing vocabulary topics and draw pictures of their own to suggest additional topics. A Checklist Version offers a more detailed format for students who have some reading ability.

A **Performance-Based Lesson Assessment** form is a tool for evaluating and documenting student participation and performance in each lesson of the *Word by Word* program. A scoring rubric provides a guide for evaluating students during each phase of a lesson: vocabulary practice, conversation practice, writing and/or discussion, and activity participation.

A **Student Name List Mask** provides a convenient way to make a list of student names and then affix it to copies of the Performance-Based Lesson Assessment form. (The CD-ROM version of this form contains text fields that enable instructors to enter student names prior to printing the form.) Many instructors like to make multiple copies of the form with the names of students filled in so that they have a convenient supply of lesson assessment forms for each class.

Lesson Planner forms enable teachers to plan and time instruction at three different levels: Low-Beginning/Literacy, Beginning, and High-Beginning/Intermediate. These forms offer a convenient framework for step-by-step planning of classroom instruction, including the key lesson stages of warm-up, introduction, presentation, practice, evaluation, extension, and application.

Instructors can complete a customized form for each lesson, writing in a particular lesson's page numbers, activities, timing suggestions, and companion materials. This is not only a convenient lesson planning tool but also an ideal way to prepare a complete lesson plan for a substitute teacher, a teaching assistant, or a co-teacher. While timing suggestions are offered for the different lesson activities, teachers are encouraged to customize these suggestions to meet the particular needs and abilities of their students. (The CD-ROM versions of these forms contain text fields that enable instructors to fill in the form prior to printing it out.)

Activity Masters include ready-to-use word cards, activity sheets, and games that are included in the *Word by Word* Teacher's Guide lesson activities.

Language & Culture Notes for each lesson are an ideal resource for teachers and reading enrichment for intermediate-level students.

Song Masters are provided for all the WordSongs in the Audio Program. For each song, there is one Song Master with the lyrics and another with a cloze exercise that enables students to fill in missing words as they listen to the song. (The Audio Program contains two versions of each song: a vocal version and an instrumental "sing-along" version.)

An additional resource is available on the CD-ROM:

An **Activity Bank of Unit Worksheets** provides valuable supplemental practice for each unit: a Vocabulary Review activity provides comprehensive practice with the unit's key words; and a Grammar Worksheet offers focused practice with important grammatical structures using the vocabulary of the unit. An Answer Key is provided.

Instructors who have access to a computer will benefit from the convenience and ease-of-use of the CD-ROM, which organizes all resources by type in a Resource Bank and also by unit and lesson folders. Instructors can therefore find the various resources related to a specific lesson quickly and easily.

Student's Name _____ I.D. Number _____

Course _____ Teacher _____ Date _____

I want to learn English words for _____.

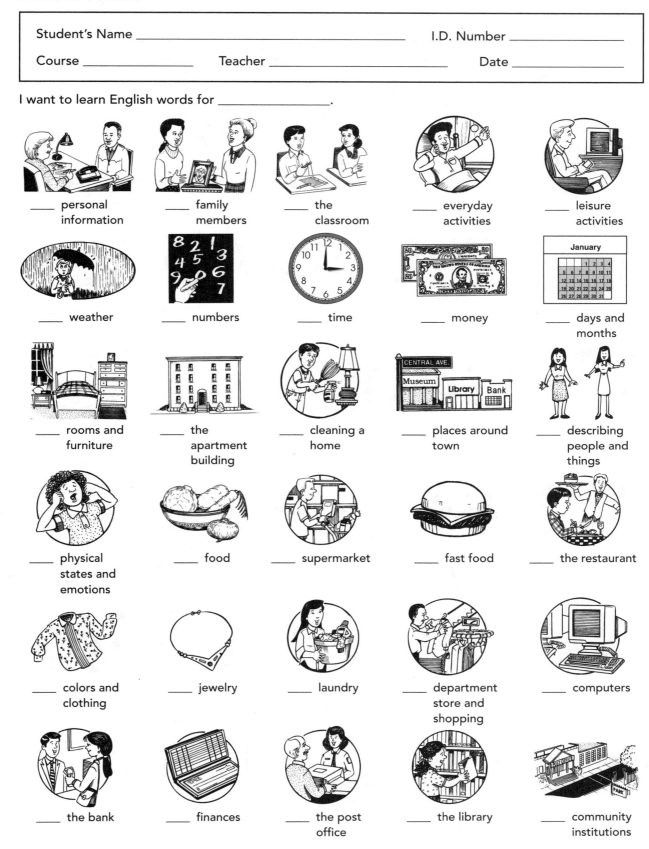

____ personal information

____ family members

____ the classroom

____ everyday activities

____ leisure activities

____ weather

____ numbers

____ time

____ money

____ days and months

____ rooms and furniture

____ the apartment building

____ cleaning a home

____ places around town

____ describing people and things

____ physical states and emotions

____ food

____ supermarket

____ fast food

____ the restaurant

____ colors and clothing

____ jewelry

____ laundry

____ department store and shopping

____ computers

____ the bank

____ finances

____ the post office

____ the library

____ community institutions

Pictorial Version

Student's Name _____ I.D. Number _____

I want to learn English words for _____.

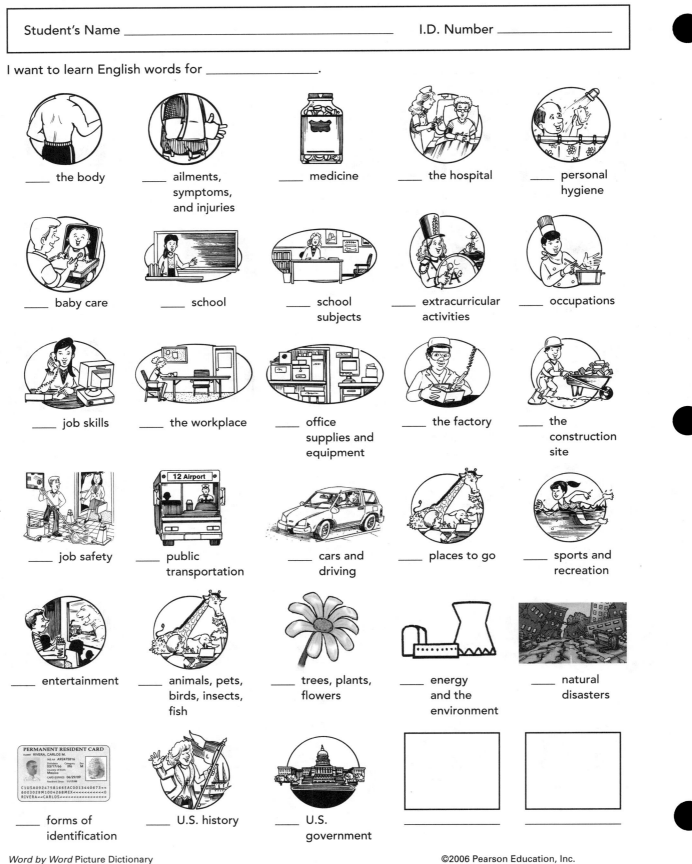

_____ the body

_____ ailments, symptoms, and injuries

_____ medicine

_____ the hospital

_____ personal hygiene

_____ baby care

_____ school

_____ school subjects

_____ extracurricular activities

_____ occupations

_____ job skills

_____ the workplace

_____ office supplies and equipment

_____ the factory

_____ the construction site

_____ job safety

_____ public transportation

_____ cars and driving

_____ places to go

_____ sports and recreation

_____ entertainment

_____ animals, pets, birds, insects, fish

_____ trees, plants, flowers

_____ energy and the environment

_____ natural disasters

_____ forms of identification

_____ U.S. history

_____ U.S. government

_____ _____

_____ _____

Student's Name _____	I.D. Number _____
Course _____ Teacher _____	Date _____

I want to learn English words for _____.

_____ personal information (name, address)
_____ family members (mother, father)

_____ classroom objects (book, pencil)
_____ classroom actions (stand up, sit down)
_____ everyday activities (brush my teeth, go to work)
_____ leisure activities (watch TV, listen to music)
_____ everyday conversation (How are you?)
_____ weather (hot, raining)

_____ numbers (one, first)
_____ time (2:00, half past three)
_____ money (dollars, cents)
_____ days of the week (Sunday, Monday)
_____ months of the year (January, February)
_____ seasons (spring, summer)

_____ types of housing (house, apartment building)
_____ rooms in a home (living room, kitchen)
_____ furniture (table, chair)
_____ the apartment building (lobby, elevator)
_____ household problems and repairs (broken, leaking)
_____ household cleaning (vacuum, wash)
_____ home supplies, tools, hardware (lightbulb, hammer)
_____ gardening (plant, shovel)

_____ places around town (library, post office)
_____ the city (police officer, fire station)

_____ describing people and things (tall, short)
_____ describing physical states and emotions (tired, happy)

_____ food (fruits, vegetables)
_____ the supermarket (aisle, cashier)
_____ preparing food and recipes (bake, boil)
_____ kitchen utensils and cookware (ladle, pot)
_____ fast food and sandwiches (hamburger, sandwich)
_____ the restaurant (waiter, menu)

_____ colors (blue, brown)
_____ clothing (shirt, pants)
_____ jewelry (ring, necklace)
_____ laundry (wash, dry)

_____ the department store (women's clothing, customer service)
_____ shopping (buy, return)
_____ video and audio equipment (TV, radio)
_____ telephones and cameras (cell phone, digital camera)
_____ computers (keyboard, monitor)
_____ the toy store (doll, game)

_____ the bank (teller, deposit slip)
_____ finances (credit card, check)
_____ the post office (stamp, money order)
_____ the library (library card, reference section)
_____ community institutions (clinic, police station)
_____ crime and emergencies (fire, burglary)

(continued)

Student's Name _____ I.D. Number _____

I want to learn English words for _____.

_____ the body (*arm, leg*)

_____ ailments, symptoms, and injuries (*cough, rash*)

_____ first aid (*bandage, ointment*)

_____ medical emergencies and illnesses (*heart attack, measles*)

_____ the medical exam (*blood pressure, stethoscope*)

_____ medicine (*aspirin, cough medicine*)

_____ medical specialists (*pediatrician, cardiologist*)

_____ the hospital (*emergency room, hospital room*)

_____ personal hygiene (*wash, shave*)

_____ baby care (*diaper, baby powder*)

_____ types of schools (*high school, college*)

_____ the school building (*classroom, office*)

_____ school subjects (*English, math*)

_____ extracurricular activities (*band, yearbook*)

_____ occupations (*cashier, teacher*)

_____ job skills and activities (*type, drive*)

_____ job search (*want ad, interview*)

_____ the workplace (*supply room, employee lounge*)

_____ office supplies and equipment (*paper clips, copy machine*)

_____ the factory (*assembly line, warehouse*)

_____ the construction site (*bulldozer, scaffolding*)

_____ job safety (*hairnet, safety glasses*)

_____ public transportation (*bus, subway*)

_____ types of vehicles (*cars, trucks*)

_____ car parts and maintenance (*engine, taillight*)

_____ highways and streets (*exit, one-way*)

_____ traffic signs and directions (*stop sign, block*)

_____ the airport and airplane travel (*gate, ticket*)

_____ the hotel (*front desk, lobby*)

_____ hobbies, crafts, and games (*collect, paint*)

_____ places to go (*park, beach*)

_____ sports and recreation (*jogging, hiking*)

_____ team sports and equipment (*baseball, soccer*)

_____ winter sports and recreation (*skating, skiing*)

_____ water sports and recreation (*swimming, sailing*)

_____ entertainment (*movies, TV programs*)

_____ musical instruments (*piano, violin*)

_____ the farm and farm animals (*barn, cow*)

_____ animals and pets (*lion, dog*)

_____ birds and insects (*crow, bee*)

_____ fish, sea animals, and reptiles (*shark, dolphin*)

_____ trees, plants, and flowers (*oak, rose*)

_____ energy, conservation, and the environment (*oil, solar energy*)

_____ natural disasters (*earthquake, hurricane*)

_____ forms of identification (*driver's license, passport*)

_____ U.S. government (*branches, representatives*)

_____ the Constitution and the Bill of Rights

_____ events in U.S. history

_____ holidays (*Valentine's Day, Thanksgiving*)

_____ the legal system (*court, lawyer*)

_____ citizenship (*application, oath*)

WORD BY WORD
Performance-Based Lesson Assessment

Lesson Page(s) _____ Date _____

Class _____ Teacher _____

Student Name	Vocabulary Practice	Conversation Practice	Writing and/or Discussion	Activity Participation
1.				
2.				
3.				
4.				
5.				
6.				
7.				
8.				
9.				
10.				
11.				
12.				
13.				
14.				
15.				
16.				
17.				
18.				
19.				
20.				
21.				
22.				
23.				

Scoring Rubric:

Score the student's performance in each section of the lesson: Vocabulary Practice, Conversation Practice, Writing and/or Discussion, and Activity Participation (Making Connections and/or Communication Activities).

5 (Excellent), **4** (Good), **3** (Fair), **2** (Poor), **1** (Unsatisfactory)

WORD BY WORD

Student Name List Mask

Student Name
1.
2.
3.
4.
5.
6.
7.
8.
9.
10.
11.
12.
13.
14.
15.
16.
17.
18.
19.
20.
21.
22.
23.

(cut or fold)

Instructions: Fill in student names on the list mask and affix to Performance-Based Lesson Assessment sheets.

Word by Word Picture Dictionary
Student Name List Mask

WORD BY WORD LESSON PLANNER
Low-Beginning/Literacy Level

Teacher _____

Class _____   Date _____

Warm-Up/Review, Completion, & Expansion of Previous Lesson(s) Time: _____ minutes

Review, complete, or expand the following *Word by Word* Picture Dictionary lesson:
(Indicate lesson pages, Teacher's Guide pages with specific teaching steps or activities, and any workbook pages to be reviewed.)

_____

_____

New Picture Dictionary Lesson

Page(s) _____   TG (Teacher's Guide) Pages _____

Introduction

State the lesson objective, and tell students what they will be doing during the lesson.

Vocabulary Preview Time: _____(5) minutes

Activate students' prior knowledge of the vocabulary using the brainstorming or picture identification activity.

Vocabulary Presentation Time: _____(5) minutes

Present the vocabulary as recommended in the TG.

Comprehension Check Time: _____(5) minutes

Check students' comprehension and pronunciation of the vocabulary.

Vocabulary Practice Time: _____(10) minutes

Have students practice the words as a class, in pairs, or in small groups as recommended in the TG.

Model Conversation Practice Time: _____(5) minutes

Have students practice the short guided conversation(s) as recommended in the TG.

Additional Conversation Practice Time: _____(5) minutes

Have students practice any additional conversations (if included in the lesson) as recommended in the TG.

Spelling Practice Time: _____(5) minutes

Have students practice spelling the vocabulary words as recommended in the TG.

Writing and Discussion Time: _____(10) minutes

Have students do the recommended activity through class discussion and/or as a writing assignment.

Evaluation (Integrated in lesson steps above)

Use the Performance-Based Lesson Assessment to evaluate class performance or individual students.

Extension Time: _____(10) minutes

Extend students' vocabulary with one or more Making Connections activities.

Selected resource(s)/community task(s): _____

Application Time: _____ minutes

Have students apply their new vocabulary by participating in new and different activities.

Selected Communication Activity number(s): _____

Workbook Skill Integration

Literacy WB Page(s)   _____

Beginning Lifeskills WB Page(s)   _____

Beginning Vocabulary WB Page(s)   _____

Teacher Reference Notes

Language & Culture Notes Page(s)   _____

Technology

WordLinks: http://www.longman.com/wordbyword

Music

WordSong

_____

*Customize lesson steps and suggested times based on students' needs and abilities and class time available for vocabulary learning. Many teachers prefer to "bridge" lessons over two or more sessions—for example, doing all lesson steps through Model Conversation Practice in a first session, then continuing with the rest of a lesson and extension/application activities in a second or later session.

WORD BY WORD LESSON PLANNER
Beginning Level

Teacher _____

Class _____ Date _____

Warm-Up/Review, Completion, & Expansion of Previous Lesson(s) Time: _____ minutes

Review, complete, or expand the following *Word by Word* Picture Dictionary lesson:
(Indicate lesson pages, Teacher's Guide pages with specific teaching steps or activities, and any workbook pages to be reviewed.)

_____

_____

New Picture Dictionary Lesson

Page(s) _____   TG (Teacher's Guide) Pages _____

Introduction

State the lesson objective, and tell students what they will be doing during the lesson.

Vocabulary Preview Time: _____(5) minutes

Activate students' prior knowledge of the vocabulary using the brainstorming or picture identification activity.

Vocabulary Presentation Time: _____(5) minutes

Present the vocabulary as recommended in the TG.

Comprehension Check Time: _____(5) minutes

Check students' comprehension and pronunciation of the vocabulary.

Vocabulary Practice Time: _____(5) minutes

Have students practice the words as a class, in pairs, or in small groups as recommended in the TG.

Model Conversation Practice Time: _____(5) minutes

Have students practice the short guided conversation(s) as recommended in the TG.

Additional Conversation Practice Time: _____(5) minutes

Have students practice any additional conversations (if included in the lesson) as recommended in the TG.

Spelling Practice Time: _____(5) minutes

Have students practice spelling the vocabulary words as recommended in the TG.

Writing and Discussion Time: _____(10) minutes

Have students do the recommended activity through class discussion and/or as a writing assignment.

Evaluation (Integrated in lesson steps above)

Use the Performance-Based Lesson Assessment to evaluate class performance or individual students.

Extension Time: _____(10) minutes

Extend students' vocabulary with one or more Making Connections activities.

Selected resource(s)/community task(s): _____

Application Time: _____ minutes

Have students apply their new vocabulary by participating in new and different activities.

Selected Communication Activity number(s): _____

Workbook Skill Integration	Technology
Beginning Lifeskills WB Page(s) _____	WordLinks: http://www.longman.com/wordbyword
Beginning Vocabulary WB Page(s) _____	**Music**
Teacher Reference Notes	WordSong
Language & Culture Notes Page(s) _____	_____

*Customize lesson steps and suggested times based on students' needs and abilities and class time available for vocabulary learning. Many teachers prefer to "bridge" lessons over two or more sessions—for example, doing all lesson steps through Model Conversation Practice in a first session, then continuing with the rest of a lesson and extension/application activities in a second or later session.

WORD BY WORD LESSON PLANNER
High-Beginning/Intermediate Level

Teacher _____

Class _____ Date _____

Warm-Up/Review, Completion, & Expansion of Previous Lesson(s) Time: _____ minutes

Review, complete, or expand the following *Word by Word* Picture Dictionary lesson:
(Indicate lesson pages, Teacher's Guide pages with specific teaching steps or activities, and any workbook pages to be reviewed.)

_____

_____

New Picture Dictionary Lesson

Page(s) _____   TG (Teacher's Guide) Pages _____

Introduction

State the lesson objective, and tell students what they will be doing during the lesson.

Vocabulary Preview Time: _____(5) minutes

Activate students' prior knowledge of the vocabulary using the brainstorming or picture identification activity.

Vocabulary Presentation Time: _____(5) minutes

Present the vocabulary as recommended in the TG.

Comprehension Check Time: _____(5) minutes

Check students' comprehension and pronunciation of the vocabulary.

Vocabulary Practice Time: _____(5) minutes

Have students practice the words as a class, in pairs, or in small groups as recommended in the TG.

Model Conversation Practice Time: _____(5) minutes

Have students practice the short guided conversation(s) as recommended in the TG.

Additional Conversation Practice Time: _____(5) minutes

Have students practice any additional conversations (if included in the lesson) as recommended in the TG.

Spelling Practice Time: _____(5) minutes

Have students practice spelling the vocabulary words as recommended in the TG.

Writing and Discussion Time: _____(10) minutes

Have students do the recommended activity through class discussion and/or as a writing assignment.

Evaluation (Integrated in lesson steps above)

Use the Performance-Based Lesson Assessment to evaluate class performance or individual students.

Extension Time: _____(10) minutes

Extend students' vocabulary with one or more Making Connections activities.

Selected resource(s)/community task(s): _____

Application Time: _____ minutes

Have students apply their new vocabulary by participating in new and different activities.

Selected Communication Activity number(s): _____

Workbook Skill Integration	**Technology**
Intermediate Lifeskills WB Page(s) _____	WordLinks: http://www.longman.com/wordbyword
Intermediate Vocabulary WB Page(s) _____	**Music**
Reading Enrichment	WordSong
Language & Culture Notes Page(s) _____	_____

*Customize lesson steps and suggested times based on students' needs and abilities and class time available for vocabulary learning. Many teachers prefer to "bridge" lessons over two or more sessions—for example, doing all lesson steps through Model Conversation Practice in a first session, then continuing with the rest of a lesson and extension/application activities in a second or later session.

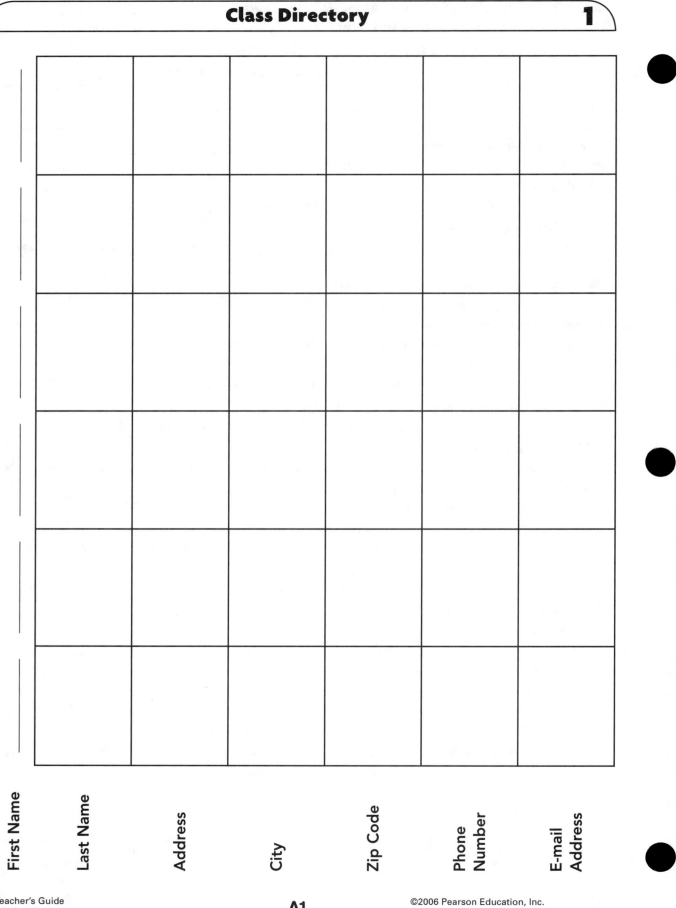

First Name	Last Name	Address	City	Zip Code	Phone Number	E-mail Address

A1

Name _____ _____ _____

            (Last)   (First)   (MI)

Address _____ _____ _____

       (Number)   (Street)   (Apartment)

_____ _____ _____

        (City)   (State)   (Zip Code)

Telephone _____

Cell Phone _____

E-Mail Address _____

Sex   Male _____   Female _____

Date of Birth _____

Place of Birth _____

Men's Names	Nicknames	Women's Names	Nicknames
Andrew	Andy	Ann	Annie
Anthony	Tony	Barbara	Barb
Christopher	Chris	Beverly	Bev
David	Dave	Catherine	Cathy
Daniel	Dan	Christine	Chris/Chrissy
Donald	Don	Deborah	Debbie
Edward	Ed/Ned	Elizabeth	Liz/Beth/Betsy
James	Jim	Jennifer	Jenny
Jeffrey	Jeff	Judith	Judy
John	Jack	Katherine	Kathy
Joseph	Joe	Kimberly	Kim
Lawrence	Larry	Margaret	Peggy/Margie/Maggie
Patrick	Pat	Megan	Meg
Richard	Rich/Richie/Dick	Pamela	Pam
Robert	Bob/Rob/Robbie	Patricia	Pat/Patty/Tricia/Trish
Samuel	Sam	Rebecca	Becky
Steven	Steve/Stevie	Sandra	Sandy
Thomas	Tom	Sarah/Sara	Sally
Timothy	Tim	Susan	Sue/Susie
William	Bill/Billy/Will	Teresa	Terry

A3

Andrew	Anthony	Christopher
David	Daniel	Donald
Edward	James	Jeffrey
John	Joseph	Lawrence
Patrick	Richard	Robert
Samuel	Steven	Thomas
Timothy	William	Ann
Barbara	Beverly	Catherine
Christine	Deborah	Elizabeth
Jennifer	Judith	Katherine
Kimberly	Margaret	Megan
Pamela	Patricia	Rebecca
Sandra	Sarah/Sara	Susan
Teresa		

Andy	Tony	Chris
Dave	Dan	Don
Ed/Ned	Jim	Jeff
Jack	Joe	Larry
Pat	Rich/Richie/Dick	Bob/Rob/Robbie
Sam	Steve/Stevie	Tom
Tim	Bill/Billy/Will	Annie
Barb	Bev	Cathy
Chris/Chrissy	Debbie	Liz/Beth/Betsy
Jenny	Judy	Kathy
Kim	Peggy/Margie/Maggie	Meg
Pam	Pat/Patty/Tricia	Becky
Sandy	Sally	Sue/Susie
Terry		

Your brother's son is your . . .	nephew.
Your wife's mother is your . . .	mother-in-law.
Your husband's father is your . . .	father-in-law.
Your uncle's daughter is your . . .	cousin.
Your mother's mother is your . . .	grandmother.
Your father's daughter is your . . .	sister.
Your mother's son is your . . .	brother.
Your sister's husband is your . . .	brother-in-law.
Your brother's daughter is your . . .	niece.
Your son's daughter is your . . .	granddaughter.

teacher	teacher's aide	student
desk	chair	teacher's desk
clock	chalkboard	whiteboard
bulletin board	P.A. system	globe
bookcase	overhead projector	map
screen	computer	wastebasket
table	pen	pencil
eraser	pencil sharpener	textbook
workbook	spiral notebook	binder
notebook paper	graph paper	ruler
calculator	chalk	eraser
marker	thumbtack	keyboard
monitor	mouse	printer

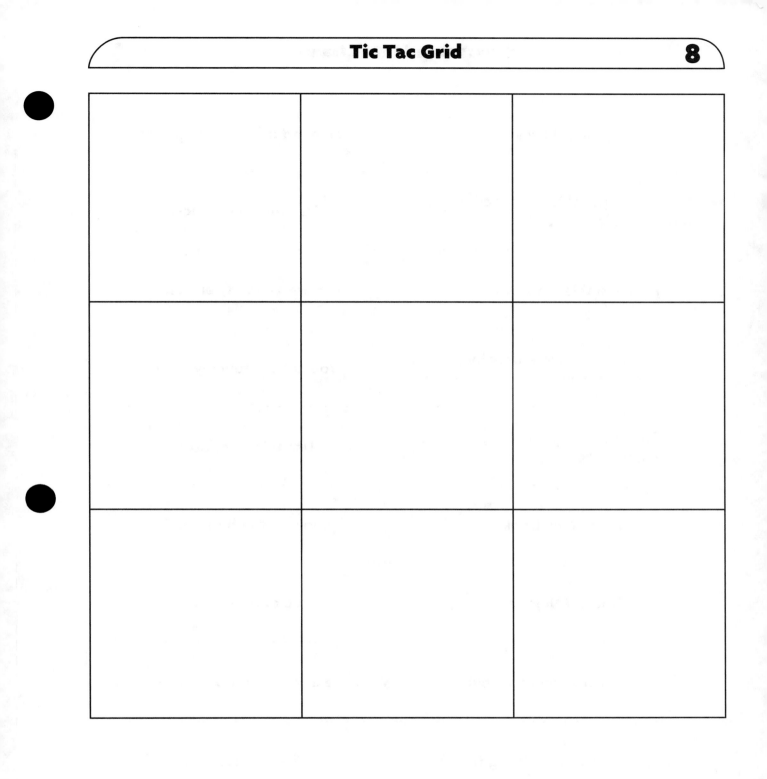

For Teacher's Guide
For Tic Tac Vocabulary Activities

My pencil broke!	You need a pencil sharpener.
How can I put this announcement on the bulletin board?	Use this thumbtack.
I spelled this word wrong!	Here. Use my eraser.
I'm having trouble drawing a straight line.	You can borrow my ruler.
This math problem is very complicated!	Use this calculator.
Where's my book?	Look on the bookshelf.
Where's Nigeria?	Look on the map.
How can we show this movie?	We have a screen in front of the room.
Where's that voice coming from?	The P.A. system.
Where can I throw out this broken pen?	In the wastebasket.

Print your name.	Sign your name.	Stand up.
Go to the board.	Write on the board.	Erase the board.
Take your seat.	Open your book.	Close your book.
Put away your book.	Raise your hand.	Go over the answers.
Correct your mistakes.	Hand in your homework.	Share a book.
Look in the dictionary.	Look up a word.	Copy the word.
Lower the shades.	Turn off the lights.	Look at the screen.
Take notes.	Turn on the lights.	Take out a piece of paper.
Pass out the tests.	Answer the questions.	Collect the tests.

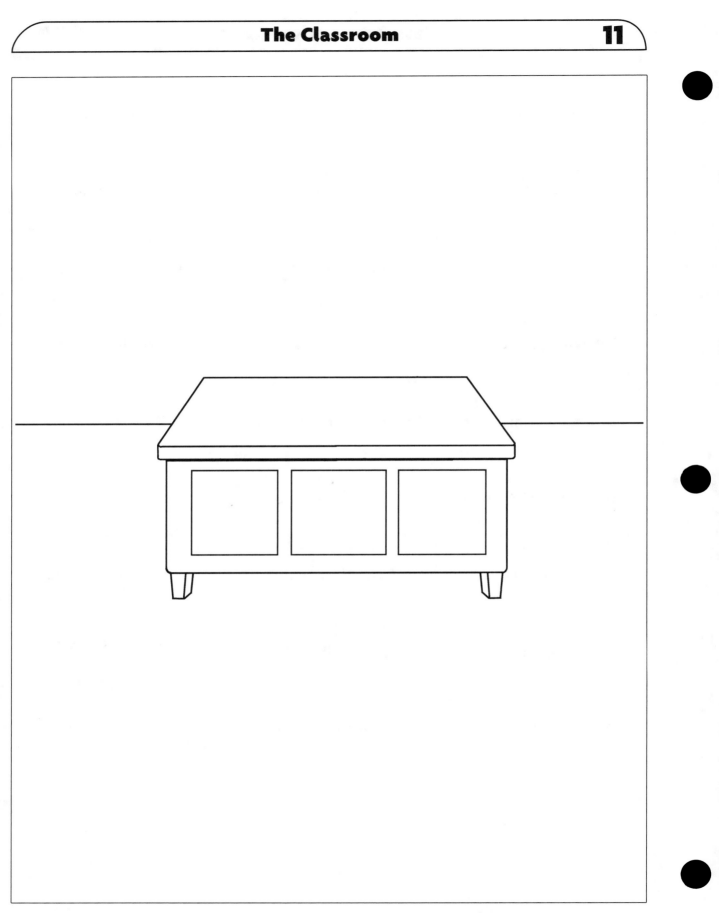

get up	take a shower	brush my teeth
shave	get dressed	wash my face
put on makeup	brush my hair	comb my hair
make the bed	get undressed	take a bath
go to bed	sleep	make breakfast
make lunch	make dinner	eat breakfast
eat lunch	eat dinner	

1. _____ gets up before 5:00 A.M. every day.

2. _____ gets up after 9:00 A.M. every day.

3. _____ eats breakfast in a coffee shop almost every day.

4. _____ makes the bed every day.

5. _____ takes a bath in the morning.

6. _____ takes a shower in the morning.

7. _____ eats lunch in a restaurant almost every day.

8. _____ takes a shower at night.

9. _____ goes to bed before 9:00 P.M.

10. _____ goes to bed after midnight.

clean the house	wash the dishes	do the laundry
iron	feed the baby	feed the cat
walk the dog	study	go to school
go to work	drive to school	take the bus to school
work	leave work	go to the store
get home		

1. _____ cleans the house more than once a week.

2. _____ washes the dishes every night.

3. _____ likes to iron.

4. _____ studies every day.

5. _____ does the laundry at a laundromat.

6. _____ takes the bus to school.

7. _____ goes to work before 7:00 A.M.

8. _____ walks the dog every day.

9. _____ walks to work.

10. _____ gets home from work after 9:00 P.M.

A15

watch TV	listen to the radio	listen to music
read a book	read the newspaper	play
play cards	play basketball	play the guitar
practice the piano	exercise	swim
plant flowers	use the computer	write a letter
relax		

For Teacher's Guide
Page 27, Activity 1
Page 28, Activities 9, 12
Page 33, Activities 1, 2, 3, 4

Do you watch TV? _____

What programs do you watch? _____

_____

Do you listen to the radio? _____

What programs do you listen to? _____

_____

Do you listen to music? _____

What do you listen to? _____

_____

Do you read? _____

What do you read? _____

_____

Do you play any games or a musical instrument? _____

What do you play? _____

_____

Do you exercise? _____

What do you do? _____

_____

How are you?	Fine, thanks.
What's new?	Not too much.
How are you doing?	Okay.
Hello. My name is Alex.	Nice to meet you, Alex.
Nice to meet you, Pat.	Nice to meet you, too.
Thank you.	You're welcome.
Hello. This is Alex. May I please speak to Robert?	Hold on a moment. Robert? Alex is on the phone.
May I please speak to Mary?	I'm sorry. Mary isn't here right now.

A. How are you?
B. Not much.

A. Good-bye. See you soon.
B. Fine, thanks.

A. Good morning.
B. Good night.

A. What's new with you?
B. Okay.

A. Thank you.
B. I'm welcome.

A. I'd like to meet my brother.
B. Nice to meet you.

A. Hello. This is Sam. May I please speak to Susan?
B. I'm sorry. Hold on a minute.

A. Sorry. I understand. Can you please repeat that?
B. Yes.

A. Excuse you. May I ask a question?
B. Sure.

A. Hello. My name is Adam.
B. Hello. Nice to meet you, too.

A. Study page ten.
B. Can I please say that again?
A. Yes. Study page ten.

A. Hi. My name is Ron.
B. Hello. This is Susan.
A. Nice to meet you, Susan.
B. Nice to meet you. too.

You're at a bus stop in the early morning. It's snowing.

You're both waiting for a train outdoors. It's 100° Fahrenheit.

You're walking your dogs in the park. It's sunny and warm.

You and a classmate see each other on the street. It's 32° Fahrenheit.

You're in the waiting area of an airport. It's hailing outside.

You're sitting next to each other on an airplane. There's a thunderstorm outside.

You're watching your children swim at a pool. Introduce yourselves. There's a heat wave.

You and your neighbor are in the elevator of your apartment building. It's smoggy outside.

1. _____ gets up before 6:00 A.M.

2. _____ goes to bed after midnight.

3. _____ eats dinner after 8:00 P.M.

4. _____ gets up after 10:00 A.M. on Sunday.

5. _____ watches TV before noon.

6. _____ is usually late for English class.

7. _____ is always on time for appointments.

$3.60	3 one-dollar bills 2 quarters 1 dime
$9.86	a five-dollar bill 4 one-dollar bills 3 quarters a dime a penny
$27.45	a twenty-dollar bill a five-dollar bill 2 one-dollar bills 1 quarter 2 dimes
$14.95	a ten-dollar bill 4 one-dollar bills 3 quarters a dime a nickel 5 pennies
$99.90	4 twenty-dollar bills a ten-dollar bill 9 one-dollar bills 8 dimes 2 nickels
$7.29	a five-dollar bill 2 one-dollar bills 1 quarter 4 pennies
$15.68	a ten-dollar bill a five-dollar bill 2 quarters a dime a nickel 3 pennies
$32.95	3 ten-dollar bills 2 one-dollar bills 3 quarters a dime a nickel 5 pennies
$56.09	a fifty-dollar bill a five-dollar bill a one-dollar bill a nickel 4 pennies

January	February
March	April
May	June
July	August
September	October
November	December

SUN	MON	TUES	WED	THURS	FRI	SAT

Wendy's Schedule A

Friday	Saturday (TODAY)	Sunday
9:00 A.M.–12:00 P.M. work at the office	*8:30 A.M.–12:30 P.M.* clean the apartment do the laundry	
		1:30 P.M. go to the supermarket
	9:00 P.M. play cards with friends at home	

Wendy's Schedule B

Friday	Saturday (TODAY)	Sunday
		9:00 A.M.–11:00 A.M. eat breakfast read the newspaper
2:30–4:30 attend a meeting	*3:30 P.M.* play basketball with friends	
7:00 P.M. have dinner with friends *9:00 P.M.* arrive home and watch TV		*6:00 P.M.* make dinner *8:00 P.M.* listen to music and study English

1. _____ cleaned his or her apartment last weekend.

2. _____ watched TV this morning.

3. _____ is going to see a movie next weekend.

4. _____ got home after 9:00 P.M. last night.

5. _____ cooks dinner every day.

6. _____ walks his or her dog twice a day.

7. _____ exercises three times a week.

8. _____ is going to go to the library tomorrow.

9. _____ used the computer yesterday evening.

10. _____ likes winter.

Main Street Bus: Schedule A

SUN	MON	TUES	WED	THURS	FRI	SAT
	7:00 A.M.		7:00 A.M.	7:00 A.M.		
	8:00 A.M.		8:00 A.M.	8:00 A.M.		8:00 A.M.
	9:00 A.M.		9:00 A.M.			
	12:30 P.M.		12:30 P.M.	12:30 P.M.		12:30 P.M.
	4:15 P.M.		4:15 P.M.			
	5:15 P.M.		5:15 P.M.	5:15 P.M.		
	6:00 P.M.		6:00 P.M.	6:00 P.M.		6:00 P.M.
	6:30 P.M.		6:30 P.M.	6:30 P.M.		
	7:00 P.M.		7:00 P.M.			
	9:00 P.M.		9:00 P.M.	9:00 P.M.		9:00 P.M.
	12:30 A.M.		12:30 A.M.	12:30 A.M.		12:30 A.M.

How many times a week is there a 7:00 A.M. bus? _____

How many times a week is there a 12:30 P.M. bus? _____

How many times a week is there a 5:15 P.M. bus? _____

Main Street Bus: Schedule B

SUN	MON	TUES	WED	THURS	FRI	SAT
		7:00 A.M.	7:00 A.M.		7:00 A.M.	
8:00 A.M.		8:00 A.M.	8:00 A.M.		8:00 A.M.	
			9:00 A.M.		9:00 A.M.	
12:30 P.M.		12:30 P.M.	12:30 P.M.		12:30 P.M.	
			4:15 P.M.		4:15 P.M.	
		5:15 P.M.	5:15 P.M.		5:15 P.M.	
		6:00 P.M.	6:00 P.M.		6:00 P.M.	
6:30 P.M.		6:30 P.M.	6:30 P.M.		6:30 P.M.	
			7:00 P.M.		7:00 P.M.	
9:00 P.M.		9:00 P.M.	9:00 P.M.		9:00 P.M.	
		12:30 A.M.	12:30 A.M.		12:30 A.M.	

How many times a week is there an 8:00 A.M. bus? _____

How many times a week is there a 4:15 P.M. bus? _____

How many times a week is there a 6:00 P.M. bus? _____

1. In the morning, people often _____
_____
_____.

2. In the afternoon, people often _____
_____
_____.

3. In the evening, people often _____
_____
_____.

4. On the weekend, people often _____
_____
_____.

5. In the summer, people often _____
_____
_____.

6. In the fall, people often _____
_____
_____.

7. In the winter, people often _____
_____
_____.

8. In the spring, people often _____
_____
_____.

coffee table	rug	floor
armchair	end table	lamp
lampshade	window	drapes
floor lamp	sofa	throw pillow
ceiling	wall	television
DVD player	wall unit	VCR
stereo system	speaker	plant
magazine holder	loveseat	painting
mantel	fireplace	fireplace screen
picture	bookcase	

dining room table	dining room chair	china cabinet
china	chandelier	platter
salad bowl	pitcher	tablecloth
candlestick	candle	vase
salt shaker	pepper shaker	butter dish
tray	teapot	coffee pot
creamer	sugar bowl	napkin
fork	plate	bowl
glass	cup	saucer
mug	knife	spoon
buffet	serving bowl	serving dish

A31

dishwasher	dishwasher detergent	dishwashing liquid
faucet	sink	garbage disposal
dish rack	paper towel holder	dish towel
trash compactor	cabinet	microwave
kitchen counter	cutting board	toaster
canister	stove	burner
tea kettle	oven	potholder
toaster oven	spice rack	can opener
cookbook	coffeemaker	refrigerator
freezer	blender	kitchen table
placemat	kitchen chair	garbage pail
food processor	electric mixer	

teddy bear	baby monitor	chest
crib	crib bumper	mobile
night light	changing table	stretch suit
changing pad	diaper pail	toy chest
doll	swing	playpen
stuffed animal	rattle	cradle
walker	car seat	stroller
baby carriage	baby backpack	food warmer
booster seat	baby seat	high chair
portable crib	baby carrier	potty
baby frontpack		

plunger	toilet	toilet seat
air freshener	toilet paper	toilet brush
towel rack	bath towel	hand towel
washcloth	hamper	scale
shelf	hair dryer	fan
mirror	medicine cabinet	sink
faucet	cup	toothbrush
toothbrush holder	soap	soap dish
soap dispenser	electric toothbrush	vanity
wastebasket	shower	shower head
shower curtain	bathtub	drain
rubber mat	sponge	bath mat

My toilet is plugged up!	You need a plunger.
The water from the shower is getting all over the floor!	Close the shower curtain.
How can I clean the tub?	Use a sponge.
I wonder how much I weigh?	Step on the scale.
I need a clean towel.	Look in the vanity.
My hair is wet.	You need a hair dryer.
Where's the aspirin?	Look in the medicine cabinet.
This hand towel is too small.	You need a bath towel.
I can't see the mirror.	Turn on the fan.
Where can I throw this out?	Here's the wastebasket.
My toothbrush doesn't clean my teeth properly.	You need an electric toothbrush.

lobby	the entrance area
landlord	the person who owns an apartment building
buzzer	bell
doorman	the employee who stands at the building entrance
smoke detector	signals when there is smoke
peephole	allows the apartment occupant to see the hallway
tenant	the person who rents an apartment
garbage chute	for moving garbage to the basement
laundry room	the area with washers and dryers
superintendent	the apartment employee who does repairs
neighbor	the person who lives next door
vacancy sign	a notice that says "Apartment for Rent"

Where's the doorman?	In the lobby.
I think I saw a cockroach!	Call the superintendent immediately.
My muscles feel tense!	Sit in the whirlpool for a while.
It's very hot in here!	Turn on the air conditioner!
Did you hear someone knock?	Maybe. Look through the peephole!
Our wastebaskets are full!	Empty them down the garbage chute!
Is this apartment safe?	Yes. It has a dead-bolt lock and a chain.
The smoke detector is going off!	Call the fire department!
I need a new apartment.	Look in the classified ads!

apartment ad	lease	lock
security deposit	moving truck	fire escape
neighbor	building manager	laundry room
parking garage	balcony	air conditioner
courtyard	trash bin	security gate
parking space	swimming pool	whirlpool
intercom	buzzer	mailbox
elevator	stairway	peephole
dead-bolt lock	door chain	smoke detector
fire alarm	fire exit	garbage chute
sprinkler system	superintendent	storage room

A. Hi. Could you press number two, please? B. Sure. No problem.	Elevator
A. This water is too cold! B. Just keep moving quickly and it won't feel so cold!	Swimming pool
A. Do you have change for a dollar bill? The machine requires six quarters and I have only two! B. There's a change machine over there, next to the dryers.	Laundry room
A. Good afternoon, Mrs. Gomez. B. Hello, Bob. Did the mailman deliver a package for me today? A. Yes. It's over there, under your mailbox.	Lobby
A. I love to come down here, sit on the bench, and watch the people walk by. B. I do, too.	Courtyard
A. Hmm. Where are those old books? I know I brought them down here a few years ago. B. I don't see your books, but look! I just found your first pair of shoes!	Storage room
A. I love to sit out here in the morning. B. It's a beautiful view. But be careful! Don't lean over too much! We're on the 12th floor!	Balcony
A. Good morning! How are you today? B. Fine, thanks. I'm getting my exercise! I'm not going to use the elevator any more! A. You're lucky you only live on the third floor!	Stairway
A. Careful! Don't look down! Just hold on and walk down carefully. The firefighters are waiting for you on the ground.	Fire escape

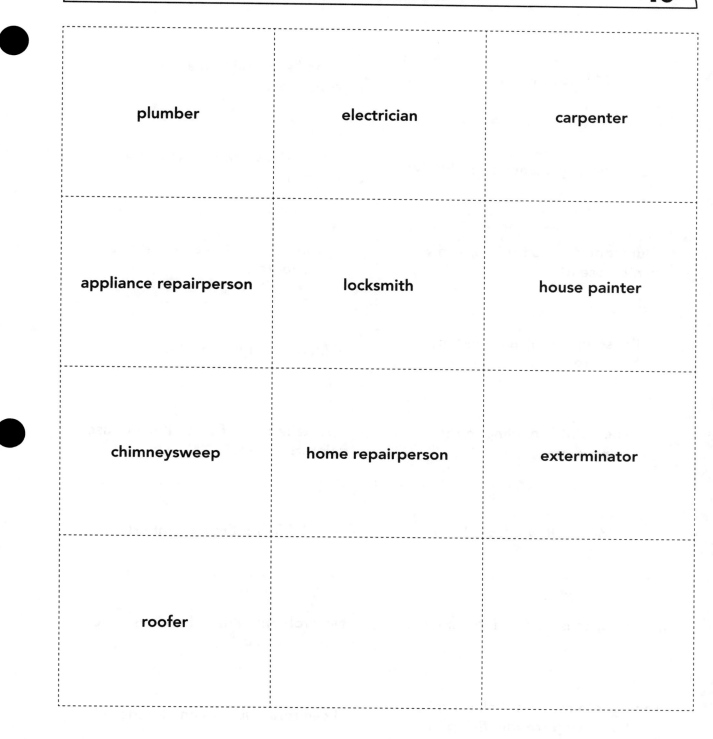

plumber	electrician	carpenter
appliance repairperson	locksmith	house painter
chimneysweep	home repairperson	exterminator
roofer		

My stove is broken!

I can help you! I'm an appliance repairperson!

I can't get any channels on the TV!

I'll fix it! I work for the cable TV company.

Our front door is broken, and we can't close it!

That's easy. I'm an excellent carpenter!

I'm so upset! I can't find my house keys!

Don't worry! I'm a locksmith!

The paint is peeling in the living room.

I can take care of that! I'm a house painter!

My toilet won't flush!

I'll fix it! I'm a plumber!

My fireplace isn't working very well!

No problem! I'm a chimneysweep!

The light in my front hall is broken, and I'm having trouble fixing it!

I can repair it! I'm an electrician!

We've got mice in our attic!

I'll take care of the problem. I'm an exterminator!

broom	dustpan	whisk broom
carpet sweeper	vacuum cleaner	vacuum cleaner attachments
vacuum cleaner bag	hand vacuum	dust mop
sponge mop	wet mop	paper towels
window cleaner	ammonia	dust cloth
feather duster	floor wax	furniture polish
cleanser	scrub brush	sponge
bucket	trash can	recycling bin

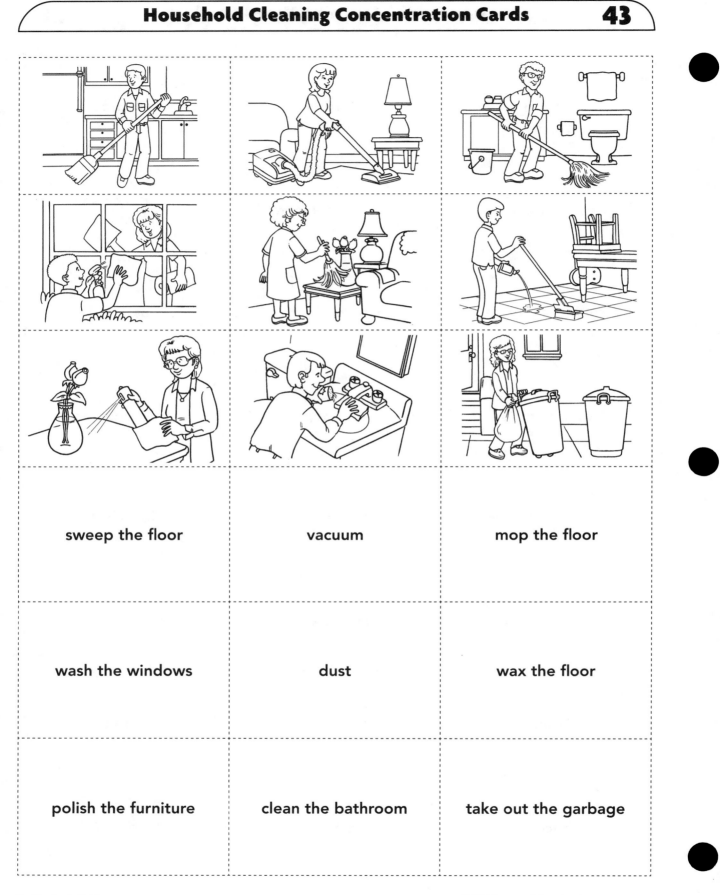

sweep the floor	vacuum	mop the floor
wash the windows	dust	wax the floor
polish the furniture	clean the bathroom	take out the garbage

yardstick	plunger	fly swatter
step ladder	tape measure	flashlight
mousetrap	extension cord	batteries
lightbulbs	fuses	masking tape
electrical tape	duct tape	oil
glue	bug spray	roach killer
work gloves	paint	paint thinner
sandpaper	paint pan	paint roller
paintbrush	spray gun	

My vacuum can't reach that part of the rug!	Use the extension cord!
There's a mouse in my house!	You need a mousetrap!
This is a big wall to paint with a small brush!	You need a paint roller!
I can't wash this paint off my hands!	You need some paint thinner!
Hmm. Will the sofa fit in this room?	You need a tape measure!
It's dark and I can't see!	You need a flashlight!
There's a bee in the house!	You need a fly swatter!
My flashlight doesn't work!	You need new batteries!
I can't reach the top cabinet!	You need a step ladder!
My toilet won't flush!	You need a plunger!
Our front door squeaks!	You need oil!
Our whole house is filled with mosquitoes!	You need bug spray!

A45

hammer	mallet	ax
saw	hacksaw	pliers
screwdriver	Phillips screwdriver	wrench
monkey wrench	hand drill	chisel
scraper	vise	level
plane	wire stripper	toolbox
electric drill	drill bit	power saw
power sander	router	wire
nail	washer	nut
wood screw	machine screw	bolt

lawnmower	gas can	line trimmer
shovel	hoe	vegetable seeds
trowel	fertilizer	wheelbarrow
hose	nozzle	sprinkler
watering can	rake	leaf blower
yard waste bag	hedge clippers	hedge trimmer
pruning shears	weeder	

mow the lawn	plant vegetables	plant flowers
water the flowers	rake leaves	trim the hedge
prune the bushes	weed	

My grass is very tall!

You need a lawnmower!

I don't like all these dead leaves here!

You need a yard waste bag!

My lawn is very dry!

Here! Use this sprinkler!

My hedges are too tall!

You need a hedge trimmer!

My plants aren't growing very well!

Use this fertilizer!

I want to plant these flowers right now.

You need a trowel and a watering can!

I can't carry all these branches!

I'll get you a wheelbarrow!

I can't stop the water!

You need a nozzle!

My arms hurt when I rake the leaves!

You can borrow my leaf blower!

things people sit on	armchair loveseat high chair
things for drinking	glass cup pitcher
things for hot drinks	creamer teapot mug
lights	chandelier floor lamp lamppost
furniture with drawers	dresser chest buffet
things that measure	scale yardstick tape measure
things with wheels	lawnmower stroller wheelbarrow
things that cut	knife pruning shears saw
repairpeople	electrician carpenter locksmith

Name four types of housing.

Name three types of tables.

Name three different things that cover windows.

Name three things that carry a baby.

Name three things that heat food.

Name two things that keep food cold.

Name two kinds of bowls.

Name four things that go on a bed.

Name two things a baby can play with.

Name three things that belong on the floor.

Name three different kinds of chairs.

Name two things that are on a roof.

Name three things in a lobby.

Name two apartment building occupations.

Name two fire safety items.

Name five kinds of repairpeople.

Name three kinds of pests you can find in a house.

Name four gardening tools.

Name four things people use to paint a room.

Name three things that give light.

Name six kinds of tools.

Name three things people use to clean the floor.

Name two things people use to clean a tub.

Name three containers for garbage.

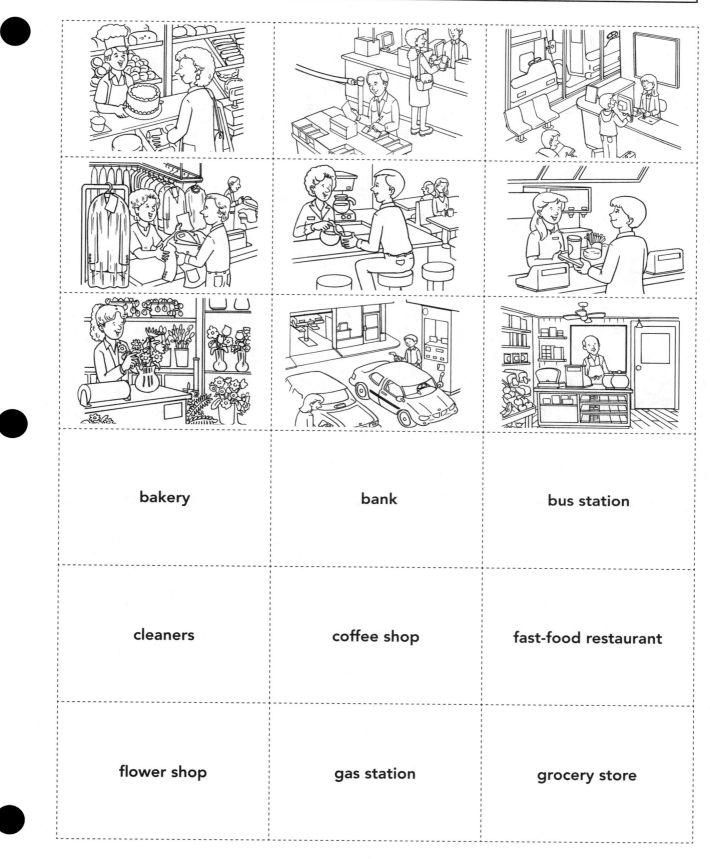

bakery

bank

bus station

cleaners

coffee shop

fast-food restaurant

flower shop

gas station

grocery store

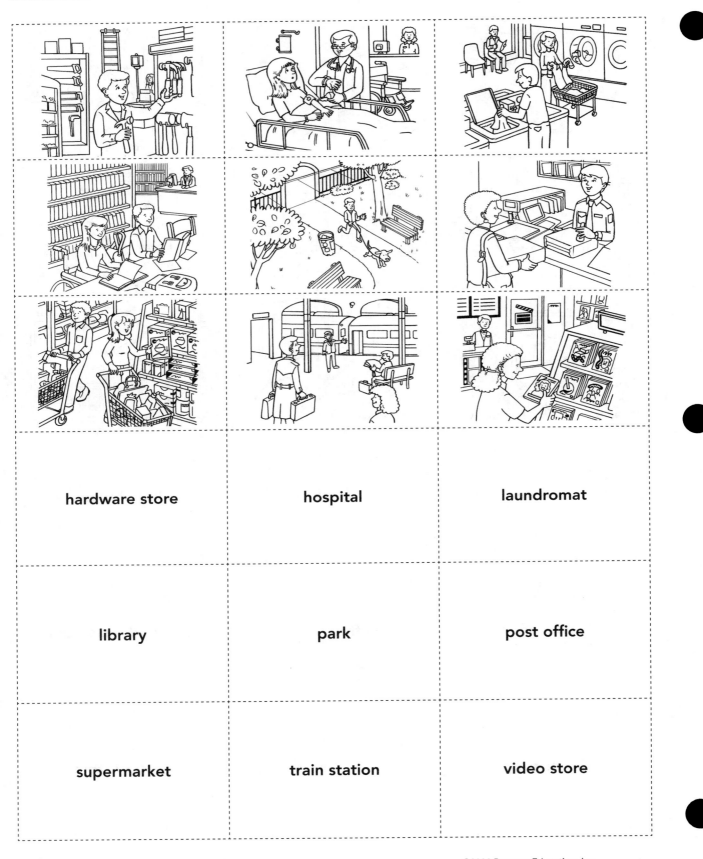

hardware store

hospital

laundromat

library

park

post office

supermarket

train station

video store

This bread looks dry and hard!

I agree. Let's not buy it!

I'd like to send something special to a friend in the hospital.

How about these beautiful yellow roses?

Do you have anything for a headache?

Look over there in the second aisle.

My sweater still has a big stain on it!

I'm sorry. We did the best we could!

This jacket doesn't fit very well.

You're right. Try on another one.

This couch is very ugly!

I know. But it's comfortable!

My car still doesn't start very well.

I'm sorry. All our mechanics are busy right now.

I'd like a hamburger and a drink.

Would you like some french fries with your meal?

I need to take a vacation!	How about a trip to Hawaii?
This movie is very boring!	You're right. Let's leave!
There's a fly in my soup!	I'm sorry. I'll get you some more from the kitchen.
You cut my hair too short!	But it's the latest style!
Shh! Please be quiet!	Sorry. We won't talk any more.
I can't find my socks!	Here they are!
Where is your homework, Alex?	I'm really sorry. I left it at home!
When is your baby due?	In one month!
Oh, Mom! It's such a sweet little dog!	Remember. You promised to take care of it and walk it every day.

A55

courthouse	taxi	taxi driver
taxi stand	street	street light
fire hydrant	sidewalk	city hall
mailbox	police station	jail
fire alarm box	sewer	parking lot
subway	subway station	meter maid
parking meter	trash container	garbage truck
newsstand	traffic light	pedestrian
crosswalk	curb	police officer
intersection	ice cream truck	parking garage
fire station	bus stop	bus
bus driver	motorcycle	public telephone
manhole	office building	street sign
street vendor	drive-through window	

I need to get this suit cleaned.	There's a dry cleaners on Main Street.
Where can I get a good cup of coffee?	At the donut shop!
I need to fill this prescription.	There's a drug store over there.
Where can I buy some fresh apples and oranges?	At Gary's Grocery Store.
I need to get a haircut.	Try the hair salon on Central Street.
I have to do research for my school project.	Go to the library. I'm sure you'll find a lot of good books there.
I have to get a birthday present for my nephew Jimmy!	Go to the new toy store on Jefferson Street.
Where can I get a magazine?	There's a newsstand on the corner.
I need to call my office.	There's a public phone over there.
Where can I get a cab?	There's a taxi stand in front of the courthouse.
Where can I throw this out?	There's a trash container next to the street light.
Where can I get a nice birthday cake?	Try Harry's Bakery on Park Street.

Name two places where you can buy items for your computer.

Name four places where you can buy food to take out.

Where can you buy a car?

Name four kinds of stores where you can buy clothes.

Name two places you can go to see a doctor.

Name two places you can stay for the night when you are traveling.

What is the name of a store that is open most hours of the day and night?

Name two places where children often spend their days.

Name two places where you can buy fresh vegetables and fruit.

Where can a pregnant woman buy clothes?

Name two kinds of public transportation.

Name two places you can park your car in the city.

What do street vendors sell?

Name five things you can buy at a hardware store.

Name two places you can go to get your clothes washed.

What is the name of a store that sells tables, chairs, and sofas?

Name two places where a person can exercise.

Where can a family buy a dog?

Where do criminals stay after they are arrested?

Where is the mayor's office?

What does a meter maid do?

What kinds of places have drive-through windows?

A58

When I'm nervous,	I bite my nails.
When I'm happy,	I smile.
When I'm thirsty,	I drink water.
When I'm angry,	I shout.
When I'm lonely,	I call a friend on the telephone.
When I'm hot,	I take a cool shower.
When I'm sick,	I take medicine and stay in bed.
When I'm embarrassed,	I blush.
When I'm worried,	I stay awake.
When I'm cold,	I put on a sweater.
When I'm bored,	I get sleepy.
When I'm confused,	I get a headache.

My legs ache, my back aches, and I've got the chills!	Uh-oh! You're probably sick.
I just won $50,000 in the lottery!	You must be very excited!
My daughter just won a piano competition!	You must be very proud!
Our teacher taught us all the English modals in one day!	You must be confused!
My doctor just told me I need surgery!	You must be upset!
I haven't heard from my son in more than six weeks!	You must be worried!
I didn't get the job I applied for!	Oh, no! I'm sure you're very disappointed!
I ate nine pieces of chicken for dinner!	You must be very full!

You just walked out of your apartment with a friend and discovered that someone stole your car!

You're in a restaurant and find a fly in your soup!

It's 2 A.M., and your son/daughter has just come home from a date!

You just won $100,000 in the lottery!

You just found out that you didn't get the job you had applied for!

You saw your boyfriend/girlfriend at the movies with someone else last night!

The telephone company overcharged you $75 on your phone bill!

You've been waiting for one week for your landlord to fix your kitchen sink!

You're awakened in the middle of the night by someone trying to open your living room window!

You see an old friend at a party and want to introduce him or her to the person you're with, but you can't remember your friend's name!

You invited a friend out to dinner. You intended to pay for the meal, but you discover that you left your wallet at home!

_____ is happy today because _____

_____ .

_____ is annoyed today because _____

_____ .

_____ is disappointed today because _____

_____ .

_____ is nervous today because _____

_____ .

_____ is worried today because _____

_____ .

_____ is unhappy today because _____

_____ .

_____ is proud today because _____

_____ .

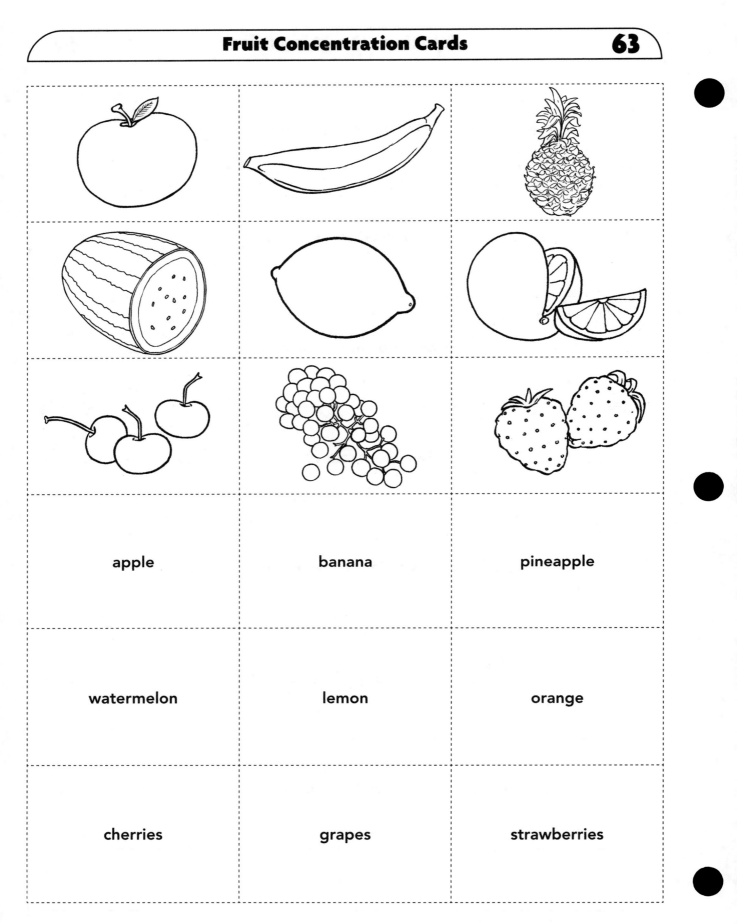

apple

banana

pineapple

watermelon

lemon

orange

cherries

grapes

strawberries

apple	peach	pear
banana	plantain	plum
apricot	nectarine	kiwi
papaya	mango	fig
coconut	avocado	cantaloupe
honeydew	watermelon	pineapple
grapefruit	lemon	lime
orange	tangerine	grapes
cherries	prunes	dates
raisins	nuts	strawberries
raspberries	blueberries	

For Teacher's Guide
Page 111, Activity 6
Page 112, Activities 9, 10, 11
Page 158, Activity 5
Page 159, Activity 8

A64

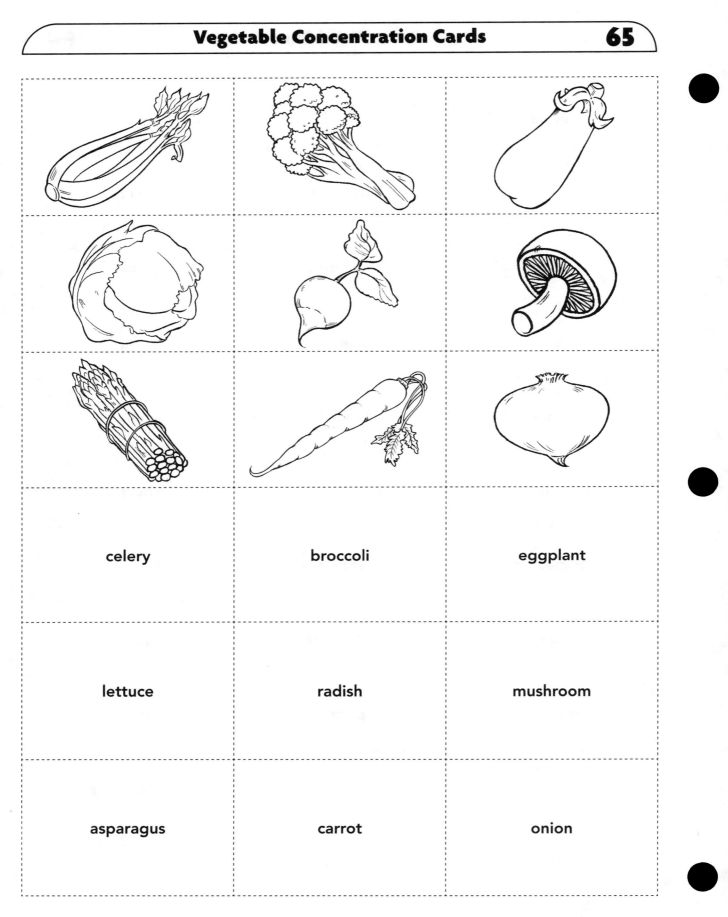

celery

broccoli

eggplant

lettuce

radish

mushroom

asparagus

carrot

onion

A65

celery	corn	broccoli
cauliflower	spinach	parsley
asparagus	lettuce	cabbage
bok choy	eggplant	zucchini
acorn squash	butternut squash	garlic
pea	green bean	lima bean
black bean	kidney bean	brussels sprout
cucumber	tomato	carrot
radish	mushroom	artichoke
potato	sweet potato	yam
green pepper	red pepper	jalapeño pepper
chili pepper	beet	onion
scallion	turnip	

milk	low-fat milk	skim milk
chocolate milk	orange juice	cheese
butter	margarine	sour cream
cream cheese	cottage cheese	yogurt
tofu	eggs	apple juice
pineapple juice	grapefruit juice	tomato juice
grape juice	fruit punch	juice paks
powdered drink mix	soda	diet soda
bottled water	coffee	decaf
instant coffee	tea	herbal tea
cocoa		

roast beef	bologna	salami
ham	turkey	corned beef
pastrami	Swiss cheese	provolone
American cheese	mozzarella	cheddar cheese
potato salad	cole slaw	macaroni salad
pasta salad	seafood salad	ice cream
frozen vegetables	frozen dinners	frozen lemonade
frozen orange juice	potato chips	tortilla chips
pretzels	popcorn	nuts

cereal	cookies	crackers
noodles	macaroni	spaghetti
rice	soup	tuna fish
canned vegetables	canned fruit	jam
jelly	peanut butter	ketchup
mustard	relish	pickles
olives	salt	pepper
spices	soy sauce	mayonnaise
cooking oil	olive oil	vinegar
salsa	salad dressing	bread
rolls	English muffins	pita bread
cake	flour	sugar
cake mix		

napkins	paper cups	tissues
straws	paper plates	paper towels
toilet paper	sandwich bags	trash bags
soap	liquid soap	aluminum foil
plastic wrap	waxed paper	baby cereal
baby food	formula	wipes
diapers	cat food	dog food

bag	bottle	box
bunch	can	dozen
container	head	jar
roll	flour	ketchup
cereal	bananas	tuna fish
eggs	yogurt	lettuce
mayonnaise	paper towels	

A71

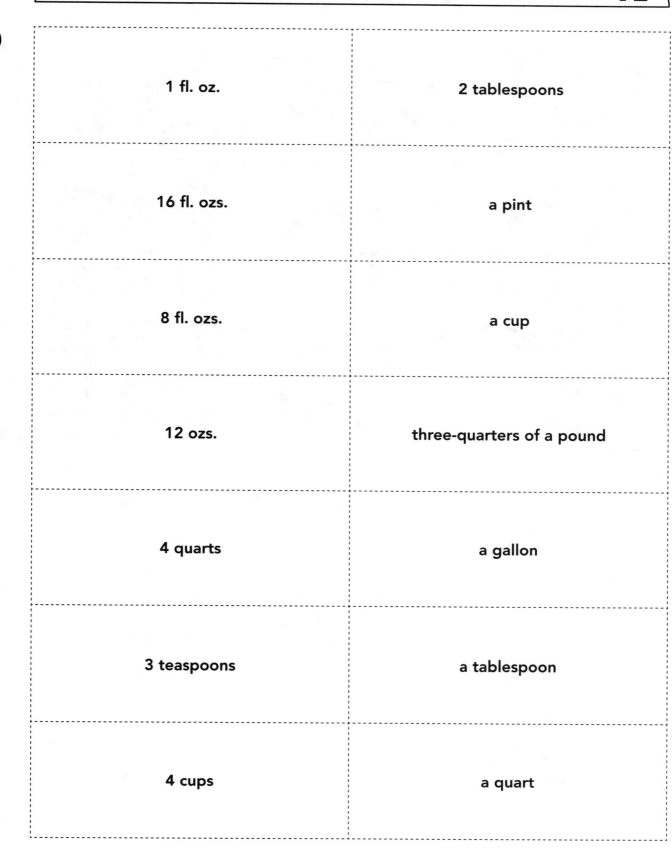

1 fl. oz.	2 tablespoons
16 fl. ozs.	a pint
8 fl. ozs.	a cup
12 ozs.	three-quarters of a pound
4 quarts	a gallon
3 teaspoons	a tablespoon
4 cups	a quart

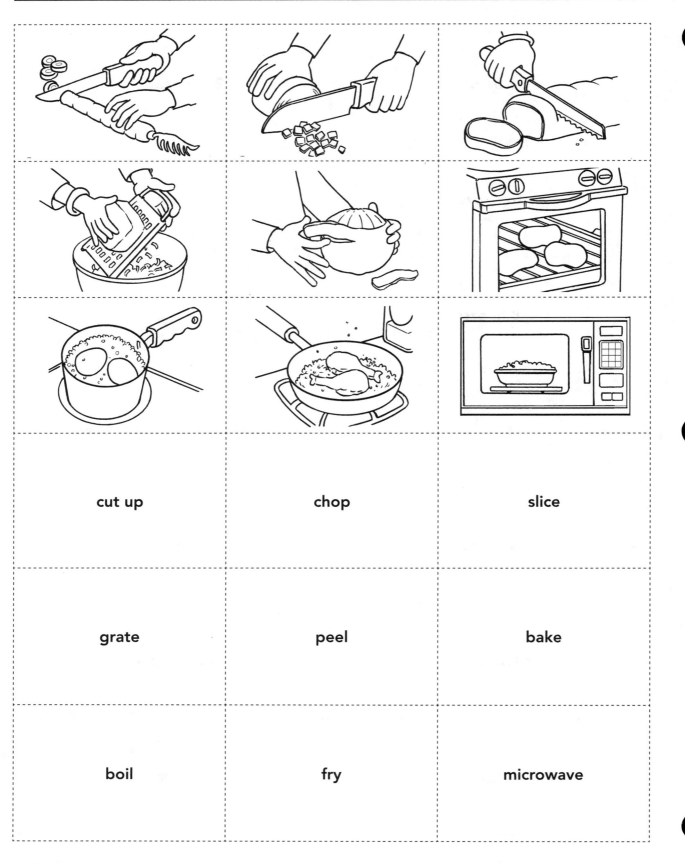

cut up	chop	slice
grate	peel	bake
boil	fry	microwave

ice cream scoop	can opener	bottle opener
vegetable peeler	egg beater	lid
pot	frying pan	double boiler
wok	ladle	strainer
spatula	steamer	knife
garlic press	grater	casserole dish
roasting pan	roasting rack	carving knife
saucepan	colander	kitchen timer
rolling pin	pie plate	paring knife
cookie sheet	cookie cutter	mixing bowl
whisk	measuring cup	measuring spoon
cake pan	wooden spoon	

hamburger	cheeseburger	hot dog
fish sandwich	chicken sandwich	fried chicken
french fries	nachos	taco
burrito	slice of pizza	bowl of chili
salad	ice cream	frozen yogurt
milkshake	soda	lids
paper cups	straws	napkins
plastic utensils	ketchup	mustard
mayonnaise	relish	salad dressing

A75

donut	muffin	bagel
bun	danish	biscuit
croissant	eggs	pancakes
waffles	toast	bacon
sausages	home fries	coffee
decaf coffee	tea	iced tea
lemonade	hot chocolate	milk
tuna fish sandwich	egg salad sandwich	chicken salad sandwich
ham and cheese sandwich	corned beef sandwich	BLT
roast beef sandwich	white bread	whole wheat bread
pita bread	pumpernickel	rye bread
roll	submarine roll	

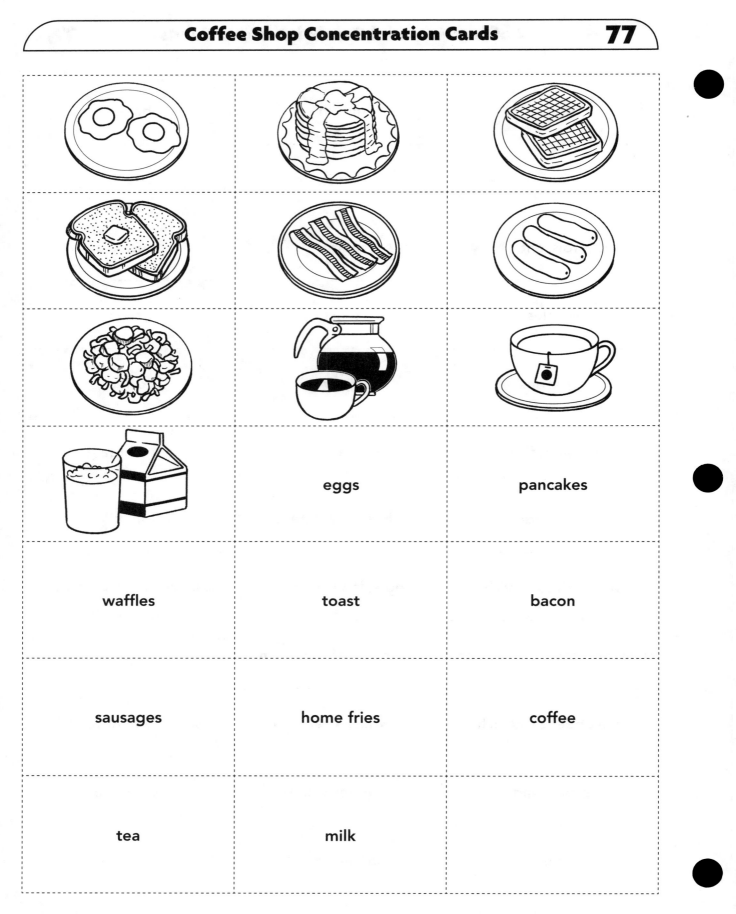

eggs

pancakes

waffles

toast

bacon

sausages

home fries

coffee

tea

milk

booth	table	high chair
booster seat	menu	bread basket
salad bar	dining room	kitchen
tray	dishroom	dessert cart
check	water glass	soup bowl
cup and saucer	napkin	knife
fork	spoon	

What's the host doing?	He's seating customers.
What's the hostess doing?	She's seating customers.
What's the customer doing?	She's paying the check and leaving a tip.
What's the busperson doing?	He's pouring water.
What's the waiter doing?	He's taking someone's order.
What's the waitress doing?	She's serving the meal.
What's the chef doing?	She's cooking the food.
What's the dishwasher doing?	He's washing the dishes.

fruit cup	tossed salad	meatloaf
baked chicken	broiled fish	baked potato
french fries	apple pie	ice cream sundae

set the table	seat a customer	pour water
take an order	serve a meal	clear the table
leave a tip	chop onions	break an egg
grate cheese	peel an apple	stir soup
barbecue hot dogs	eat pizza	drink a cup of hot tea
stir-fry vegetables	eat a banana	make a sandwich

1. _____ eats fast food twice a week.

2. _____ likes to eat fruit.

3. _____ likes to eat shellfish.

4. _____ leave big tips in restaurants.

5. _____ likes tomato juice.

6. _____ eats eggs for breakfast.

7. _____ eats lunch in a restaurant almost every day.

8. _____ doesn't eat meat.

9. _____ drinks three cups of coffee a day.

10. _____ doesn't like french fries.

Things that are green.

grass

broccoli

lettuce

Things that are red.

a stop sign

a tomato

spaghetti sauce

Things that are white.

snow

vanilla ice cream

teeth

Things that are blue.

blueberries

the sky

the ocean

Things that are yellow.

corn

a banana

a lemon

Things that are purple.

an eggplant

a cabbage

a plum

Things that are orange.

a carrot

an apricot

fire

A83

blouse	skirt	shirt
pants	sport shirt	jeans
jersey	dress	sweater
jacket	sport jacket	suit
three-piece suit	tie	uniform
T-shirt	shorts	maternity dress
jumpsuit	vest	jumper
blazer	tunic	leggings
overalls	turtleneck	tuxedo
bow tie	evening gown	

1. _____ wears a suit often.

2. _____ has a bow tie.

3. _____ has an evening gown.

4. _____ likes to wear neckties.

5. _____ likes to wear a tuxedo.

6. _____ wears shorts often.

7. _____ doesn't like to wear turtlenecks.

8. _____ wears a uniform to work.

9. _____ wears sport shirts to work.

10. _____ doesn't like to wear skirts.

coat	overcoat	hat
jacket	scarf	sweater jacket
tights	cap	leather jacket
baseball cap	windbreaker	raincoat
rain hat	trench coat	umbrella
poncho	rain jacket	rain boots
ski hat	ski jacket	gloves
ski mask	down jacket	mittens
parka	sunglasses	ear muffs
down vest		

pajamas	nightgown	nightshirt
bathrobe	slippers	blanket sleeper
undershirt	jockey shorts	boxer shorts
athletic supporter	long underwear	socks
bikini panties	briefs	bra
camisole	full slip	half slip
stockings	pantyhose	tights
knee socks	knee-highs	

tank top	running shorts	sweatband
jogging suit	sweatshirt	sweatpants
T-shirt	lycra shorts	leotard
swimsuit	cover-up	swimming trunks
shoes	high heels	pumps
loafers	sneakers	tennis shoes
running shoes	high-tops	sandals
thongs	boots	work boots
hiking boots	cowboy boots	moccasins

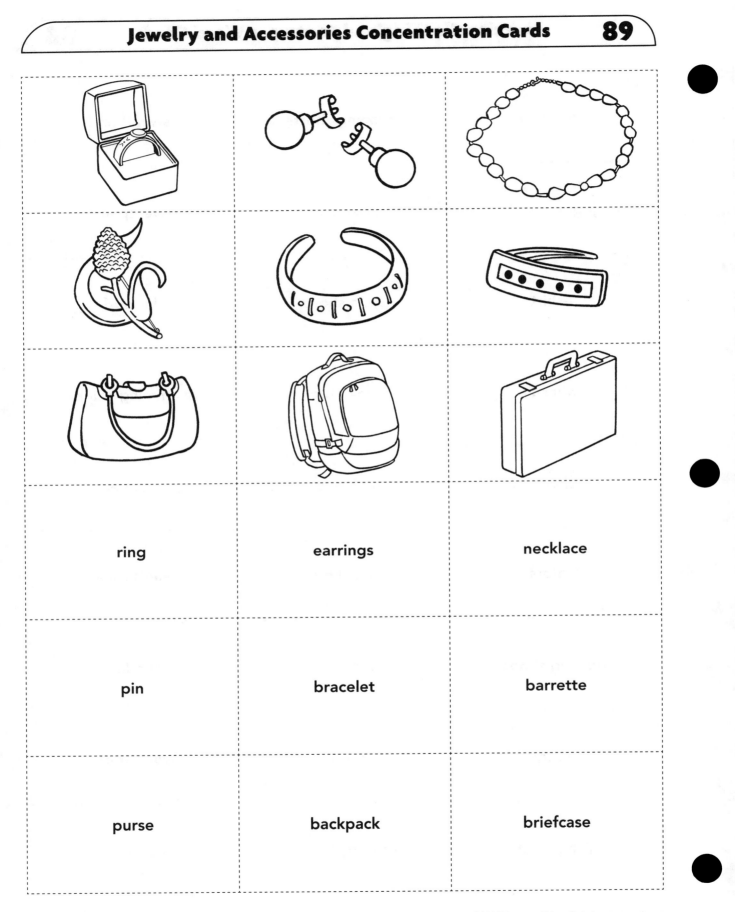

ring	earrings	necklace
pin	bracelet	barrette
purse	backpack	briefcase

ring	engagement ring	wedding ring
earrings	necklace	pearls
chain	beads	pin
locket	bracelet	cuff links
barrette	suspenders	handkerchief
belt	watch	key ring
wallet	change purse	purse
shoulder bag	tote bag	book bag
backpack	makeup bag	briefcase

long-sleeved shirt	short-sleeved shirt	sleeveless shirt
turtleneck	V-neck sweater	cardigan sweater
crewneck sweater	turtleneck sweater	knee-high socks
ankle socks	crew socks	pierced earring
clip-on earrings	striped	checked
plaid	polka-dotted	print
flowered	paisley	solid

long	short
tight	baggy
large	small
high	low
fancy	plain
heavy	light
dark	light
wide	narrow

The sleeves on your shirt are too long.

The sleeves on your shirt are too short.

Your pants are too long.

Your pants are too short.

Your pants are too baggy.

Your pants are too tight.

Your heels are too high.

The buttonholes on your shirt are too small.

Your collar is stained.

Your sleeve is stained.

The pocket on your pants is torn.

The pocket on your shirt is torn.

Your gloves are too large.

Your gloves are too small.

The zipper on your coat is broken.

A button on your shirt is missing.

These sleeves are too long!	You need to shorten them.
These sleeves are too short!	You need to lengthen them.
This jacket is too tight!	You need to let it out.
This jacket is too loose!	You need to take it in.
These shorts are stained!	You need to take them to the cleaners.
This suit is too dark!	Try this one. It's lighter.
This tie is too wide!	Try this one. It's narrower.
This coat is too light!	Try this one. It's heavier.
This shirt is too fancy!	Try this one. It's plainer.
These shoes are too small!	Try these. They're bigger.

laundry	laundry basket	laundry bag
washer	laundry detergent	fabric softener
bleach	dryer	lint trap
static cling remover	clothesline	clothespins
iron	ironing board	spray starch
closet	hanger	drawer
shelf		

sort the laundry

load the washer

unload the washer

put the clothes in the dryer

iron the clothes

fold the laundry

put the clothing away

1. _____ has a missing button.

2. _____ likes to wear jewelry.

3. _____ carries a briefcase to school or to work.

4. _____ likes paisley patterns.

5. _____ likes the color purple.

6. _____ never wears a tie.

7. _____ likes to wear baggy pants.

8. _____ irons long-sleeved shirts in less than three minutes.

9. _____ has a pair of overalls.

10. _____ never wears sandals.

I don't like the smell of this one.	Try *Delirious!* I think you'll find the smell more pleasant.
I want to return this shirt. The collar is stained.	No problem. I can give you a refund.
Can you please wrap this bathrobe?	Certainly. What kind of paper would you like?
I need something for a two-month-old baby.	How about this bib?
I'd like a cup of coffee, please.	Do you take it black, or with cream and sugar?
Women's Clothing. Second floor.	Excuse me. This is where I get off.
Are the gold ones on sale?	No. Just the silver.
Do you sell pots and pans in this department?	No. We sell stoves. You need to go to the second floor.

You can't find the Men's Clothing Department.

The sweater you bought has a hole in it.

The TV you bought is very heavy.
You can't carry it to your car.

You need a box for a gift you bought.

You want to buy a toaster.

You have to go to the bathroom.

You're shopping at the department store,
and you're very thirsty.

You want to buy a necklace.

You want to buy a jumper for your daughter.

You want to go upstairs to the third floor.

1. _____ goes shopping for clothes about once a week.

2. _____ goes shopping for clothes about once a month.

3. _____ never returns things to a store.

4. _____ likes to shop.

5. _____ shops only when there are sales.

6. _____ always keeps receipts.

7. _____ never keeps receipts.

8. _____ exchanged something last month.

9. _____ always tries on clothes before buying them.

10. _____ never tries on clothes before buying them.

TV	plasma TV	projection TV
LCD TV	portable TV	remote control
DVD player	DVD	VCR
video	video camera	battery pack
battery charger	radio	clock radio
shortwave radio	tape recorder	microphone
sound system	turntable	record
tuner	CD player	CD
tape deck	cassette	speakers
boom box	personal CD player	personal cassette player
headphones	personal digital audio player	video game system
video game	hand-held video game	

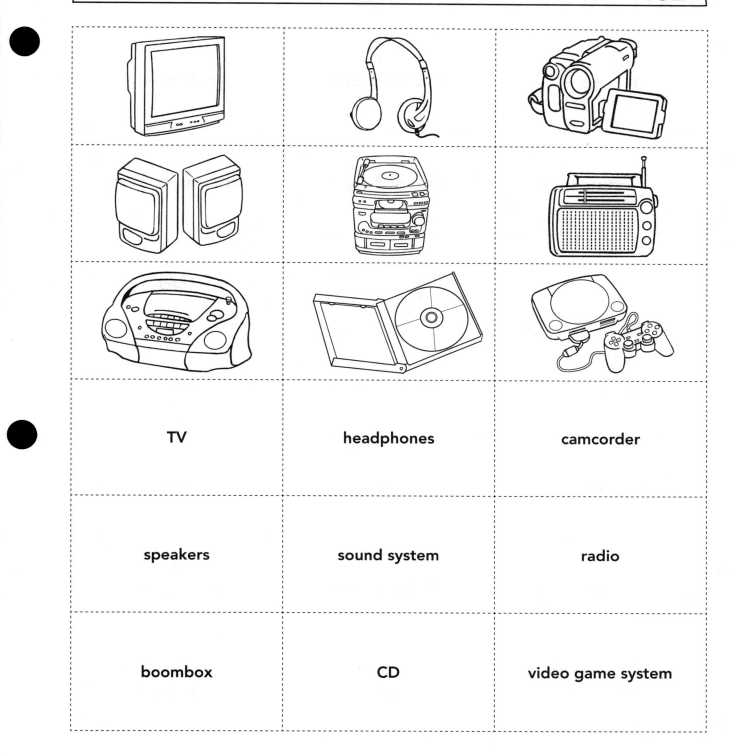

TV	headphones	camcorder
speakers	sound system	radio
boombox	CD	video game system

telephone	cordless phone	cell phone
battery	battery charger	answering machine
pager	electronic personal organizer	fax machine
calculator	adding machine	adapter
voltage regulator	camera	lens
film	digital camera	memory disk
zoom lens	flash	camera case
tripod	slide projector	screen

For Teacher's Guide
Page 194, Activities 1, 6
Page 195, Activities 8, 13
Page 201, Activity 4
Page 202, Activity 6

A103

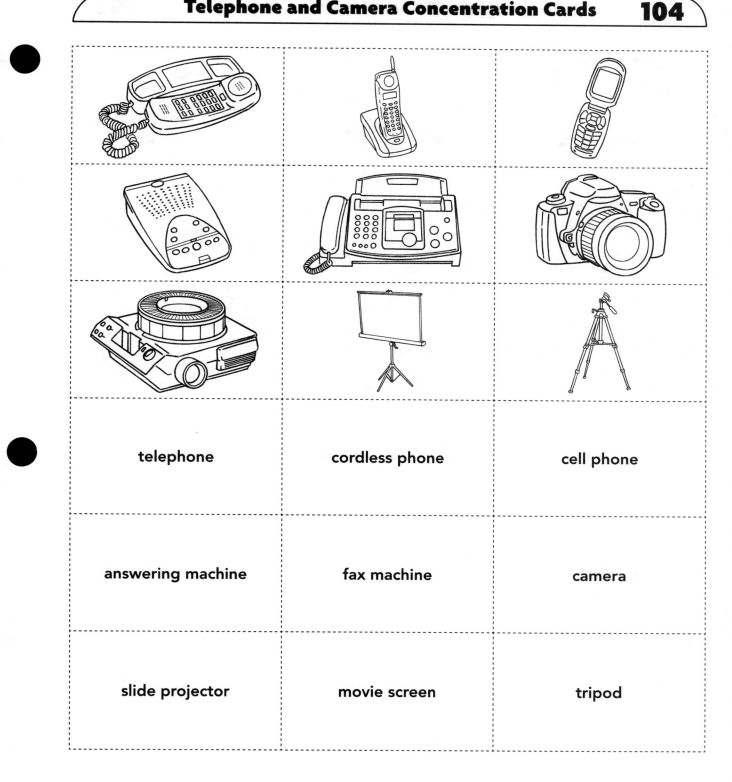

telephone	cordless phone	cell phone
answering machine	fax machine	camera
slide projector	movie screen	tripod

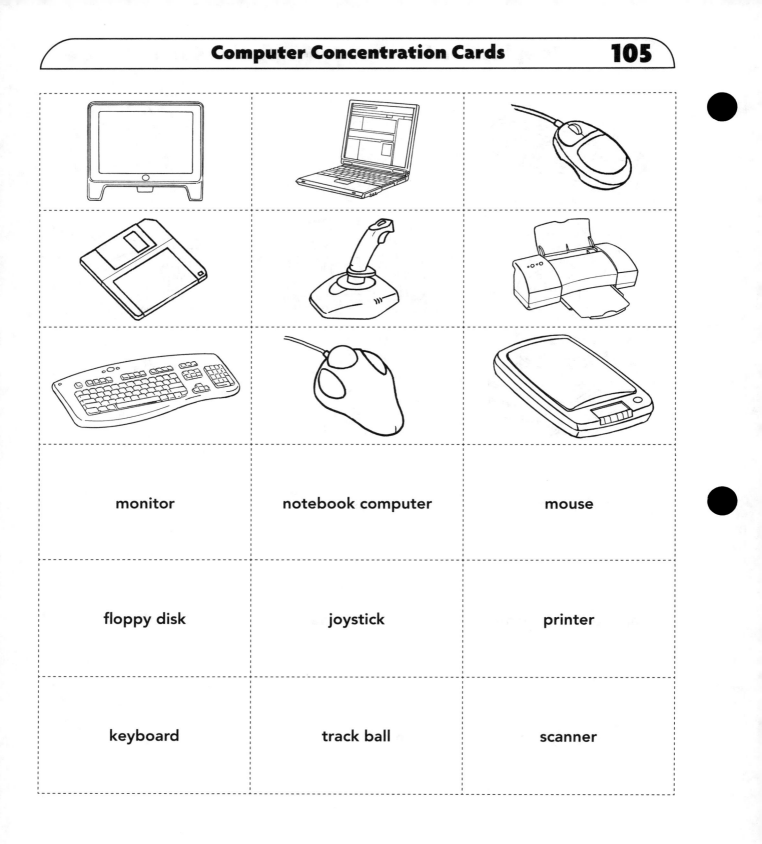

monitor	notebook computer	mouse
floppy disk	joystick	printer
keyboard	track ball	scanner

1. _____ uses a computer for work.

2. _____ plays games on the computer.

3. _____ uses a track ball.

4. _____ has a notebook computer.

5. _____ spends at least twenty hours a week on the computer.

6. _____ doesn't like to use computers.

7. _____ uses educational software.

8. _____ uses spreadsheet software.

9. _____ prefers to use a desktop computer.

10. _____ spends less than two hours a week at a computer.

board game	puzzle	construction set
blocks	rubber ball	beach ball
pail and shovel	doll	doll clothing
doll house	doll house furniture	action figure
stuffed animal	matchbox car	toy truck
racing car set	train set	model kit
science kit	walkie-talkie	hula hoop
jump rope	bubble soap	trading cards
crayons	markers	coloring book
construction paper	paint set	clay
stickers	bicycle	tricycle
wagon	skateboard	swing set
play house	kiddie pool	

For Teacher's Guide
Page 199, Activities 4, 6
Page 200, Activities 8, 9
Page 201, Activity 4
Page 202, Activity 6

A107

action figure	jump rope	doll
toy truck	markers	tricycle
wagon	swing set	stuffed animal

It's 10:00 at night, and I need some money.

Use your ATM card!

I want to take a course at a local university, but I don't have enough money.

Here's a loan application for you to fill out!

I want to send in a fee with my school application, but the university won't accept personal checks.

How about a money order?

I have a very expensive ring that I don't want to keep in my apartment.

You should rent a safe deposit box!

I'd like to put my paycheck in the bank.

Here's a deposit slip!

I'm going on a trip, and I really don't want to take a lot of cash.

How about traveler's checks?

I have a question about the balance in my bank account.

Ask me! I'm a bank teller!

I want to change this money from my trip to Asia.

Ask the teller to exchange your currency!

Insert the ATM card.

Enter your PIN number.

Select the transaction: "Make a deposit."

Enter the money amount to be deposited.

Put the deposit into the ATM.

Remove your card.

Take your receipt.

I'm moving next week.	You need to fill out this change-of-address form.
I have to a pay a bill, and I don't have a checking account.	Buy a money order.
This letter has to get to San Francisco by tomorrow.	Send it by overnight mail.
I need to send these heavy books, but it doesn't matter if it takes a week or two.	Send them by parcel post.
This letter is very important. How can I know the person received it?	Send it by certified mail.
The line for the postal clerk is too long! I only need two stamps!	Use the stamp machine.
How much does this parcel weigh?	Let's put it on the scale.
How do I know when the person mailed this letter?	Look at the postmark.
How do I know who sent me this letter?	Look at the return address.

police station	fire station	hospital
town hall	recreation center	dump
child-care center	senior center	church
synagogue	mosque	temple
police officer	emergency operator	police car
firefighter	fire engine	EMT
emergency room	ambulance	mayor
meeting room	activities director	gym
game room	swimming pool	sanitation worker
recycling center	child-care worker	nursery
playroom	eldercare worker	

I need to talk to the mayor!	Go to city hall.
Where can my son play basketball?	Call the recreation center.
Where can I take my garbage?	Go to the dump.
I cut my finger very badly!	I'll take you to the emergency room.
My elderly mother is lonely and bored at home.	Call the senior center.
Where do the firefighters sleep?	In the fire station.
I need to find someone to take care of my two-year-old daughter.	Call the child-care center.

What do you need if you want to check out a book at the library?

Name a periodical that is published every day.

Where do you find books in other languages in the public library?

Where do many children go after school?

Who drives a fire engine?

Where is the city manager's office?

Where can young children go while their parents work?

What is the name of a Hindu's place of worship?

What is the difference between a mugging and a robbery?

Name four kinds of crime.

Name three forms of payment.

What is the name of a Christian's place of worship?

What do you need to make a deposit in a bank?

What should you write on an envelope before you send it?

Describe the steps when you use an ATM machine.

What is a parcel?

Name three kinds of emergencies.

Name five different kinds of bills.

Name three post office occupations.

What is an online catalog in a library?

Name three bank occupations.

Where do you get a passport application in the United States?

head	hair	forehead
face	eye	eyebrow
eyelid	eyelashes	iris
pupil	cornea	ear
nose	cheek	jaw
mouth	lip	tooth
gums	tongue	chin
neck	shoulder	chest
abdomen	breast	back
arm	elbow	waist
hip	buttocks	leg

thigh	knee	calf
shin	hand	wrist
thumb	finger	palm
fingernail	knuckle	skin
foot	ankle	heel
toe	toenail	brain
throat	esophagus	lungs
heart	liver	gallbladder
stomach	large intestine	small intestine
pancreas	kidneys	bladder
veins	arteries	

I can't talk!	No wonder! You have laryngitis!
I can't lift any heavy things!	I know. You have a terrible backache!
I'm having trouble breathing!	That's because you're congested.
My whole body is itchy!	I'm not surprised. You have a terrible rash!
My dentist says I have a big cavity.	That's probably why you have a bad toothache.
I sat in the sun too long this afternoon.	You must have a terrible sunburn!
I don't feel very good. It must be something I ate.	Do you have a bad stomachache?
My head hurts!	That's a shame. You must have a very bad headache!
I was playing tennis, and I hurt my foot very badly.	Did you sprain your ankle?
The room is spinning around and around!	Oh, no! You must be terribly dizzy!

What should you do when you are in a park and . . .

your friend starts choking on some food? _____

_____

you cut your foot on a rock? _____

_____

you get a blister from new hiking boots? _____

_____

your friend gets a piece of glass in his hand? _____

_____

you twist your ankle? _____

_____

your friend faints? _____

_____

your friend is swimming and stops breathing? _____

_____

your friend falls and breaks her arm? _____

_____

you have a terrible headache? _____

_____

you get a bee sting? _____

_____

you get a rash on your arms? _____

_____

you break a tooth? _____

_____

first-aid manual	first-aid kit	bandage
antiseptic cleansing wipe	sterile pad	hydrogen peroxide
antibiotic ointment	gauze	adhesive tape
tweezers	antihistamine cream	Ace™ bandage
aspirin	non-aspirin pain reliever	CPR
rescue breathing	the Heimlich maneuver	splint
tourniquet		

| measure *your* height and weight | take *your* temperature | check *your* blood pressure |

| draw some blood | ask *you* some questions about *your* health | examine *your* eyes |

| listen to *your* heart | take a chest X-ray | |

A120

scale	thermometer	blood pressure gauge
needle	examination room	examination table
eye chart	stethoscope	X-ray machine

For Teacher's Guide
Page 232, Activity 5
Page 252, Activity 8

I cut my foot on a piece of glass!	You might need some stitches.
I fell down and twisted my shoulder!	You should keep your arm in a sling.
The doctor gave me a prescription.	Then let's go to the pharmacy!
Why do you have a cast on your leg?	I broke my ankle!
Is it going to hurt?	No. We'll give you a shot of Novocaine first.
The wound is swelling a lot.	Here's an ice pack!
What does the dentist do after he drills the cavity?	He fills the tooth.
Who's going to clean my teeth?	The dental hygienist.
I need to make another appointment.	Why don't you speak to the receptionist?
This bandage is falling off!	Here's some more tape.

clean the wound	close the wound	dress the wound
clean *your* teeth	examine *your* teeth	give *you* a shot of anesthetic
drill the cavity	fill the tooth	waiting room
receptionist	insurance card	medical history form
examination room	doctor	patient
nurse	alcohol	cotton balls
stitches	gauze	tape
shot	crutches	ice pack
prescription	sling	cast
brace	dental hygienist	mask
gloves	dentist	dental assistant
drill	filling	

What should I do?

I have asthma. _____

_____

I'm sad all the time. _____

_____

I'm too heavy. _____

_____

I have a stiff neck. _____

_____

I twisted my ankle. _____

_____

I'm exhausted. _____

_____

I get ear infections all the time. _____

_____

I have a sore throat. _____

_____

I have the flu. _____

_____

I'm allergic to dust. _____

_____

I have a broken ankle, and I can't walk! | You should get a wheelchair.

My back hurts! | You should use a heating pad.

My throat hurts! | Try gargling. That should help.

I don't like to eat fruit or vegetables. | Then you should take a vitamin every day.

I don't feel like eating! | Okay, but you should drink plenty of fluids.

I work at a desk all day. | You should get some exercise.

I gained twenty pounds this year. | You need to go on a diet.

My husband and I aren't happy together anymore. | Maybe you should get some counseling.

I have terrible allergies at home. | Maybe you should get an air purifier.

rest in bed	drink fluids	gargle
go on a diet	exercise	take vitamins
see a specialist	get acupuncture	heating pad
humidifier	air purifier	cane
walker	wheelchair	blood work
tests	physical therapy	surgery
counseling	braces	

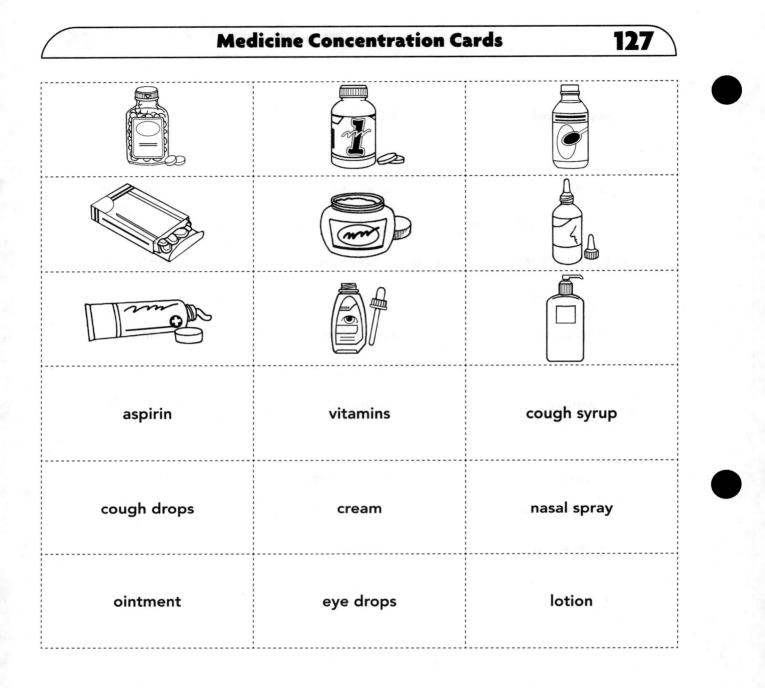

aspirin	vitamins	cough syrup
cough drops	cream	nasal spray
ointment	eye drops	lotion

A127

My skin is very itchy!	You should use this lotion.
I can't stop coughing!	Why don't you get some cough drops?
I've been feeling very tired recently.	Maybe you should take some vitamins.
How many aspirin should I take for my headache?	Two tablets.
How much cough syrup should I take?	Two teaspoons.
My eyes are red and itchy.	Maybe you need eye drops!
I ate too much!	Here! I have some antacid tablets.
My nose is terribly stuffy!	You should try some nasal spray.
I have a headache and a stomachache.	Why don't you take some non-aspirin pain reliever?
I have a headache, a cough, and a sore throat.	You need some cold tablets!

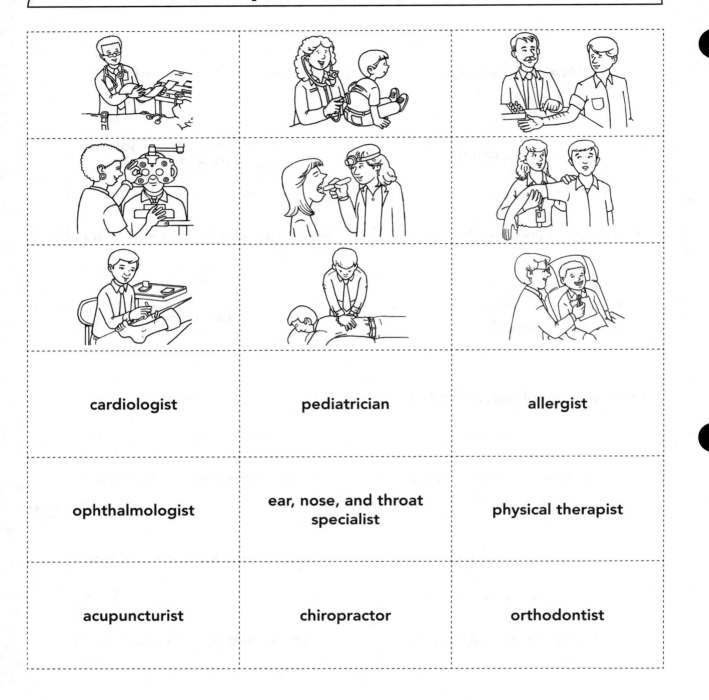

cardiologist	pediatrician	allergist
ophthalmologist	ear, nose, and throat specialist	physical therapist
acupuncturist	chiropractor	orthodontist

toothbrush	toothpaste	dental floss
mouthwash	teeth whitener	soap
bubble bath	shower cap	shampoo
conditioner	hair dryer	comb
hair brush	curling iron	hairspray
hair gel	bobby pin	barrette
hairclip	shaving cream	razor
razor blade	electric shaver	styptic pencil
aftershave	nail file	emery board

nail clipper	nail brush	scissors
nail polish	nail polish remover	deodorant
hand lotion	body lotion	powder
cologne	sunscreen	blush
foundation	moisturizer	face powder
eyeliner	eye shadow	mascara
eyebrow pencil	lipstick	shoe polish
shoelaces		

brush *my* teeth	floss *my* teeth	gargle
whiten *my* teeth	take a bath	take a shower
wash *my* hair	dry *my* hair	comb *my* hair
brush *my* hair	style *my* hair	shave
do *my* nails	put on deodorant	put on makeup
polish *my* shoes		

baby food	bib	bottle
nipple	formula	vitamins
disposable diaper	cloth diaper	diaper pin
baby wipes	ointment	baby powder
training pants	baby shampoo	cotton swab
baby lotion	pacifier	teething ring
child-care center	child-care worker	rocking chair
cubby	toys	

Name four parts of a hand.	Name four internal organs.
Name three parts of a leg.	What parts of the body does a gastroenterologist treat?
Name three parts of the eye.	Name five parts of the face.
Name five items in a first-aid kit.	Name three symptoms of the flu.
Name two symptoms of strep throat.	Name one symptom of asthma.
Tell three things a doctor does during a medical exam.	How does a doctor take care of a sprained ankle?
Why does a dentist give a patient a shot of Novocaine?	When does a doctor prescribe physical therapy?
Who puts braces on a patient?	Name six medical specialists.
What's the difference between a counselor and a psychiatrist?	Name four kinds of medicine.
Name three occupations in a hospital.	Name four things you can find in a hospital room.
Name three things a person can use to shave.	Name five baby-care items.
Name four things a woman uses to do her nails.	Name three kinds of makeup.

My best friend is feeling depressed.	I can recommend a good psychiatrist.
I hurt my back while I was lifting a heavy box.	You should go to a chiropractor.
I get ear infections all the time.	You should see an ENT specialist.
I have a toothache.	You should see a dentist.
I have chest pains a lot these days	You should see a cardiologist!
I have a stomachache all the time.	You should see a gastroenterologist.
I'm going to have a baby!	Do you have a good obstetrician?
My child needs to see a doctor.	I can recommend a good pediatrician.
My daughter has terrible allergies.	I can recommend a good allergist.
I think I need to see an eye doctor.	I can recommend a good ophthalmologist.

I want my child to get to know other children and learn songs and art.	Send your child to preschool!
I want to become a doctor.	You need to go to medical school!
I want to learn English for my job.	You should study in an adult school.
I don't want to go to college. I want to learn how to fix computers now.	You should go to vocational school!
I want to go to college.	Study hard! You have to get good grades in high school.
I want to become a lawyer.	You need to go to law school!
I just finished elementary school.	Junior high school is next!
I just completed middle school!	High school is next!
I'm almost finished with college!	Graduate school is next!
I want to get a two-year degree in nursing.	Look at the community college. They have a health program.

Type of School	Name and Location of School	Dates of Attendance

main office	principal's office	nurse's office
guidance office	classroom	hallway
locker	science lab	gym
locker room	track	bleachers
field	auditorium	cafeteria
library		

Excuse me. Where's the locker room?	It's right next to the gym.
I'm hungry.	I am, too! Let's go to the cafeteria.
I think someone took my wallet.	You should go to the principal's office.
I need to find some books for my research project.	Go to the school library.
I want to find out about different universities.	Go to the guidance office. You'll find a lot of information there.
I want to run a mile today.	I do, too. Let's go over to the track.
Where is the best place to watch the game?	Sit in the bleachers.
I can't find my books!	They're probably in your locker.
I'd love to play soccer now.	Let's go over to the field!
I think I have a fever.	You should go to the nurse's office.
Where is the school play going to be?	In the auditorium.

math	English	history
geography	government	science
biology	chemistry	physics
health	computer science	Spanish
French	home economics	industrial arts
business education	physical education	driver's education
art	music	

1. _____ likes math.

2. _____ never studied computer science.

3. _____ speaks French.

4. _____ speaks Spanish.

5. _____ never studied chemistry.

6. _____ studied business education.

7. _____ liked music class the best.

8. _____ liked art class the best.

9. _____ liked history the best.

10. _____ never studied driver's education.

band	orchestra	chorus
drama	football	cheerleading
student government	community service	school newspaper
yearbook	literary magazine	A.V. crew
debate club	computer club	international club
chess club		

Extracurricular Activity Questionnaire   143

1. _____ plays/played in the school band.

2. _____ sings/sang in the chorus.

3. _____ participates/participated in drama productions.

4. _____ plays/played on the football team.

5. _____ does/did community service.

6. _____ writes/wrote articles for the school newspaper.

7. _____ serves/served in student government.

8. _____ is/was in the computer club.

9. _____ has a school yearbook.

height	width	depth
length	inch	foot
yard	centimeter	meter
distance	mile	kilometer
straight line	curved line	parallel lines
perpendicular lines	square	rectangle
right triangle	isosceles triangle	circle
ellipse	cube	cylinder
sphere	cone	pyramid

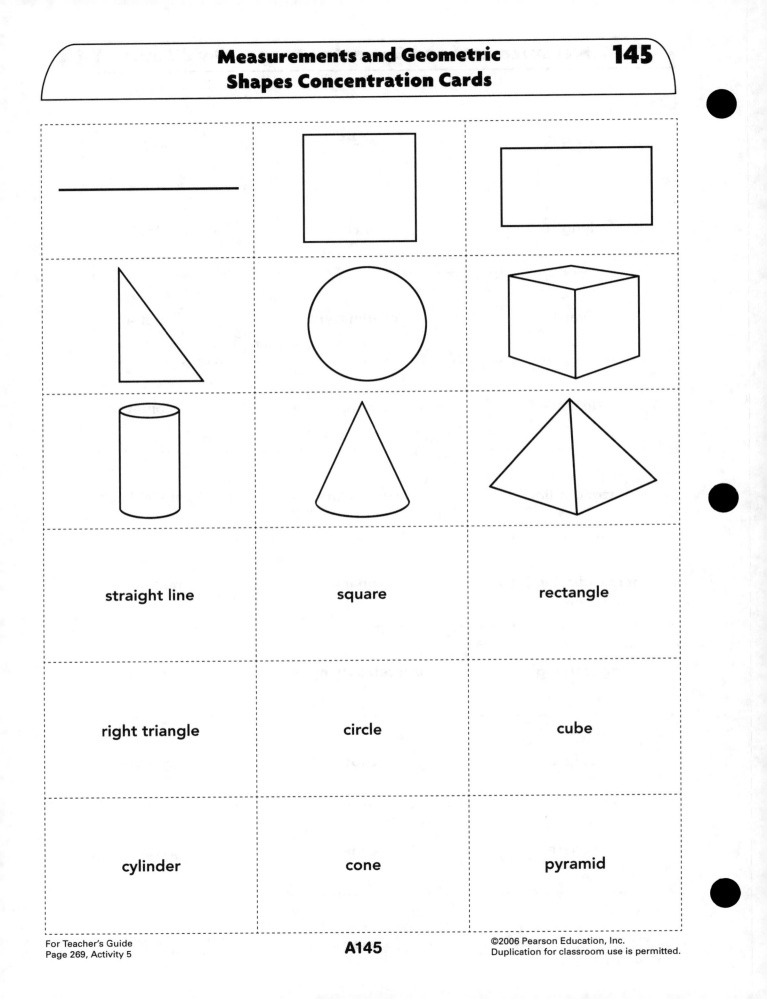

straight line	square	rectangle
right triangle	circle	cube
cylinder	cone	pyramid

A145

declarative sentence	interrogative sentence	imperative sentence
exclamatory sentence	noun	verb
preposition	article	adjective
pronoun	adverb	period
question mark	exclamation point	comma
apostrophe	quotation marks	colon
semi-colon		

1. _____ writes e-mails every day.

2. _____ writes instant messages every day.

3. _____ writes a letter at least once a month.

4. _____ reads the newspaper almost every day.

5. _____ received a thank-you note this year.

6. _____ likes to read magazines more than newspapers.

7. _____ reads at least two novels a year.

8. _____ reads at least one non-fiction book a year.

9. _____ likes poetry.

10. _____ likes biographies.

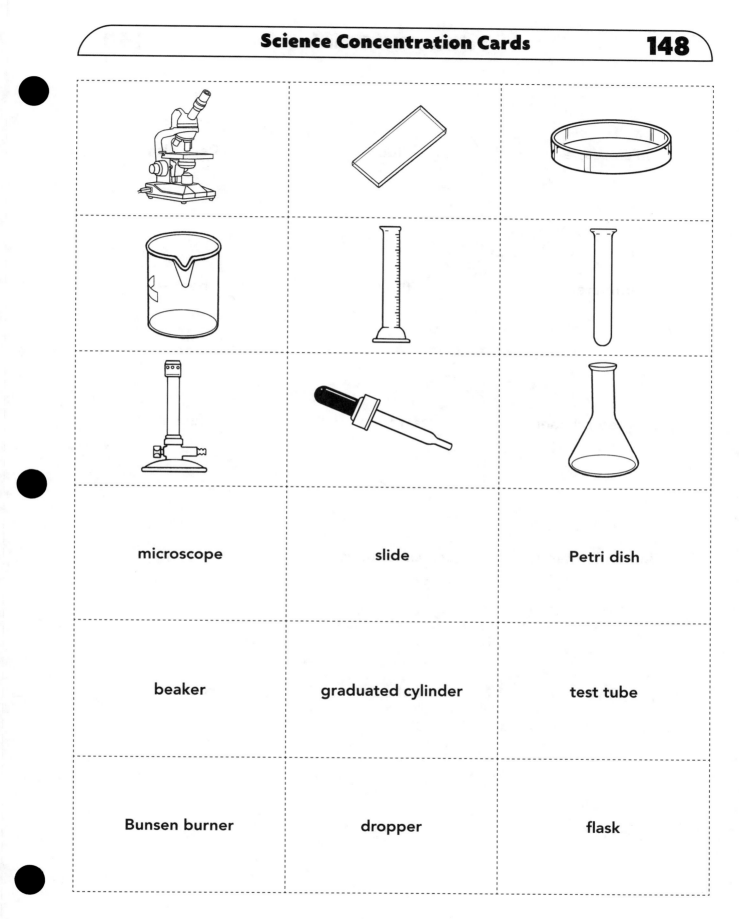

microscope

slide

Petri dish

beaker

graduated cylinder

test tube

Bunsen burner

dropper

flask

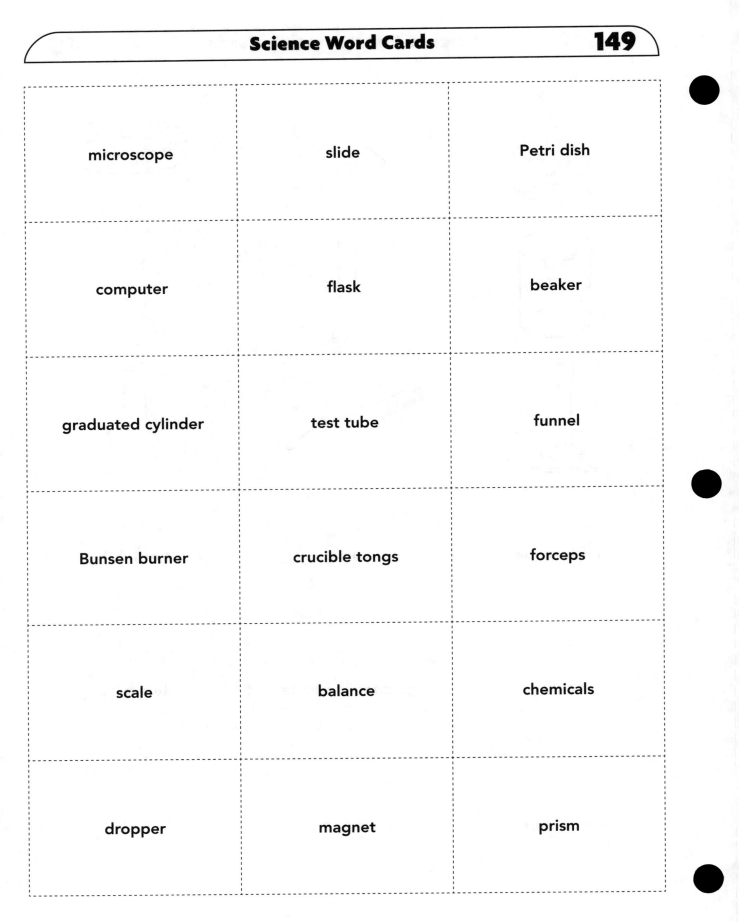

microscope	slide	Petri dish
computer	flask	beaker
graduated cylinder	test tube	funnel
Bunsen burner	crucible tongs	forceps
scale	balance	chemicals
dropper	magnet	prism

State the problem.

Form a hypothesis.

Plan a procedure.

Do the procedure.

Record observations of the experiment.

Draw conclusions.

Name three types of schools for adults.	Name three types of schools for children and teenagers.
Name four parts of a high school.	Name five extracurricular activities.
Name seven school subjects.	Name three types of math.
Name four fractions.	Name three units of measurement.
Name three geometric shapes.	Name two kinds of lines.
Name four kinds of punctuation marks.	Name four parts of speech.
Name the steps in the writing process.	Name four different ways to write to a friend.
Name three kinds of books.	Name four kinds of bodies of water.
Name three things in a mountain range.	Give the name of an important river, desert, rainforest, and peninsula.
Name six things you can find in a science classroom.	Name the steps of the scientific method.
Name two things in space exploration.	Name five planets.

A151

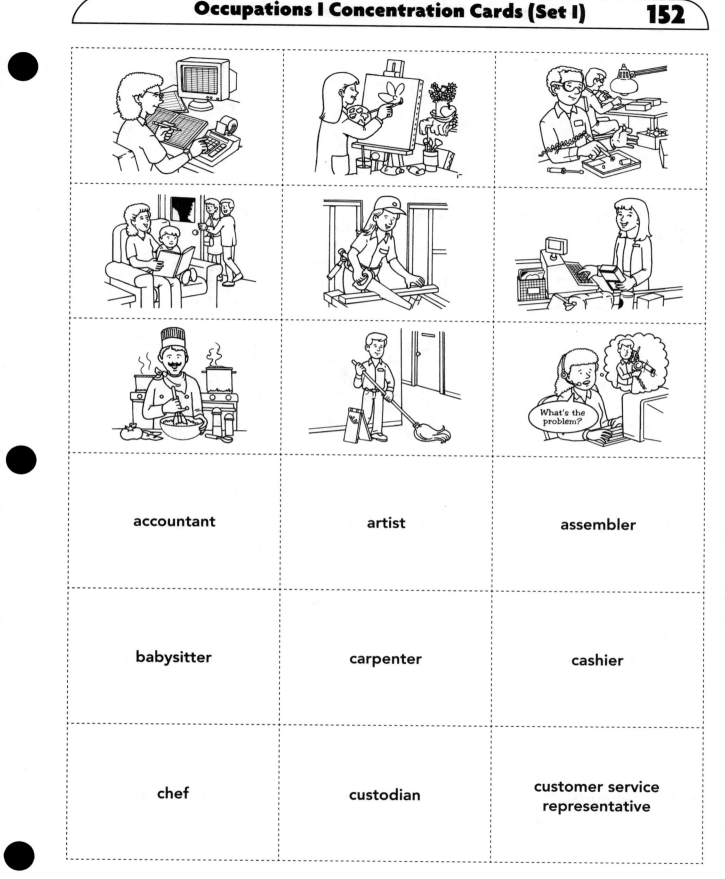

accountant	artist	assembler
babysitter	carpenter	cashier
chef	custodian	customer service representative

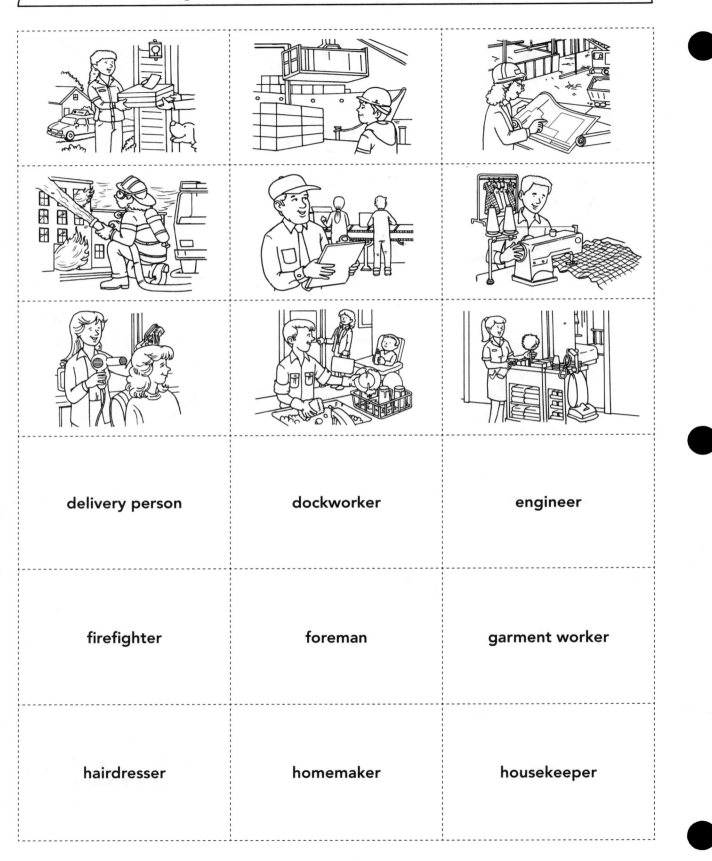

delivery person	dockworker	engineer
firefighter	foreman	garment worker
hairdresser	homemaker	housekeeper

A153

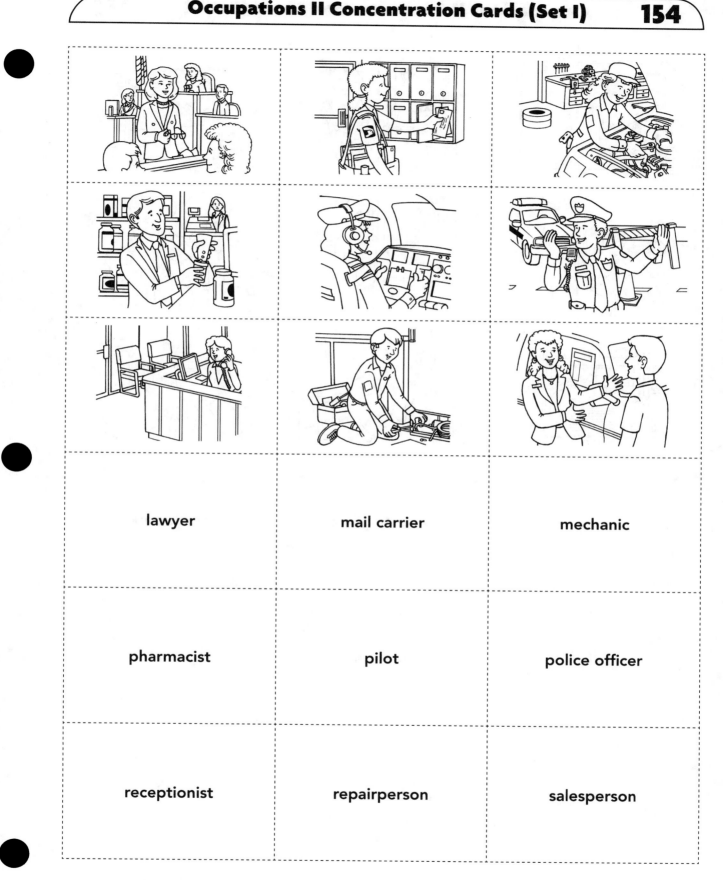

lawyer	mail carrier	mechanic
pharmacist	pilot	police officer
receptionist	repairperson	salesperson

secretary

security guard

stock clerk

tailor

teacher

translator

truck driver

veterinarian

welder

accountant	actor	actress
architect	artist	assembler
babysitter	baker	barber
bricklayer	businessman	businesswoman
butcher	carpenter	cashier
chef	child day-care worker	computer software engineer
construction worker	custodian	

customer service representative	data entry clerk	delivery person
dockworker	engineer	factory worker
farmer	firefighter	fisher
food-service worker	foreman	gardener
garment worker	hairdresser	health-care aide
home health aide	homemaker	housekeeper

journalist	lawyer	machine operator
mail carrier	manager	manicurist
mechanic	medical assistant	messenger
mover	musician	painter
pharmacist	photographer	pilot
police officer	postal worker	receptionist
repairperson	salesperson	

sanitation worker	secretary	security guard
serviceman	servicewoman	stock clerk
shopkeeper	supervisor	tailor
teacher	telemarketer	translator
travel agent	truck driver	veterinarian
waiter	waitress	welder

accountant	a calculator
baker	an oven
carpenter	a hammer
hairdresser	a hairbrush
custodian	a broom
gardener	a rake
butcher	a knife
fisher	a boat

journalist	a notebook
mechanic	a wrench
painter	a brush
photographer	a camera
pilot	an airplane
tailor	a tape measure
teacher	a textbook
waiter	a tray

act	assemble	assist
bake	build	clean
cook	deliver	design
draw	drive	file
fly	grow	guard
manage	mow	operate
paint	play	prepare
repair	sell	serve
sew	sing	speak
supervise	take care of	take inventory
teach	translate	type
use a cash register	wash dishes	write

So you want to be an architect with our company?	Yes. I design buildings very well.
So you want to be a pilot for our company?	Yes. I fly airplanes very well.
So you want to be a musician in our band?	Yes. I play the guitar very well.
So you want to be a landscaper?	Yes. I mow lawns very well.
So you want to be a delivery person?	Yes. I drive very well.
So you want to be a chef in our kitchen?	Yes. I cook very well.
So you want to be a translator?	Yes. I speak Chinese and English very well.
So you want to be a tailor?	Yes. I sew very well.
So you want to be a secretary?	Yes. I type and file very well.

1. _____ has a resume.

2. _____ filled out a job application.

3. _____ had a job interview.

4. _____ found a job through a want ad in the newspaper.

5. _____ works part-time.

6. _____ works full-time.

7. _____ gets good benefits.

8. _____ is looking for a job right now.

9. _____ reads the classified ads almost every day.

10. _____ works Monday through Friday.

reception area	conference room	mailroom
work area	office	supply room
storage room	employee lounge	coat rack
coat closet	conference table	presentation board
postal scale	postage meter	mailbox
cubicle	swivel chair	typewriter
adding machine	photocopier	paper shredder
paper cutter	filing cabinet	computer workstation
supply cabinet	storage cabinet	vending machine
water cooler	coffee machine	message board

Where's the coat rack?	It's in the reception area.
Where's the presentation board?	It's in the conference room.
Where's the postal scale?	It's in the mailroom.
Where's the photocopier?	It's in the work area.
Where's the boss?	She's in her office.
Where's the supply cabinet?	It's in the supply room.
Where's the storage cabinet?	It's in the storage room.
Where's the vending machine?	It's in the employee lounge.

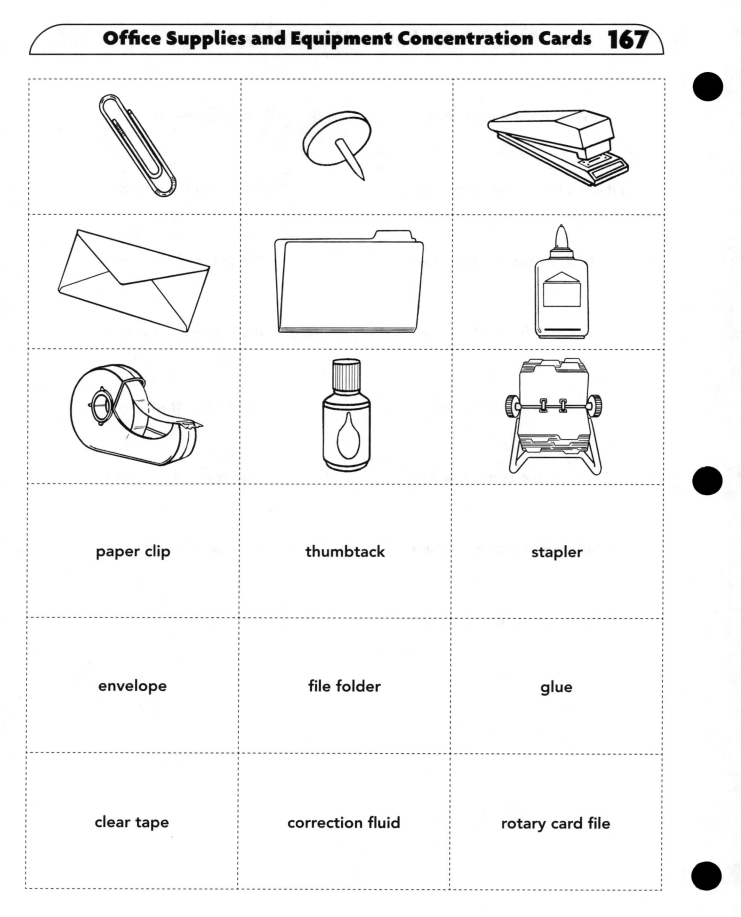

paper clip	thumbtack	stapler
envelope	file folder	glue
clear tape	correction fluid	rotary card file

A167

stapler	letter tray	rotary card file
desk pad	appointment book	clipboard
note pad	electric pencil sharpener	desk calendar
Post-It note pad	personal planner	paper clip
rubber band	staple	thumbtack
pushpin	legal pad	file folder
index card	envelope	stationery
mailer	mailing label	typewriter cartridge
ink cartridge	rubber stamp	ink pad
glue stick	glue	rubber cement
correction fluid	cellophane tape	packing tape

I need that big box on the top shelf. | I'll get the forklift.

My friend is looking for a job. | Tell her to go to the personnel office.

Where do I put my personal belongings? | In the locker room.

Where does the factory keep its merchandise? | In the warehouse.

We need to send these toys to our customers right away! | I'll take them to the shipping department immediately!

I need to take these toys to the loading dock. | Use this hand truck.

My finger is bleeding! | I'll get the first-aid kit!

I have to leave a little early today for an appointment. | You need to speak to the line supervisor.

I found a mistake on my paycheck. | The payroll office can help you.

These teddy bears have only one eye! | You should tell the quality control supervisor!

shovel	wheelbarrow	blueprints
jackhammer	sledgehammer	pickax
ladder	toolbelt	tape measure
trowel	scaffolding	cement mixer
cement	dump truck	front-end loader
cherry picker	crane	bulldozer
backhoe	concrete mixer truck	concrete
pickup truck	trailer	drywall
lumber	plywood	wire
insulation	brick	shingle
pipe	girder	

I have to remove a large piece of that rock.

Here's a pneumatic drill!

I need something to apply the cement between the bricks.

I have a trowel you can use.

We have to move some more girders to the top of the building.

No problem. I'll get the crane started.

I want to see what my new house is going to look like.

I have the blueprints right here.

We need to dig a deep hole for the foundation.

I'll get the backhoe started.

How will they move all this dirt away from the foundation?

With a bulldozer.

How can he get up to work on those high wires?

He uses a cherry picker.

Where's my hammer?

Look in your toolbelt!

How long is this piece of lumber?

Here! Use my tape measure.

These bricks are too heavy to carry.

Use that wheelbarrow over there.

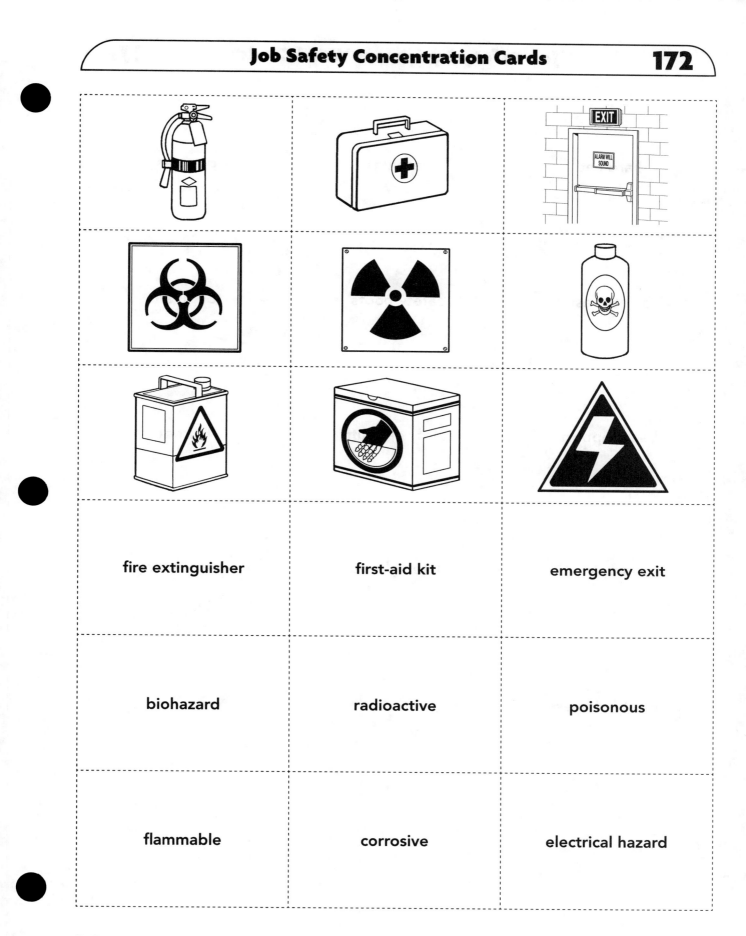

fire extinguisher

first-aid kit

emergency exit

biohazard

radioactive

poisonous

flammable

corrosive

electrical hazard

hard hat	earplugs	goggles
safety vest	safety boots	toe guard
back support	safety earmuffs	hairnet
mask	latex gloves	respirator
safety glasses		

1. _____ wears latex gloves at work.

2. _____ wears a hairnet at work.

3. _____ wears a mask at work.

4. _____ occasionally wears back support.

5. _____ never wears earplugs.

6. _____ knows the location of all the emergency exits in the school.

7. _____ has a first-aid kit at work.

8. _____ knows the location of the fire extinguisher at work.

9. _____ saw an accident at work.

Name three office occupations.

Name four outdoor occupations.

Name three occupations that require a college degree.

Name three factory occupations.

Name six job skills.

Name four steps in a job search.

Name three areas in a factory.

Name three areas in an office workplace.

Name six kinds of office supplies.

Name three office machines.

Name four construction vehicles.

Name three kinds of hazards.

Name six pieces of job safety equipment.

Name three occupations that use a computer.

Name three health occupations.

Name five occupations in the food preparation or food-service industry.

Name two types of job ads.

Name three occupations related to children.

Name four occupations related to constructing an office building.

Name three occupations that require travel.

Name two public safety occupations.

Explain what a landscaper, an architect, and a cashier do.

ticket window	platform	bus stop
ferry	bus route	fare
token	taxi stand	subway station
where passengers purchase tickets	where passengers wait for a train	where passengers wait for a bus
a boat that travels back and forth between two points	where the bus goes	the price passengers pay
a coin passengers use in some subway systems	where passengers can get a cab	where passengers wait for a subway

bus stop	bus route	passenger
bus fare	transfer	bus driver
baggage compartment	ticket counter	ticket
train station	ticket window	arrival and departure board
information booth	schedule	track
conductor	platform	subway station
subway token	fare card	fare card machine
turnstile	taxi stand	taxi
meter	cab driver	ferry

A177

Do you know where Bus 88 goes?	Let's look at the bus route.
I think my brother's train is late, but I'm not sure.	Check the arrival and departure board.
I need to take two buses to get there.	Don't forget to get a transfer!
I don't want to take this suitcase on the bus with me!	Put it in the baggage compartment!
How do I know how much the taxi ride costs?	Look at the meter!
I need to be in Cleveland by noon.	Then don't take the bus. Take a train!
How do people get on and off the island?	They take the ferry.
I think I'm on the wrong train!	Go ask the conductor.
I can't find a cab anywhere!	There's a taxi stand over there!
Why can't I get through this turnstile?	You need a fare card!

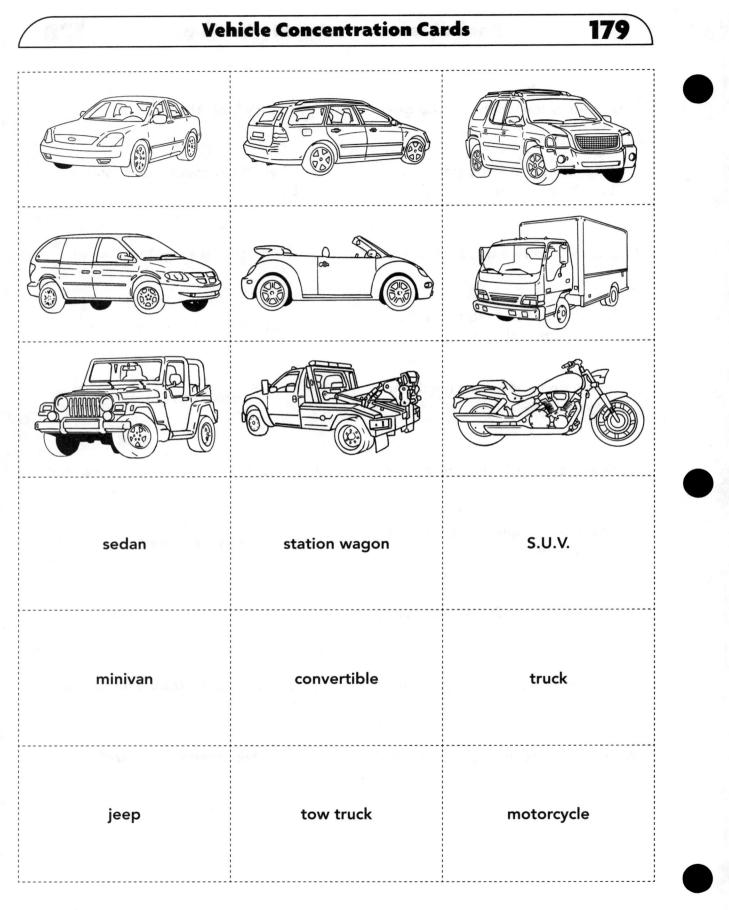

sedan	station wagon	S.U.V.
minivan	convertible	truck
jeep	tow truck	motorcycle

sedan	hatchback	convertible
sports car	hybrid	station wagon
S.U.V.	jeep	van
minivan	pickup truck	limousine
tow truck	camper	moving van
truck	tractor trailer	bicycle
moped	motor scooter	motorcycle

antenna	muffler	jack
battery	radiator	gas gauge
odometer	glove compartment	trunk
receives radio signals	reduces engine noise	lifts the car to change a flat tire
stores electricity	cools the engine	indicates fuel level
indicates miles the car has gone	provides storage space inside the car	storage area in the back of a sedan

headlight	bumper	turn signal
parking light	fender	tire
hubcap	hood	windshield
windshield wipers	side mirror	antenna
sunroof	roof rack	rear window
rear defroster	trunk	taillight
brake light	backup light	license plate
tailpipe	muffler	transmission
gas tank	jack	spare tire
lug wrench	flare	jumper cables
engine	spark plugs	air filter
fuel injection system	battery	dipstick
alternator	radiator	fan belt
radiator hose	air pump	gas pump

nozzle	gas cap	gas
oil	coolant	air
visor	rearview mirror	dashboard
gas gauge	temperature gauge	power outlet
speedometer	odometer	warning lights
vent	turn signal	steering wheel
air bag	horn	ignition
radio	CD player	air conditioning
heater	defroster	navigation system
glove compartment	emergency brake	brake
accelerator	gearshift	automatic transmission
clutch	stickshift	manual transmission
door lock	door handle	shoulder harness
armrest	headrest	seat belt

There's ice on my windshield!	Turn on the defroster!
It's raining!	Turn on your windshield wipers!
It's really cold in this car!	Turn on the heater!
I can't believe how hot it is!	Turn on the air conditioner!
I want to pass that car.	Put on your turn signal!
The sun is in my eyes!	Lower your visor!
I think we need gas!	Check the gas gauge!
Are we low on oil?	I'm not sure. I'll look at the dipstick.
I need to change a flat tire!	I'll get the spare and the jack!
I'm afraid the car might roll down the hill!	Put on the emergency brake!
Is the car ahead of us going to stop?	Don't you see the brake lights on?
Uh-oh! The car won't slow down!	The accelerator is probably stuck!

no left turn	no right turn	no U-turn
right turn only	pedestrian crossing	railroad crossing
school crossing	merging traffic	slippery when wet

ticket counter	X-ray machine	boarding pass
ticket	immigration officer	claim check
customs officer	gate	baggage carousel
where passengers purchase tickets	inspects carry-on luggage	indicates a passenger's seat number
indicates the flight number, destination, and fare	checks passports	identifies baggage
checks merchandise passengers have in their luggage	where passengers board a plane for a flight	where passengers pick up their luggage

ticket	ticket counter	ticket agent
suitcase	arrival and departure monitor	security checkpoint
security officer	X-ray machine	carry-on bag
metal detector	check-in counter	boarding pass
gate	boarding area	baggage claim area
baggage carousel	baggage	baggage cart
luggage carrier	garment bag	baggage claim check
customs	customs officer	customs declaration form
immigration	immigration officer	passport
visa		

cockpit	pilot	co-pilot
lavatory	flight attendant	overhead compartment
aisle	window seat	middle seat
aisle seat	Fasten Seat Belt sign	No Smoking sign
call button	oxygen mask	emergency exit
tray table	emergency card instruction	air sickness bag
life vest	runway	terminal
control tower	airplane	

take off your shoes

empty your pockets

put your bag on the conveyor belt

put your computer on a tray

walk through the metal detector

check in at the gate

get your boarding pass

board the plane

stow your carry-on bag

find your seat

fasten your seat belt

1. _____ likes an aisle seat.

2. _____ likes a window seat.

3. _____ likes the middle seat.

4. _____ has been in the cockpit of an airplane.

5. _____ never takes a carry-on bag.

6. _____ doesn't like to travel in airplanes.

7. _____ likes to travel in airplanes.

8. _____ travels in an airplane at least once a year.

9. _____ always looks for the emergency exits on an airplane.

front desk	concierge desk	restaurant
lobby	pool	ice machine
room service	valet parking	guest room
where guests check in	where guests get information about the area	where guests can eat breakfast
where guests can meet people	where guests can swim	where guests can get ice
brings food to the room	a service that parks the car for a hotel guest	where the guest stays

A191

doorman	valet parking	parking attendant
bellhop	luggage cart	bell captain
lobby	front desk	desk clerk
guest	concierge desk	concierge
restaurant	meeting room	gift shop
pool	exercise room	elevator
ice machine	hallway	room key
housekeeping cart	housekeeper	guest room
room service		

Name three types of public transportation.

Name three types of cars.

Name three types of trucks.

Name three types of cars that carry more than four passengers.

Name five car engine parts.

Name five instruments on a car dashboard.

Name three parts of a seat in a car.

Name three things a car needs.

Name six things you see on a highway.

Name six different traffic signs.

Name six different prepositions of motion. Give an example for each.

Name the four compass directions.

Name three road test instructions.

Name four areas in an airport.

Name five things you see in an airplane.

Name three safety devices on an airplane.

Name four hotel occupations.

Name three things you must do to go through a security checkpoint in an airport.

Name four parts of a hotel.

Name two windows on a car.

sew	knit	crochet
paint	draw	do embroidery
do needlepoint	do woodworking	do origami
make pottery	collect stamps	collect coins
build models	go bird-watching	play cards
play board games	go online	photography
astronomy		

stamp album	magnifying glass	coin collection
coin catalog	model kit	glue
acrylic paint	binoculars	field guide
deck of cards	club	diamond
heart	spade	chess
checkers	backgammon	Monopoly
dice	Scrabble	web browser
web address	camera	telescope

1. _____ likes to sew.

2. _____ knows how to knit.

3. _____ likes to paint with watercolor.

4. _____ can draw a good picture of an animal.

5. _____ does origami.

6. _____ has a collection.

7. _____ goes online every day.

8. _____ plays chess often.

9. _____ knows how to play Scrabble.

museum	art gallery	concert
play	amusement park	historic site
national park	craft fair	yard sale
flea market	park	beach
mountains	aquarium	botanical gardens
planetarium	zoo	movies
carnival	fair	

1. _____ went to a museum recently.

2. _____ went to an art gallery last month.

3. _____ went to a concert last month.

4. _____ saw a play this year.

5. _____ went to an amusement park recently.

6. _____ went to a U.S. national park a few years ago.

7. _____ went to an aquarium this year.

8. _____ bought something at a yard sale.

9. _____ went to a planetarium this year.

10. _____ went to the movies last week.

bicycle path	duck pond	picnic area
trash can	grill	picnic table
water fountain	jogging path	bench
tennis court	ballfield	fountain
bike rack	merry-go-round	skateboard ramp
playground	climbing wall	swings
climber	slide	seesaw
sandbox	sand	

lifeguard	lifeguard stand	life preserver
snack bar	rock	swimmer
wave	surfer	vendor
sunbather	sand castle	seashell
beach umbrella	beach chair	beach towel
boogie board	surfboard	kite
beach blanket	sun hat	sunglasses
sunscreen	pail	shovel
beach ball	cooler	

1. _____ doesn't like to go to the beach.

2. _____ likes to sunbathe.

3. _____ likes to build sand castles.

4. _____ collects shells or rocks.

5. _____ likes to walk on the beach.

6. _____ knows how to surf.

7. _____ always wears sunscreen at the beach.

8. _____ likes to fly kites.

9. _____ went to the beach last weekend.

10. _____ never wears a sun hat.

camping	tent	sleeping bag
tent stakes	hatchet	lantern
camping stove	Swiss army knife	insect repellant
matches	hiking	backpack
hiking boots	canteen	trail map
compass	GPS device	rock climbing
rope	harness	mountain biking
mountain bike	bike helmet	picnic
picnic blanket	thermos	picnic basket

I'm afraid I might fall!	Don't worry! You'll have a rope and harness!
How will we be able to cook?	We'll take a camping stove!
I'm afraid I might be cold at night!	You'll have a nice warm sleeping bag! Don't worry!
What if it rains?	We'll stay dry in the tent!
I can't go hiking in my regular shoes!	You'll wear hiking boots!
We'll need to drink water!	Don't worry! I have two canteens!
We'll probably get lost!	No, we won't. We'll have a trail map!
How will we know what direction we're walking in?	Don't be so nervous! We'll use a compass!
I'm sure I won't be able to bring everything I need!	Of course you will! You'll have a large backpack!
It's very dark in the woods!	Don't get so upset! We'll take a lantern with us!

jogging	running	walking
inline skating	cycling	skateboarding
bowling	horseback riding	tennis
badminton	racquetball	ping pong
golf	Frisbee	billiards
martial arts	gymnastics	weightlifting
archery	box	wrestle
work out		

For Teacher's Guide
Page 354, Activity 2
Page 355, Activities 10, 11

A204

©2006 Pearson Education, Inc.
Duplication for classroom use is permitted.

jogging shoes	inline skates	knee pads
bicycle	helmet	skateboard
elbow pads	bowling ball	bowling shoes
saddle	reins	stirrups
tennis racket	tennis ball	badminton racket
birdie	safety goggles	racquetball
racquet	paddle	ping pong table

net	ping pong ball	golf clubs
golf ball	flying disc	pool table
billiard balls	pool stick	balance beam
parallel bars	mat	horse
trampoline	barbell	weights
bow and arrow	target	boxing gloves
wrestling mat	exercise equipment	exercise bike
rowing machine	treadmill	

baseball	softball	football
lacrosse	hockey	basketball
volleyball	soccer	

1. _____ likes to watch baseball.

2. _____ likes to watch football.

3. _____ likes to watch ice hockey.

4. _____ likes to watch basketball.

5. _____ likes to play soccer.

6. _____ likes to play volleyball.

7. _____ likes to play softball.

8. _____ knows the rules of baseball.

9. _____ knows the rules of football.

10. _____ knows the rules of lacrosse.

baseball	bat	batting helmet
baseball uniform	catcher's mask	baseball glove
catcher's mitt	softball	softball glove
football	football helmet	shoulder pads
lacrosse ball	face guard	lacrosse stick
hockey puck	hockey stick	hockey mask
hockey glove	hockey skates	basketball
backboard	basketball hoop	volleyball
volleyball net	soccer ball	shinguards

downhill skiing	skis	ski boots
bindings	ski poles	cross-country skiing
cross-country skis	skating	ice skates
blade	skate guards	figure skating
figure skates	snowboarding	snowboard
sledding	sled	saucer
bobsledding	bobsled	snowmobiling
snowmobile		

sailing	canoeing	rowing
kayaking	white-water rafting	swimming
snorkeling	scuba diving	surfing
windsurfing	waterskiing	fishing

sailboat	life jacket	canoe
paddles	rowboat	oars
kayak	raft	swimsuit
goggles	bathing cap	mask
snorkel	fins	wet suit
air tank	diving mask	surfboard
sailboard	sail	water skis
towrope	fishing rod	reel
fishing line	fishing net	bait

hit	pitch	throw
catch	pass	kick
serve	bounce	dribble
shoot	stretch	bend
walk	run	hop
skip	jump	reach
swing	lift	swim
dive	shoot	push-up
sit-up	jumping jack	deep knee bend
somersault	cartwheel	handstand

A213

play	theater	actor
actress	concert	concert hall
orchestra	musician	conductor
band	opera	opera singer
ballet	ballet dancer	ballerina
music club	singer	movies
movie theater	movie screen	comedy club
comedian		

violin	viola	cello
bass	acoustic guitar	electric guitar
banjo	harp	piccolo
flute	clarinet	oboe
recorder	saxophone	bassoon
trumpet	trombone	French horn
tuba	drums	cymbals
tambourine	xylophone	piano
electric keyboard	organ	accordion
harmonica		

Name three types of crafts.

Name two kinds of collections.

Name three board games.

Name three suits in a deck of cards.

Name five places to go on the weekend.

Name five parts of a park and playground.

Name six things people take with them to the beach.

Name three pieces of camping equipment.

Name four kinds of outdoor recreation.

Name eight kinds of individual sports.

Name four team sports.

Name three pieces of baseball equipment.

Name three pieces of hockey equipment.

Name five winter sports.

Name five water sports.

Name sport and exercise actions for a basketball player.

Name sport and exercise actions for a baseball player.

Name four kinds of entertainment.

Name six kinds of music.

Name five kinds of movies.

farmhouse	farmer	garden
scarecrow	hay	hired hand
barn	stable	horse
barnyard	turkey	goat
lamb	rooster	pig pen
pig	chicken coop	chicken
hen house	hen	crop
irrigation system	tractor	field
pasture	cow	sheep
orchard	fruit tree	farm worker
alfalfa	corn	cotton
rice	soybeans	wheat

moose	polar bear	deer	wolf
black bear	mountain lion	grizzly bear	buffalo
coyote	fox	skunk	porcupine
rabbit	beaver	raccoon	possum
horse	pony	donkey	armadillo
bat	worm	slug	monkey
anteater	llama	jaguar	mouse
rat	chipmunk	squirrel	gopher
prairie dog			

cat	kitten	dog	puppy
hamster	gerbil	guinea pig	goldfish
canary	parakeet	antelope	baboon
rhinoceros	panda	orangutan	panther
gibbon	tiger	camel	elephant
hyena	lion	giraffe	zebra
chimpanzee	hippopotamus	leopard	gorilla
kangaroo	koala	platypus	

robin

hummingbird

seagull

pigeon

eagle

duck

fly

bee

butterfly

robin	blue jay	cardinal	crow
seagull	woodpecker	pigeon	owl
hawk	eagle	swan	hummingbird
duck	sparrow	goose	penguin
flamingo	crane	stork	pelican
peacock	parrot	ostrich	fly
ladybug	firefly	moth	caterpillar
butterfly	tick	mosquito	dragonfly
spider	praying mantis	wasp	bee
grasshopper	beetle	scorpion	centipede
cricket			

A221

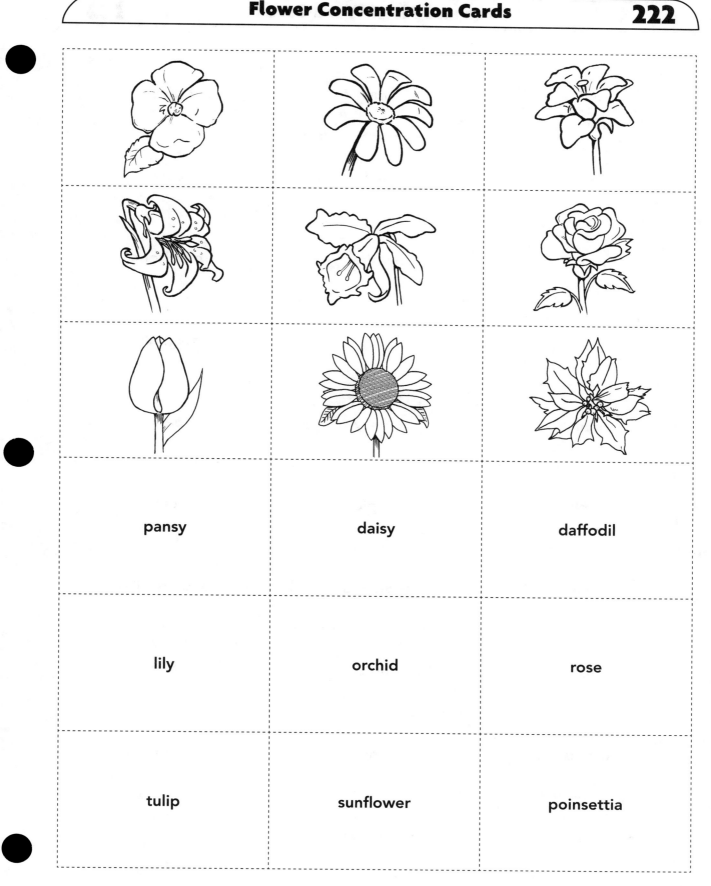

pansy	daisy	daffodil
lily	orchid	rose
tulip	sunflower	poinsettia

leaf	twig	branch
limb	trunk	bark
root	needle	pine cone
dogwood	holly	magnolia
elm	cherry	palm
birch	maple	oak
pine	redwood	weeping willow
bush	shrub	fern
cactus	vine	poison ivy
poison sumac	poison oak	

petal	stem	bud
thorn	bulb	chrysanthemum
daffodil	daisy	marigold
carnation	gardenia	lily
iris	pansy	petunia
orchid	rose	sunflower
crocus	tulip	geranium
violet	poinsettia	jasmine
hibiscus		

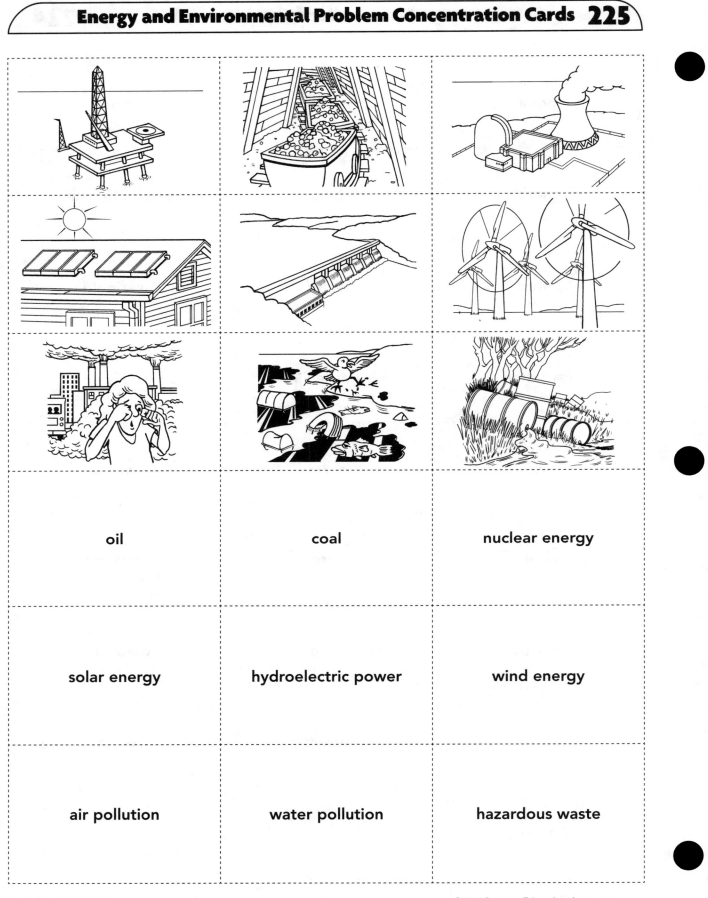

oil	coal	nuclear energy
solar energy	hydroelectric power	wind energy
air pollution	water pollution	hazardous waste

oil	natural gas	coal
nuclear energy	solar energy	hydroelectric energy
wind energy	geothermal energy	recycle
save energy	conserve water	carpool
air pollution	water pollution	hazardous waste
acid rain	radiation	global warming

earthquake	hurricane	tornado
flood	tsunami	forest fire
avalanche	blizzard	volcanic eruption

earthquake	hurricane	typhoon
blizzard	tornado	flood
tsunami	drought	forest fire
wildfire	landslide	mudslide
avalanche	volcanic eruption	

Name four parts of a farm.

Name five farm animals.

Name five animals in North America.

Name three animals in Asia.

Name four animals in Africa.

Name two animals that have spots.

Name three parts of a bird.

Name ten kinds of birds.

Name two birds that can't fly.

Name four insects that fly.

Name five kinds of fish.

Name seven sea animals.

Name two kinds of snakes.

Name two kinds of lizards.

Name six kinds of trees.

Name eight kinds of flowers.

Name three parts of a flower.

Name four sources of energy.

Name two types of conservation.

Name five natural disasters.

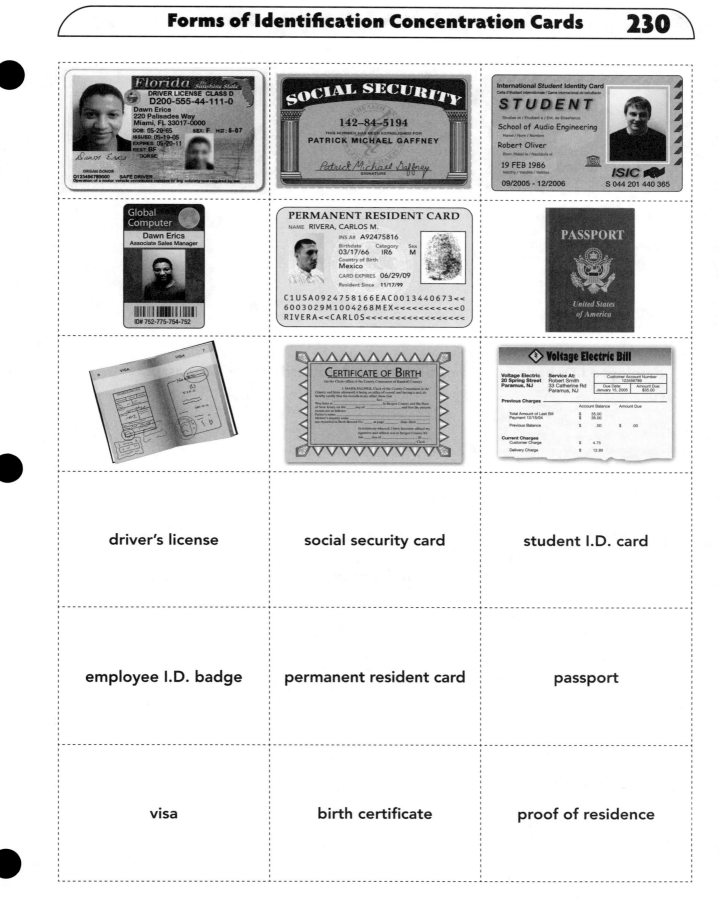

driver's license	social security card	student I.D. card
employee I.D. badge	permanent resident card	passport
visa	birth certificate	proof of residence

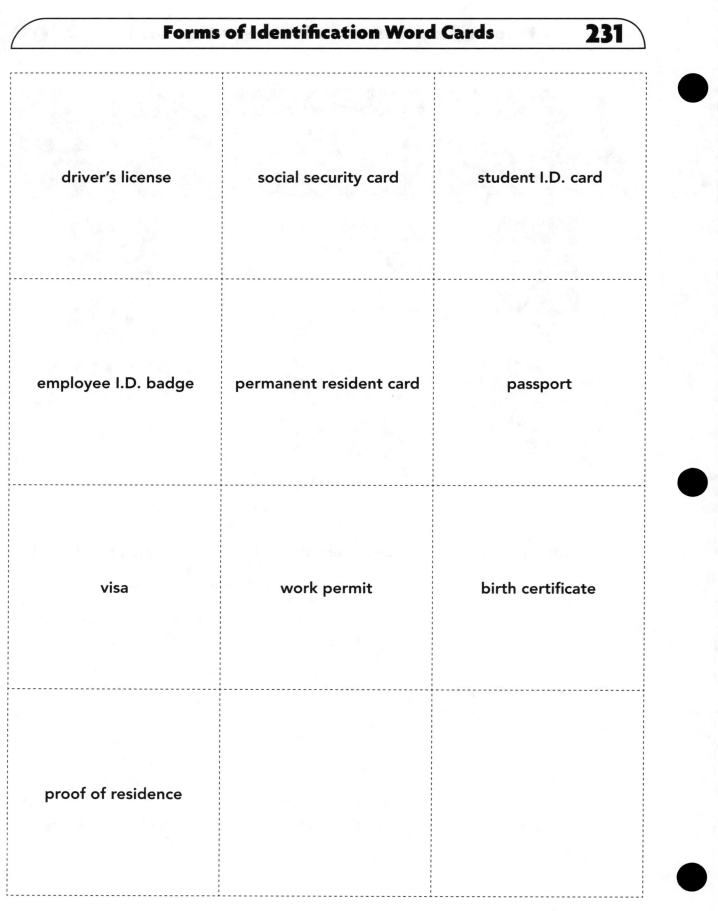

driver's license

social security card

student I.D. card

employee I.D. badge

permanent resident card

passport

visa

work permit

birth certificate

proof of residence

legislative branch	makes the laws	house of representative
representative	senate	senator
Capitol Building	executive branch	enforces the laws
president	vice-president	cabinet
White House	judicial branch	explains the laws
Supreme Court	Supreme Court justices	chief justice
Supreme Court Building		

Colonists come to Jamestown, Virginia.

The colonies declare independence.

The Revolutionary War ends.

Representatives write the U.S. Constitution.

George Washington becomes the first U.S. president.

The Civil War begins.

President Lincoln signs the Emancipation Proclamation.

World War I begins.

The Great Depression begins.

World War II begins.

The civil rights movement begins.

The Vietnam War begins.

The Persian Gulf War begins.

The man is arrested.

The man is booked at the police station.

The suspect hires an attorney.

The suspect appears in court.

The suspect stands trial.

The defendant is convicted.

The convict is sentenced.

The convict goes to jail.

The convict is released.

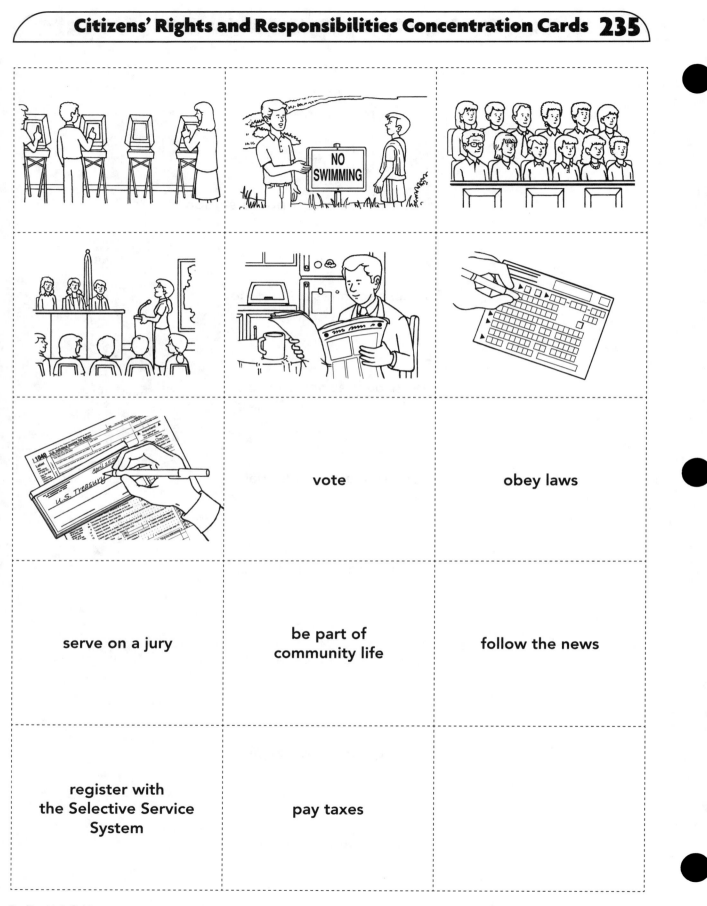

	vote	obey laws
serve on a jury	be part of community life	follow the news
register with the Selective Service System	pay taxes	

You apply for citizenship.

You learn about U.S. government and history.

You take the citizenship test.

You have a naturalization interview.

You attend a naturalization ceremony.

You recite the Oath of Allegiance.

Name six forms of identification.

Name one occupation in the legislative branch of the U.S. government.

Name one occupation in the judicial branch of the U.S. government.

Name one occupation in the executive branch of the U.S. government.

Name two important buildings in Washington, D.C.

Name three freedoms that are guaranteed under the First Amendment.

Describe three amendments to the U.S. Constitution.

What is the "supreme law of the land"?

Name two religious holidays.

Name three U.S. national holidays.

Explain what happens after a person is arrested. (at least four steps)

Name three occupations of people who work in the U.S. courts.

Describe four steps on the path to citizenship.

Name one American inventor.

Name the three branches of the U.S. government.

What is the Bill of Rights?

Name two important events in the US in the 1800s.

Name two important events in the US in the 1900s.

1 **name:** In most situations, when someone asks a person for his or her name, that person gives the first and last name. When someone is filling out a form or in official situations, a person gives his or her full name: first, middle, and last.

2 **first name:** Many first names have nicknames—informal versions of the first name that friends or family members use. Nicknames are usually shorter forms of the full name and many times have the ending *y* or *ie*. For example:

Steven	Steve/Stevie
Robert	Bob/Bobbie
Stanley	Stan
Judith	Judy
Deborah	Debbie
Katherine/Kathleen	Kathy

Some names have both male and female versions. For example:

Male	*Female*
Robert	Roberta
Samuel	Samantha
Patrick	Patricia
Christopher	Christine

3 **middle initial:** People often use an initial instead of a full middle name—for example, Carla A. Martino, Carla G. Martino. In the United States, parents often give their children a middle name that is the first or last name of an important family member.

4 **last name/family name/surname:** When a woman gets married, she often changes her last name to her husband's last name. Therefore, if Susan Carter marries John Gray, her name becomes Susan Gray. Her *maiden name* (her last name before she got married) was Carter, and her *married name* is Gray. However, many married women prefer to keep their maiden names or hyphenate the two last names (Susan Carter-Gray).

5 **address:** This is a general term that includes the street number, street name, apartment number, city, state, and zip code. Many forms ask for a *present* address and a *permanent* address. A college student who is living away from home, for example, has a present or temporary college address and a permanent home address, which is his or her official residence.

6 **street number:** In spoken English, you give your street address in single-digit or two-digit combinations, such as:

136 Elm Street—one thirty-six Elm Street/ one three six Elm Street

1438 Maple Street—fourteen thirty-eight Maple Street

7 **street:** There are many different words for *street*. For example:

Jefferson Street	Jefferson Drive
Jefferson Road	Jefferson Circle
Jefferson Avenue	Jefferson Lane
Jefferson Boulevard	

The following abbreviations are common for written street names:

Street – St.	Drive – Dr.
Road – Rd.	Circle – Cir.
Avenue – Ave.	Lane – La.
Boulevard – Blvd.	

8 **apartment number:** The typical sequence is first a number, which gives the floor of the building, and then a letter that gives the unit on that floor—e.g., 10A, 5B.

10 **state:** The U.S. Postal Service uses the following abbreviations with zip-code addresses for the 50 U.S. states:

AL (Alabama)	CO (Colorado)
AK (Alaska)	CT (Connecticut)
AZ (Arizona)	DE (Delaware)
AR (Arkansas)	FL (Florida)
CA (California)	GA (Georgia)

HI (Hawaii)
ID (Idaho)
IL (Illinois)
IN (Indiana)
IA (Iowa)
KS (Kansas)
KY (Kentucky)
LA (Louisiana)
ME (Maine)
MD (Maryland)
MA (Massachusetts)
MI (Michigan)
MN (Minnesota)
MS (Mississippi)
MO (Missouri)
MT (Montana)
NE (Nebraska)
NV (Nevada)
NH (New Hampshire)
NJ (New Jersey)

NM (New Mexico)
NY (New York)
NC (North Carolina)
ND (North Dakota)
OH (Ohio)
OK (Oklahoma)
OR (Oregon)
PA (Pennsylvania)
RI (Rhode Island)
SC (South Carolina)
SD (South Dakota)
TN (Tennessee)
TX (Texas)
UT (Utah)
VT (Vermont)
VA (Virginia)
WA (Washington)
WV (West Virginia)
WI (Wisconsin)
WY (Wyoming)

(11) zip code: This is the number that the U.S. Postal Service gives a geographical region, such as 02145-3617. All addresses must include the first five digits of the zip code.

(12) area code: Each geographical area in the US has its own three-digit area code, such as 212. You have to use these numbers when you call someone in a different area. These days, in crowded metropolitan areas, callers have to use area codes even when they call someone within their own area. For example, a person who is calling another person within the 212 calling area has to dial 212, then the seven-digit phone number. There is a list of area codes in telephone books, or you can call a long-distance operator.

(13) telephone number/phone number: All U.S. telephone numbers have seven digits for a local call, such as 267-9325. Most

cities in the US now require all local calls to include the three-digit area code, for example 617-267-9325. When you say a telephone number, you say each digit individually, such as two–six–seven [pause] nine–three–two–five.

(15) e-mail address: The names for e-mail address symbols are *dot* for (.) and *at* for @. When you give an e-mail address, you usually say the address in whole words whenever possible. You also say the domain names as complete words. For example, you say the address kmjones@yahoo.com as *k-m Jones at yahoo dot com.*

(16) social security number: The social security program is a national program of old-age pension payments. Anyone who earns money must report these earnings to the government. The employer deducts a portion of an employee's earnings and pays it to the government. Each person receives a social security number at birth and will receive monthly social security payments that start at age 62 for women and age 65 for men. It is common to use your social security number as an identification number in other situations, for example in bank transactions.

(17) sex: This refers to a person's gender. On forms it is common to see the abbreviations M for male and F for female.

(18) date of birth: When you abbreviate dates, you write the month first, then the day, and then the year. For example, the abbreviation for February 11, 2009, is 2/11/09.

(19) place of birth: A person from the US writes both the town and state name.

The *nuclear* or *immediate* family refers to a father, mother, and their children who are living as a unit.

A *blended* family may occur when a divorced parent remarries. The blended family may include children from previous marriages of both the husband and wife and any children the new partners have. *Step-* is added to names of family members when they remarry and shows that the relationship is legal rather than biological (e.g., *stepmother, stepfather, stepdaughter, stepson, stepchild*).

When a child is adopted, the terms *natural/biological/birth mother* and *natural/biological/birth father* refer to the child's biological parents. The terms *adoptive mother* and *adoptive father* refer to the parents who raise the child.

(1) husband: If a couple divorces, the husband becomes the *ex-husband* or *former husband*. If a man's wife dies, he is a *widower*.

(2) wife: If a couple divorces, the wife becomes the *ex-wife* or *former wife*. If a woman's husband dies, she is a *widow*.

(3) father: There are a number of informal ways for a child to address his or her father: *Dad, Daddy, Papa, Poppa, Pop, Pa.*

(4) mother: There are a number of informal ways for a child to address his or her mother: *Mom, Mommy, Momma, Mama, Mum, Mummy, Ma.*

children: A very common informal synonym for children is *kids*.

(7) baby: a term for children under a year old. It is also common to refer to the baby as a *baby boy* or *baby girl*. Children

between the ages of one and three are *toddlers*. People also use *baby* to refer to the youngest child of the generation ("I'm 45 years old, but I'm the baby of my family").

siblings: *Sibling* is a general term for both sisters and brothers. ("How many siblings do you have?" "I have three siblings—one brother and two sisters.") *Sibling rivalry*, or jealousy between siblings, is a problem in many families.

(10) grandmother: There are a number of informal ways for a child to address his or her grandmother: *Grandma, Gramma, Granny, Grammie, Grandmommie, Gran, Nana, Nannie.*

(11) grandfather: There are a number of informal ways for a child to address his or her grandfather: *Grandpa, Grampa, Grampie, Gramps, Gramp, Granddad, Granddaddy.*

LANGUAGE & CULTURE NOTES

(1) uncle: the brother of a person's mother or father. A *great-uncle* is the brother of a person's grandmother or grandfather.

(2) aunt: the sister of a person's mother or father. A *great-aunt* is the sister of a person's grandmother or grandfather.

(3) niece: the daughter of a person's sister or brother.

(4) nephew: the son of a person's sister or brother.

(5) cousin: the son or daughter of a person's aunt or uncle.

(6–11) in-law: The phrase *in-law* shows that the relation is based on legal rather than biological ties. It is common to refer to the mother-in-law and father-in-law collectively as *in-laws* ("My in-laws are coming for dinner this Sunday").

LC3

U.S. public school systems typically assign children to classes or grades by age. Children must attend school until the age of sixteen. *Preschool* is for children who are three and four years old. *Elementary school* includes a *kindergarten* class for five-year-olds and first through fifth or sixth grades for six- to ten- or eleven-year-olds. Some school systems have a separate school, a *middle school* or *junior high school*, for grades six or seven through grade eight. *High school* includes ninth through twelfth grades for teenagers fourteen to eighteen years old.

The school year usually includes about 180 days, with a ten-week summer vacation. The average school day is six hours long. Most children eat their lunch at school. They can bring a lunch from home or buy their lunch in the school cafeteria.

(1) teacher: Students usually call their teacher *Mr./Mrs./Miss/Ms.* and the teacher's last name.

(2) teacher's aide: Many classrooms have a teacher's aide who helps the teacher. The aide works with individual students or with small groups.

(3) student: In elementary schools, it is common to use the word *pupil* instead of *student*. Teachers usually call their students by their first names.

(4) desk: The desks in this classroom are movable. Teachers can arrange the desks in rows, in a circle, or in groups. Other classrooms have desks in stationary rows.

(10) chalkboard/board: A *blackboard* is a board that is black. People write on a board with white and colored chalk.

(13) bulletin board: Teachers typically display a variety of things on their classroom bulletin boards such as newspaper clippings, announcements, and examples of students' work.

(14) P.A. system/loudspeaker: *P.A.* is an abbreviation for *public address*. Announcements of interest to the whole school come through the P.A. system at the beginning of each school day.

(15) whiteboard/board: This is a more contemporary addition to the classroom. You write on the board only with *dry-erase markers*, which you can easily wipe away.

(21) pencil: There two types of pencils: traditional *wood pencils* and *mechanical pencils*. You refill a mechanical pencil with *lead*.

(24) book/textbook: *Book* refers to any kind of book, such as a novel, a picture book, or a textbook. A *textbook* is a book for classroom learning.

(27) binder/notebook: a hard-sided book with rings so it's possible to add or take out papers. There are *three-ring* binders and *two-ring* binders.

(28) notebook paper: Notebook paper can be lined or unlined. It has holes in it so it's possible to insert it through the rings in the notebook.

(29) graph paper: Graph paper has a lined grid.

(34) marker: There are many types of markers: *broad tip markers* for younger children, *fine tip markers* for more detailed work, *permanent markers* for clothing and other non-traditional materials, and *dry-erase markers* for a *whiteboard* (15).

The following verbs on *Picture Dictionary* pages 6–7 are irregular:

bring	brought	brought
break	broke	broken
choose	chose	chosen
do	did	done
go	went	gone
put	put	put
read	read	read
say	said	said
sit	sat	sat
stand	stood	stood
take	took	taken
write	wrote	written

(12) **read / (13)** **study:** When you study, you read the pages carefully and take notes on the information to help you remember it.

(16) **Raise your hand.** In most U.S. classrooms, students raise their hands when they want to say something. The teacher will then *call on* them to give their answers.

(21) (22) (25) **homework:** This is a general term for any work that the teacher assigns a student to do outside of class time.

(36–40) There are many possible ways for students to work on classroom assignments—independently, with a partner, in groups, or as a class.

(47) (50) **tests:** Teachers in the US usually give *closed-book* tests during which the student may not look at notes or the textbook. An *open-book* test means a student may look at notes or the textbook during the test. A *take-home* test means that the student can do the test outside the class with the help of notes or the textbook.

LANGUAGE & CULTURE NOTES

The prepositions in this lesson are all prepositions of place or prepositions of location. A noun, or an article and a noun, follows the preposition. The combination is a "prepositional phrase." A preposition of place plus a noun tells where something is.

A sentence can have more than one prepositional phrase. Each phrase gives a little more information. For example:

The clock is on the wall.
The clock is on the wall over the table.

The milk is in the refrigerator.
The milk is in a pitcher in the refrigerator.
The milk is in a pitcher on the top shelf in the refrigerator.

(1) **above:** A synonym for *above* is *over.* For example: *The clock is above the bulletin board. = The clock is over the bulletin board.*

(2) **below:** A synonym for *below* is *beneath.* For example: *The bulletin board is below the clock. = The bulletin board is beneath the clock.*

(4) **behind:** A synonym for *behind* is *in back of.* For example: *The chalkboard is behind the map. = The chalkboard is in back of the map.*

(6) **on:** A synonym for *on* is *on top of.* For example: *The computer is on the table. = The computer is on top of the table.*

(7) **under:** Two synonyms for *under* are *below* and *beneath.* For example: *The wastebasket is under the table. = The wastebasket is below the table. = The wastebasket is beneath the table.*

(10) **in:** A synonym for *in* is *inside.* For example: *The pencil is in the pencil sharpener. = The pencil is inside the pencil sharpener.*

The following verbs on *Picture Dictionary* page 9 are irregular:

eat	ate	eaten
get	got	gotten
go	went	gone
have	had	had
make	made	made
put	put	put
sleep	slept	slept
take	took	taken

(2) **take a shower /** (12) **take a bath:** Americans typically bathe (*take a shower* or *take a bath*) once a day.

(3) *Teeth* is the irregular plural of the noun *tooth.*

(7) **put on makeup:** *Makeup* is a general term that includes any combination of base or foundation, blush or rouge, lipstick, eye shadow, eye liner, and mascara. (See *Picture Dictionary* page 99.)

(15–20): There is no article before *breakfast/lunch/dinner* unless you're talking about a specific meal. ("George ate *dinner* at a new restaurant. *The dinner* was very good.")

(15) (18) **breakfast:** American breakfasts may include fruit or fruit juice; bread or toast; eggs; bacon, ham, or sausage; potatoes; cereal; yogurt; and a beverage (coffee, tea, milk, cocoa). Americans typically eat breakfast between 6:00 A.M. and 9:00 A.M.

(16) (19) **lunch:** Lunch is not the main meal of the day for Americans. They typically eat something light, such as a sandwich, salad, soup, and a beverage (coffee, tea, milk, or a soft drink). Americans typically eat lunch between 11:30 A.M. and 1:30 P.M.

(17) (20) **dinner:** Dinner is usually the main meal of the day. It may include soup; a salad; an entree of meat or fish; potatoes, pasta, or rice; a dessert such as a fruit or sweet; and a beverage (coffee, tea, or milk). Americans typically eat dinner between 5:30 and 7:00 P.M. A light dinner is a *supper.*

Activities 1–7 are household *chores*—daily household responsibilities or work. Traditionally in American culture, women were responsible for these activities. Now, however, it is common for men and women to share the household chores.

The following verbs on *Picture Dictionary* page 10 are irregular:

come	came	come
do	did	done
drive	drove	driven
feed	fed	fed
get	got	gotten
go	went	gone
leave	left	left
take	took	taken

(1) **clean the apartment/clean the house:** This includes such activities as sweeping, dusting, and vacuuming.

(2) **wash the dishes:** See *Picture Dictionary* page 24 for related vocabulary: *dishwasher, dishwasher detergent, dishwashing liquid, dish rack, dish towel, sink, faucet.*

(3) **do the laundry:** This includes both washing and drying clothes, bedding, towels, and sheets. People do their laundry at home or at a laundromat. See *Picture Dictionary* page 73 for related vocabulary: *laundry detergent, fabric softener, bleach, starch, static cling remover, laundry basket, laundry bag, clothesline, clothespins, washer, dryer.*

(4) **iron:** See *Picture Dictionary* page 73 for related vocabulary: *iron* (noun), *ironing board. Permanent press* clothes are popular because people don't have to iron them.

(5) **feed the baby:** The baby in the illustration is sitting in a *high chair,* a chair where babies sit when someone is feeding them.

(6) **feed the cat:** Dogs and cats are popular pets in the US. People often treat them like members of the family. Some people feed their pets scraps of leftover food. Others go to supermarkets and buy *cat food* and *dog food* (see *Picture Dictionary* page 54). The cat in the illustration is ready to eat from a special pet food bowl.

(7) **walk the dog:** People *walk their dogs* so that the dogs can get some exercise and have an opportunity to *go to the bathroom* outside the house.

(11) **drive to work:** Many people drive to work in the US. Others take buses, trains, or subways. A *commute* is the trip to and from work. For example: Jim has a short *commute* on the subway, but his wife has a long *commute* in her car. She drives 50 miles a day.

(12) **take the bus to school:** Most public school districts in the US provide school buses to transport children who live a mile or more away from the schools they attend. In busy urban areas, older children sometimes take public transportation to school instead.

(15) **go to the store:** A person can *go to the store, pick something up at the store,* or *go shopping.* All three expressions mean to buy something at a supermarket or grocery store. Many people stop at a store on their way home from work to buy the food they need for dinner. Others go shopping once a week, often on the weekend, to buy all the food they'll need for the upcoming week.

(6) play: This general term includes activities children do for fun. In the illustration, the girl on the left is playing with a *jump rope,* and the girl on the right is playing *hopscotch* (a game in which a player throws a stone on one of the squares of a chalk grid on a pavement and the child hops on each square except the one that has the stone).

(8) play basketball: Basketball is a popular American sport that people play informally or formally in two teams of five members each. A team scores points when a player throws a ball through a round metal circle called a *hoop* that hangs on a pole (see *Picture Dictionary* pages 142 and 143).

There is no article (*a/an/the*) with the names of games or sports after *play* —e.g., *play basketball, play baseball, play hopscotch.*

(9) play the guitar / (10) practice the piano: The article *the* comes before the names of musical instruments.

(11) exercise: This can be any kind of activity that strengthens muscles and raises the heartbeat. Popular forms of exercise today are walking, jogging, bicycling, yoga, pilates, and aerobics.

(13) plant flowers: A more general term is *to garden* (flowers or vegetables). When someone *gardens,* he or she *plants, weeds* (pulls out bad plants), and *prunes* (cuts back plants to promote healthy growth).

(14) use the computer: There are many ways people use the computer for leisure. They use *software* programs to play games. They communicate with others online through the Internet by *e-mail, instant messaging,* or in *chat rooms.* They read the news on a *website* or visit a store website to *shop online.*

(1) Hello./Hi. *Hi* is a shorter and more informal version of *Hello*. In the United States people say *Hello* to acknowledge another person, but it isn't required. For example, in the illustration on *Picture Dictionary* page 12, the person who is approaching the bus stop says *Hello* to greet another person who is waiting there. It is equally common for a person to approach the bus stop and say nothing at all to the other person, especially if they aren't acquainted.

(2) Good morning. a common greeting in the morning, which is from the beginning of the day until 12:00 noon. It is interchangeable with *Hello*. People do not say both *Good morning* and *Hello*.

(3) Good afternoon. a greeting in the afternoon hours between noon and 6:00. It is interchangeable with *Hello*. People do not say both *Good afternoon* and *Hello*.

(4) Good evening. a greeting in the evening hours between 6:00 and 11:00. Because *Good evening* is a greeting, people use it even late at night if they are just meeting each other.

(5–6) How are you?/How are you doing?/ Fine./Fine, thanks./Okay. After a greeting, it is customary to ask a person you know, *How are you?* This question is part of the greeting. No one expects a long or honest answer. "Fine," "Fine, thanks," or "Okay" are appropriate responses even when the person isn't feeling *fine* or *okay*.

(7–8) What's new?/What's new with you?/ Not much./Not too much. When someone stops briefly to greet a person he or she knows, it is customary to ask *What's new?* or *What's new with you?* This often takes place after the routine greeting *How are you?/Fine, thanks.*

A long or elaborate response is not necessary, but a conversation of one or two minutes is possible.

(9) Good-bye./Bye. It is not customary to say *Good-bye* when two people didn't have a real conversation. For example, when a person greets a friend on the way to class, it is appropriate to say *Hello. How are you?* but not to add *Good-bye*. When two people are concluding a conversation, before they actually say *Good-bye*, they often give a reason to end the conversation—for example, *It's getting late. I have to get home now.*

(10) Good night. At the end of the day, whatever the hour, when people take leave, they say *Good night*. It doesn't necessarily have to be nighttime, though. For example, when two people are leaving their office at 5:00 in the afternoon, they might say *Good night* to one another.

(11) See you later./See you soon. These expressions are slightly more informal than *Good-bye*. People also commonly say *See you tomorrow/next week/on Monday.*

(12) Hello. My name is _____./Hi. I'm _____. Self-introductions are common and appropriate in the United States. When both men and women introduce themselves, they usually give a brief handshake (two shakes).

(13–14) Nice to meet you./Nice to meet you, too. When someone introduces two people to each other, it is appropriate for one person to say *Nice to meet you* (a shortened version of *It's nice to meet you*) and for the other to respond *Nice to meet you, too*. People also commonly say *It's a pleasure to meet you.*

LANGUAGE & CULTURE NOTES

15 **I'd like to introduce _____./This is _____.** These phrases are common during introductions. A typical exchange:

A. I'd like to introduce *my husband.* (or) *This is my husband.*

B. Nice to meet you. [They shake hands.]

C. Nice to meet you, too.

16 **Excuse me.** People commonly use this polite expression to attract someone's attention.

17 **May I ask a question?** Before a person asks a question, it is common and polite to begin with *May I ask a question?* or *Can I ask you a question?*

18 **Thank you./Thanks.** *Thanks* is less formal than *Thank you.* In the US, people express gratitude frequently, even to those who are only doing their jobs. For example, in the situation on *Picture Dictionary* page 13, the supermarket bagger is doing what he normally does, but still the customer says, *Thank you.*

19 **You're welcome.** This is the most common response after someone expresses thanks. Another common and more informal response is *No problem.*

20 **I don't understand./Sorry. I don't understand.** It is best to be direct and to state when you don't understand something. Both of these phrases are common and appropriate.

21 **Can you please repeat that?/Can you please say that again?** It is appropriate to ask for repetition when something is not clear. People in the US appreciate it when others are candid and direct.

22 **Hello. This is _____. May I please speak to _____?** When you call someone on the telephone, it is appropriate to greet the person who answers and identify yourself. If the person you are calling doesn't answer the phone, the most common polite way to ask to speak to that person is to say *May I please speak to _____?* A more informal way is to say *Is _____ there?*

23 **Yes. Hold on a moment.** It is also common to say *Yes. Just a minute, please.*

24 **I'm sorry. _____ isn't here right now.** It is common and appropriate to apologize in this situation and offer to take a message (*Can I give him/her a message?*).

LANGUAGE & CULTURE NOTES

> The weather is a favorite topic of *small talk* in the US. People often use the weather as a conversation starter. Typical questions and comments are "What's it like out?," "Nice day today, isn't it!," or "It sure is raining hard today!"

Weather: *Weather* describes the atmospheric situation on a particular day or the average conditions of a region. *Climate* refers only to the average conditions of a region.

(2) **cloudy:** When the sky is totally covered with clouds, people say it's *overcast*. If there is part-sun and part-clouds, people say it's *partly cloudy*.

(3) **clear:** People often use this when they want to say it's *sunny* or *fair*.

(4) **hazy:** not clear, with enough light vapor or pollution in the atmosphere so that the air is not transparent.

(5) **foggy:** when moisture in the air makes it difficult to see.

(6) **smoggy:** *Smog* is a combination of fog and local air pollution. It is a very unhealthy mix that hangs low over a city.

(8) **humid/muggy:** warm, moist air that makes the heat seem uncomfortable or even oppressive.

(9) **raining:** Forecasters refer to *light* or *heavy* rain.

(10) **drizzling:** *Drizzle* is a light, fine, misty rain.

(11) **snowing:** Forecasters refer to *light* or *heavy snow* or *snowfalls*. People use the word *flurries* to refer to light, intermittent snow.

(12) **hailing:** *Hail* is small balls of compact ice and snow that fall like rain.

(13) **sleeting:** *Sleet* is frozen or partly frozen rain. Often a weather forecast will say *sleet and freezing rain*.

(15) **thunderstorm:** thunder and lightning usually with heavy rain.

(16) **snowstorm:** snow together with wind. A *blizzard* is intense snow with high winds

that make it difficult to see and make roads impassable.

(17) **dust storm:** In dry climates, strong and persistent winds can blow sand and dirt to create dust storms.

(18) **heat wave:** a period of very hot weather that lasts for more than three days.

Temperature: All temperatures are relative, and their description depends on what the individual is accustomed to.

(19) **thermometer:** an instrument that measures heat. Two scales register heat—the *Fahrenheit* scale and the *Centigrade* or *Celsius* scale.

(20) **Fahrenheit:** the scale that people in the US use to measure temperature. The boiling point of water is 212 degrees Fahrenheit (above zero), and the freezing point is 32 degrees (above zero).

(21) **Centigrade/Celsius:** the scale that people in most of the world outside the US use. The boiling point of water is 100 degrees. The freezing point is 0 degrees.

212°F = 100°C		100°C = 212°F	
100	37.8	40	104
90	32.2	30	86
80	27	20	68
70	21.1	10	50
60	15.6	0	32
50	10.0	−10	14
40	4.4		
32	0		
20	−6.6		
10	−12.3		
0	−17.8		

Conversion:

Fahrenheit − 32 × 5 divided by 9 = Centigrade
Centigrade × 9 divided by 5 = Fahrenheit

(26) **freezing:** This literally means "below 32° Fahrenheit." However, many people say, "It's freezing!" to mean "It's very cold."

LANGUAGE & CULTURE NOTES

Cardinal numbers tell *how many* (4, 25, 10,000). You use cardinal numbers when you count.

In American English, when you say *zero* in a series of numbers, you usually pronounce it as "oh." For example:

1909 = "one nine oh nine"

In large numbers, it is common to add *and* between the hundreds and the tens. For example:

283 = two hundred *and* eighty-three
283,000 = two hundred *and* eighty-three thousand
1,495 = one thousand four hundred *and* ninety-five

If there is a zero in the tens place, you usually say *and* before the ones. For example:

203 = two hundred *and* three
1,405 = one thousand, four hundred, *and* five
1,005 = one thousand *and* five

Ordinal numbers indicate order or rank in a series. You use ordinals for dates (February *6th*), for locations (the *8th* floor of a building), for centuries (the *21st* century), and for series (the *2nd* book in a series).

LANGUAGE & CULTURE NOTES

To express hourly time, you say *o'clock*—one o'clock, two o'clock, etc. It is also common to express hourly time by just the hour—for example, "I'll meet you at two."

To express time from one minute until nine minutes after the hour, you say *oh* plus the number of minutes—*two oh one, two oh two, . . . two oh nine.*

To express time from ten minutes after the hour until one minute before the next hour, you say the hour plus the number of minutes—*two ten, two eleven, . . . two fifty-nine.* This is especially common when someone is telling time from a digital clock or watch.

To express quarter hours, you say *a quarter after/a quarter past, half past,* and *a quarter to/a quarter of* the hour.

To express time until the half-hour, you say the number of minutes after the hour—*five after two, ten after two*—or by *past*—*five past two, ten past two.*

To express time from the half hour until the next hour, you say the number of minutes to the next hour—*twenty-five to three, ten to three*—or by *of*—*twenty-five of three, ten of three.*

A.M. refers to the time from midnight until noon.
P.M. refers to the time from noon until midnight.

When you refer to noon and midnight, it is not possible to express time with *midnight/noon* plus the number of minutes (i.e., *noon ten, midnight fifteen*). Instead, use *after/past/to/of* (i.e., *ten after midnight, twenty past midnight*).

Many countries use a *twenty-four hour clock* to express times of transportation and other schedules—e.g., *fourteen o'clock, sixteen o'clock.* In the United States, this method is only for military time.

Time in the US is an important concept. It is common to keep personal calendars and organize one's days around plans for specific times. People expect others to be *on time* or even early for most meetings and events. Expressions such as *three o'clock sharp* or *four thirty on the dot* reflect the importance of time and promptness.

MONEY

LANGUAGE & CULTURE NOTES

In the United States, the unit of money is the *dollar*. Money comes in two forms—metal *coins* and paper *bills*.

There are six denominations of coins—dollar, half dollar, quarter, dime, nickel, and penny. The date the US made (minted) the coin appears on its front, along with the picture of one of the presidents of the United States. The value of the coin and the inscription THE UNITED STATES OF AMERICA appear on the back of the coin.

Bills are all the same size paper. They have the number of the value of the bill in all four corners on the front and back. Bills come in denominations of one, five, ten, twenty, fifty, and one hundred dollars. The U.S. government issued a two-dollar bill in 1966, but there are very few in circulation. The largest bill most Americans typically carry is a twenty-dollar bill.

The following pictures appear on the front and back respectively of the bills:

one-dollar bill	George Washington/The Great Seal
two-dollar bill	Thomas Jefferson/Monticello
five-dollar bill	Abraham Lincoln/Lincoln Memorial
ten-dollar bill	Alexander Hamilton/U.S. Treasury Building
twenty-dollar bill	Andrew Jackson/The White House
fifty-dollar bill	Ulysses S. Grant/U.S. Capitol
one-hundred dollar bill	Benjamin Franklin/Independence Hall

(1) **penny:** The copper penny or *cent* is worth 1/100 of a dollar. It is bigger than a dime, but worth less. The picture of Abraham Lincoln appears on the front of the penny, and the Lincoln Memorial is on the back.

(2) **nickel:** This silver-colored five-cent coin is bigger and thicker than a penny and smaller than a quarter. Thomas Jefferson appears on the front, and Monticello, Jefferson's famous home in Virginia, is on the back.

(3) **dime:** This silver-colored ten-cent coin is the smallest in size. Dimes are convenient to have for vending machines, parking meters, and public telephones. Franklin D. Roosevelt is on the front of the dime, and a torch, laurel wreath, and oak leaves are on the back.

(4) **quarter:** This silver-colored twenty-five-cent coin is larger than a nickel. Quarters are convenient for parking meters, public telephones, vending machines, and fares on public transportation. George Washington is on the front of the quarter, and the eagle, the U.S. national symbol, is on the back.

(5) **half dollar:** The U.S. government often issues this silver-colored fifty-cent coin as a special coin to honor an outstanding individual such as Booker T. Washington or John F. Kennedy, whose faces appear on the front of their coin.

(6) **silver dollar:** This silver-colored one-dollar coin is not very common. One reason is the U.S. government doesn't issue very many. Another reason is that people save them as souvenirs.

LANGUAGE & CULTURE NOTES

In the United States, the calendar week begins with Sunday.

To express a date, you give the month, day (with an ordinal number), and year—for example, "March tenth, two thousand and nine."

When you say most years, you divide the year by the first two and the last two numbers—for example, 1999 is *nineteen ninety-nine* and 1277 is *twelve seventy-seven*. The only exception to this is in the early years of the millennium, when you say the dates in the full number. For example, for 2008, you say *two thousand eight* or *two thousand and eight* rather than *twenty, eight*.

A common way to abbreviate dates is with the number of the month/day/year—for example, 3/10/09.

You often abbreviate many of the months when you write them—for example, Jan./Feb./Mar./Apr./Aug./Sept./Oct./Nov./Dec.

When you write the year, you often abbreviate it as follows: '08.

Here are some common ways to express time:

in (year)	in 2009
in (month)	in March
on (day)	on Tuesday
on (date)	on March 10, 2009

(5) **weekend:** The weekend is from Friday evening to Sunday night. Most U.S. businesses and public buildings are closed on the weekend. Throughout the US, stores are open all day Saturday. They open for more restricted hours on Sunday. These Sunday hours vary, depending on local state laws. It is typical for people to ask each other on a Thursday or Friday, "What are your plans for the weekend?" and on a Monday, "What did you do over the weekend?"

(27) **anniversary:** Most married couples celebrate their wedding anniversary. Traditionally, a couple's 25th anniversary is their "silver anniversary" and their 50th is their "golden anniversary." In the past, friends and family of the couple often gave gifts of silver or gold on these anniversaries. People don't usually do this now, but the names of the anniversaries remain. Businesses, schools, and other institutions also announce and celebrate the anniversaries of their founding.

(28) **appointment:** Appointments are usually for medical or business situations. Friends and romantic partners do not make appointments. They make *dates*.

LANGUAGE & CULTURE NOTES

(4) **morning:** Technically, morning begins after 12 midnight, but most people refer to morning as the early part of the day until 12:00 noon.

(5) **afternoon:** the time between 12:00 noon and 6:00 P.M.

(6) **evening /** (7) **night:** *Evening* is the last part of the day between 6:00 P.M. and bedtime. *Night* is the time in the evening when the sun no longer shines or when a person sleeps. There are no certain hours to distinguish between *evening* and *night*. The only difference is that *evening* is the beginning and *night* is the middle and end.

(20–26) These expressions are for months, years, or any other period of time—for example: *last (year), this (month), next (summer), once a (week), once a (century), twice a (month), every (millennium).*

(23) **once a week /** (24) **twice a week:** It is not common to say *one time* or *two times* (a week), but it is grammatically correct.

(25) **three times a week:** This expression refers to more than two events (twice) in a time period — for example: *ten times a day, twenty-six times a week,* etc.

Seasons

There are no rainy and dry seasons in the United States. Instead there are the four conventional seasons: spring, summer, winter, and fall. Although there is a range of climates in the US from tropical Florida to artic Alaska, the descriptions below fit most of the United States.

(27) **spring:** from about March 21 to June 21. The temperature ranges from cool to warm.

(28) **summer:** from about June 21 to September 21. The temperature is usually hot.

(29) **fall/autumn:** from about September 21 to December 21. The temperature is warm at the beginning and becomes cold.

(30) **winter:** from about December 21 to March 21. The temperature is cold to freezing and below.

LANGUAGE & CULTURE NOTES

(1) **apartment building:** There are many types of apartment buildings, from two floors to multilevel structures. Multilevel buildings (*high rise* apartments) are more common in urban areas.

(2) **house:** Single-family houses are usually in suburban and rural areas. Many have an attached garage. Houses in northern regions usually have basements.

(3) **duplex/two-family house:** The house on *Picture Dictionary* page 20 is a side-by-side duplex where two families live next to each other. A duplex or two-family house can also be a house in which one family lives on the first floor and the other lives on the second floor.

(4) **townhouse/townhome:** An individual townhouse or townhome is normally in an attached group of several identical two-story structures.

(5) **condominium/condo:** This term refers to a type of ownership rather than a type of housing. Individuals own the houses or apartments in a condominium complex, and there is an owners' association that manages the common areas and services, such as yard maintenance and garbage collection for all the units.

(6) **dormitory/dorm:** This is housing that colleges provide for students. Students may live alone in a single (room), or with one or more *roommates* in a double, triple, or quad room. A dormitory often has a cafeteria or dining room and special study rooms, social lounges, and laundry facilities.

(7) **mobile home:** Mobile homes are self-contained units that have kitchens, bathrooms, bedrooms, and living/dining rooms. They may be on an individual plot

of land or together in a group in *trailer parks* in suburban and rural areas.

(8) **nursing home:** This facility gives medical care and daily help to the elderly or anyone who needs long-term medical care. In the US, elderly people do not typically live with their married children. They usually live with their spouses or by themselves in houses or apartments, and often move into nursing homes when they become too old to care for themselves. As a result, nursing homes very often have long waiting lists of people who want to move in.

(9) **shelter:** A shelter provides care for homeless people. This may include sleeping facilities, medical attention, food, and education or employment support services.

(11) **ranch:** A ranch is an animal farm, usually for cattle, but also for sheep and horses. In the US, most ranches are in the West, where there is a lot of undeveloped land.

(13) **the city:** This refers to the urban center of a metropolitan area.

(14) **the suburbs:** These are the outlying districts of a metropolitan area. Suburbs typically consist of residential neighborhoods of (single-family) homes often with large yards.

(15) **the country:** This refers to rural areas that are not connected economically or socially to any metropolitan area. *The country* typically consists of farms and undeveloped land.

(16) **a town/village:** This is a small community in a country setting. A *village* is smaller than a *town*.

The living room is a room where people socialize and relax. Many houses have two living rooms—a more formal living room that adults use for themselves or to entertain guests, and a less formal *family room* that all family members use for everyday activities.

(6) fireplace screen: It is common to have this screen in front of a fireplace so sparks from the fire don't go into the room.

(7) DVD player: *DVD* stands for *Digital Video Disc.*

(8) television/TV: People usually say *TV* rather than *television.*

(12) drapes: curtains that go from the top of the window to the floor.

(14) loveseat: a couch with space for two people to sit. Loveseats typically match the style of the sofa.

(15) wall unit: a large set of shelves that hold a stereo system, books, decorative objects, and other miscellaneous items.

(17) stereo system: A stereo system includes any of the following music-playing devices: a tape deck, a CD (compact disc) player, a tuner (radio), a record player, and a receiver that coordinates all the components. (See *Picture Dictionary* page 76.)

(19) (throw) pillow: a small pillow that people usually place in the corner(s) of a sofa both for decoration and to lean against.

(22) coffee table: a low table that stands in front of a sofa. It is usually the same length or a little shorter than the sofa. It holds decorative objects, magazines, and food for guests.

(23) rug: a general term for floor covering. A rug that covers an entire floor of a room is a *carpet* or *wall-to-wall carpet.* A rug that covers just an area of the floor (as the one on *Picture Dictionary* page 21) is an *area rug.*

(24) lamp: The lamp on *Picture Dictionary* page 21 is a *table lamp,* as opposed to a *floor lamp* (28), which is free-standing on a long pole.

(26) end table: People sometimes call this a *side table.* There is often a pair of matching end tables at either end of a sofa.

(28) floor lamp: any lamp that stands on the floor rather than on a table.

(29) armchair: a tall upholstered chair with arms.

THE DINING ROOM

LANGUAGE & CULTURE NOTES

In some houses and apartments, the dining area and the living room are a single living room and *dining area*. People sometimes call this a *great room*.

Even though many homes have dining rooms, families often eat in the kitchen every day and use their dining rooms only when they have guests.

When people serve food *family style*, they put the food in large bowls and platters that they pass around so others can serve themselves.

When people serve *buffet style*, they put the food in large bowls and platters on the buffet (item 3 in the illustration) and allow everyone to serve themselves. *Buffet style* is the only possible way to entertain a large group of guests since there isn't enough room for everyone around the table. The guests help themselves at the buffet and then find a place to sit, perhaps in the living room.

(3) buffet: a long piece of dining room furniture that displays decorative objects or that people typically use to put food on. If you are serving *buffet style,* you also have plates on the buffet that guests fill with portions they take from the various containers of food.

(8) creamer: a container that holds cream for coffee or tea.

(12) china: People often call their china their *best dishes* because these are the dishes they use for special occasions and for company.

(13) salad bowl: Most salad bowls are wooden.

(14) serving bowl: a large bowl that you use to serve foods such as vegetables and potatoes.

(15) serving dish: a large dish, often with a lid.

(16) vase: For formal dinners, it is common to put a flower arrangement in a *vase* in the center of the dining room table. *Vases* may also hold arrangements of flowers in other rooms.

(18) candlestick: A candlestick that holds more than one candle is a *candelabra*.

(19) platter: an oval or rectangular dish with a rim that you use to serve foods such as meat, chicken, and fish.

(21) salt shaker / (22) pepper shaker: In the United States, it is common to sprinkle salt and/or pepper on food to enhance its flavor. Shakers are the containers that hold the salt and pepper.

(25)(27)(28) fork, knife, and spoon: Silverware (or flatware) is a general term that includes knives, forks, spoons, and serving utensils. Today silverware is often stainless steel rather than silver.

(26)(29) plate and bowl: Plates are generally flat with only a slightly raised edge. Bowls have deep sides. You use them to serve soups, salads, cereal, ice cream, and other desserts. (See *Picture Dictionary* page 63 for a full place setting.)

(30) mug / (32) cup: When Americans drink tea or coffee, they often use a mug (no saucer) in informal situations and a cup and saucer in more formal situations.

(1) **bed:** This is a general term. The terms *twin bed, double bed, queen-size bed,* and *king-size bed* tell the size of a particular bed.

(4) **pillowcase:** a cotton or silk cover that protects the pillow.

(5) **fitted sheet:** a piece of cotton or silk material that has elastic at the corners to keep it in place on the mattress. A fitted sheet is the *bottom sheet* since it goes next to the mattress.

(6) **(flat) sheet:** This is also a piece of cotton or silk. It can be a *bottom sheet* next to the mattress or a *top sheet* under the blankets.

(7) **blanket:** People usually sleep with one or more wool, cotton, or polyester blankets.

(8) **electric blanket:** a blanket that has electrical wires in the material and a *control* that regulates the amount of heat the wires produce.

(11) **comforter/quilt:** a bed covering with feathers or polyester material inside.

(13) **chest (of drawers):** a vertical set of drawers that people typically use to store clothing.

(14) **blinds:** a set of plastic or metal strips on a pulley that allows a person to regulate the amount of sunlight in a room. The word *blinds* is a plural noun.

(15) **curtains:** *Curtains* is a general term for fabric window coverings of any length. In contrast, *drapes* (*Picture Dictionary* page 21) are curtains that go from the top of the window to the floor and are a more formal window treatment.

(22) **dresser/bureau:** a piece of furniture to store clothing. A dresser often has a mirror over it.

(23) **mattress:** a thick pad of rubber, feathers, or synthetic material that rests on top of the box spring (24) and provides a soft surface to sleep on. A mattress pad is a quilted cover that protects the mattress.

(24) **box spring:** a box with fabric around it that contains wire coils. It rests on the bed frame and supports the mattress.

(25) **bed frame:** a wooden or metal support for the box spring and mattress.

LANGUAGE & CULTURE NOTES

> The kitchen on *Picture Dictionary* page 24 is an *eat-in kitchen,* a kitchen that is large enough to hold a table and chairs where people can eat.

(3) garbage pail: Some people call this a *wastebasket.* A garbage pail always has a lid.

(4) (electric) mixer: an appliance that combines foods at various speeds.

(5) cabinet: Another word for *cabinet* is *cupboard.*

(7) canister: a container that you use to store foods such as flour, sugar, or cookies.

(9) dishwasher detergent: soap for a dishwasher. It comes in two forms—a granular powder and a liquid.

(10) dishwashing liquid: soap in liquid form that you use when you wash dishes by hand.

(14) (garbage) disposal: an electrical appliance that chops up food scraps so they can pass through sewer pipes.

(19) blender: an appliance that mixes ingredients at various speeds and produces a liquid.

(20) toaster oven: an electrical appliance that can toast, bake, and reheat small portions of food.

(21) microwave (oven): an electrical appliance that uses electromagnetic waves to cook food internally. A microwave may also be free-standing, a separate unit that goes on a counter.

(22) potholder: a cotton mitt to protect the hands when someone is holding hot cooking utensils or pots.

(23) tea kettle: a pot that you use to heat water to boiling. A whistling tea kettle produces a whistle sound when the water boils.

(25) burner: the heating unit on the top surface of a stove. Stoves can have from four to eight burners.

(26) oven: the interior compartment of a stove where you bake and broil food.

(27) toaster: an electrical appliance that browns slices of bread.

(28) coffeemaker: an electrical appliance that heats water and prepares coffee. The heated water drips through the ground coffee beans and into the pot. The surface below the pot heats to keep the coffee hot.

(29) trash compactor: an electrical appliance that compresses kitchen trash.

(30) cutting board: a block of wood or plastic that protects the surface when someone is cutting food.

(32) food processor: an appliance with different blades that cuts foods in a variety of thicknesses.

(35) placemat: a rectangular piece of material or plastic that you put under a place setting to protect the table or for decoration.

THE BABY'S ROOM

LANGUAGE & CULTURE NOTES

> *Baby* or *infant* is the general term for children under a year old. *Toddler* is for children one to three years old. *Preschooler* is for four- and five-year-old children. It is common to refer to children colloquially as *kids*.
>
> Many items that people use for a baby begin with the word *baby*—for example, *baby spoon, baby quilt, baby clothes, baby food.*

(2) **baby monitor/intercom:** a microphone and speaker system that allows the parent in another room to monitor the baby's noises. One unit of the system stays in the baby's room, and the parent can carry the other unit from room to room.

(4) **crib:** a special bed for babies with high sides that raise and lower so the baby doesn't fall (or an older baby doesn't climb) out of the crib.

(5) **crib bumper/bumper pad:** a cloth or plastic-covered soft pad that fits inside the crib so the baby doesn't bump the crib frame.

(6) **mobile:** a toy that hangs over the crib for the baby to look at. Many doctors feel that the visual stimulation of a mobile is important for a baby's development.

(7) **changing table:** a table on which someone *changes* (puts clean diapers on) a baby.

(8) **stretch suit:** a one-piece outfit of *stretch* (elasticized) material.

(10) **diaper pail:** a container for soiled diapers.

(11) **night light:** a small light that plugs into a socket. Parents often keep a night light on in their baby's room so that the room won't be completely dark at night.

(19) **cradle:** a special small bed for very young babies. It is often on poles or has curved feet that allow the parent to *rock* (move gently) the cradle back and forth. To *cradle* a baby means to hold and/or rock the baby in your arms.

(24) **food warmer:** a hollow double dish with an interior that you fill with hot water to keep the food in the top dish warm. Stores also sell electric food warmers.

(25) **booster seat:** a small seat that sits on a chair to raise the child to the height of a table top. It's common to use booster seats at home. Most restaurants also have them.

(29) **potty:** a child-size portable toilet.

(30) **baby frontpack:** a cloth harness to carry a young baby in which the baby faces forward. Many parents like these because the baby can see the world and not just the adult's chest.

(31) **baby backpack:** a padded frame so that an adult can carry a baby aged six months to two years on his or her back.

LANGUAGE & CULTURE NOTES

(2) **vanity:** the cabinet that contains the sink and storage areas.

(5) **soap dispenser:** a container for liquid soap.

(8) **medicine cabinet:** a cabinet where people put personal care products such as those on *Picture Dictionary* pages 98 and 99.

(16) **hamper:** a container for dirty clothes and towels.

(19) **hand towel:** When Americans have guests come to their home, they often put out *guest towels*, decorative *hand towels* that are paper, cotton, or linen.

(22) **plunger:** a tool that you use to unplug a blocked toilet.

(23) **toilet brush:** a brush with a long handle that you use to clean toilets.

(25) **air freshener:** a container of liquid scent that removes odors. Spray cans of air freshener in many scent varieties are common.

(26) **toilet:** A toilet in North America has a *seat* (27) that raises and lowers.

(28) **shower:** Some bathrooms contain only a shower that is not part of a bathtub. The term for a separate shower is *shower stall*.

OUTSIDE THE HOME

DICTIONARY PAGE 27

LANGUAGE & CULTURE NOTES

The grassy area around a house is a *yard* in American English and a *garden* in British English. In American English, a *garden* is a plot of land where people grow flowers, fruits, or vegetables. The area in front of the house is the *front yard,* and the area behind the house is the *backyard.* The word for the grass around the house is *lawn.* People often have gardens in their backyards and use their backyards to entertain guests at barbecues.

(2) mailbox: Some homes have a mailbox such as the one on *Picture Dictionary* page 27 in front of the house at the end of the front walk. This is common in suburban and rural communities. Other houses have a *mail slot*, an opening in the front door. In the United States, there is home delivery of mail Monday through Saturday. The mail carrier brings the mail to the house and leaves it in the mailbox or puts it in the mail slot.

(5) (front) porch: a roofed, wooden platform in the front of some houses. People often place chairs and tables on the porch during warm weather.

(6) storm door: a metal or wooden door with glass or a clear-plastic window that protects the wooden front door from the weather and provides insulation. During warm weather, a screen replaces the window of a storm door.

(11) (window) screen: a wire mesh that people put on their windows in warm weather so they can open the windows to let air in and keep bugs out.

(12) shutter: In the past, people closed their shutters during cold weather to provide insulation for the house. Nowadays, shutters are purely decorative, except in areas where there are hurricanes, tornadoes, and other severe weather conditions.

(17) lawn chair: an outdoor chair of weather-resistant materials, such as aluminum, plastic, or wrought iron.

(18) lawnmower: a machine that you use to mow the lawn (*cut the grass*). There are hand-pushed, electrical, and gasoline-powered lawnmowers.

(19) tool shed: a small building where you store equipment and products you use outside the home.

(20) screen door: a door with a wire mesh screen that you use in warm weather so you can keep the door open to let air in, but not insects.

(23) deck: a wooden platform at the back of a house. People often place chairs and tables on the deck during warm weather.

(24) barbecue/(outdoor) grill: an outdoor stove that you heat with charcoal or propane gas, over which you *barbecue* meat, fish, and vegetables.

(26) gutter: an open metal tube that collects rainwater and diverts it to the ground through a drainpipe (27).

(27) drainpipe: a metal tube that carries rainwater from the gutter to the ground.

(28) satellite dish: a receiver for satellite TV channels.

(29) TV antenna: a wire frame that receives television signals from TV stations. Some communities offer cable TV service, for which viewers pay a monthly fee to receive television channels over cable wires.

(32) fence: Fences can be wood, plastic, brick, metal, or stone.

> In the United States many people locate apartments through newspaper or Internet listings. It is also common to go to a real estate agent and pay a fee to find an apartment.

Looking for an Apartment

(1–2) apartment ads/classified ads/ apartment listings: Apartment owners and real estate firms advertise apartments for rent in newspapers or on Internet websites. Another word for these ads is *listings*.

(3) vacancy sign: Apartment owners sometimes put up a sign to indicate an apartment for rent.

Signing a Lease

(4) tenant: A person who lives in an apartment is the *occupant* or the *tenant*.

(5) landlord: an owner of an apartment or of an entire building.

(6) lease: the written contract between a tenant and a landlord. It defines the cost of the rent, the requirements for payment, the responsibilities for care and maintenance of the apartment, and the duration of the rental period.

(7) security deposit: Some landlords require tenants to put down a security deposit when they sign the lease. This is often equal to one month's rent. The money goes into a bank account and collects interest until the tenant moves out. If the tenant damages any part of the apartment, the landlord takes money for the repairs from the security deposit.

Moving In

(8) moving truck/moving van: People can hire a company to help them move to a new home, or they can do it themselves with a truck that they rent for a day or two. A moving van is much larger than a moving truck.

(10) building manager: the person who manages a building. Unlike the superintendent (41), the manager does not do repairs. He or she collects the rent, oversees large renovations, and intervenes when there are disputes among neighbors.

(11) doorman: Some apartment buildings have a doorman at the entrance for security reasons. The doorman lets people into the building, checks to make sure that only tenants and their guests are entering, may assist people when they load or unload their cars, and may hail a taxi for a tenant or visitor.

(14) first floor: In the United States the first floor is the entry-level floor or the *ground floor*.

(19) fire escape: Apartment buildings in the US are required to have two stairways. Many older buildings have outdoor metal stairways that serve as an emergency escape route.

(26) whirlpool: a small hot tub with a motor that makes the water bubble and swirl around. It helps people to relax their aching muscles.

(27) trash bin: a large container for large items and in some cases for all the tenants' garbage.

Lobby: the entrance area of an apartment building.

(29) intercom/speaker: a speaker system that allows people in the lobby to talk to people in their apartments.

LANGUAGE & CULTURE NOTES

(30) **buzzer:** a bell that rings in the apartment to let occupants know that someone wants to speak to them on the intercom. In apartment buildings that do not have a doorman but have locked entrance doors, the buzzer alerts the resident that someone wants to enter the building. Each apartment has a buzzer that unlocks the entrance door.

Doorway

(34) **peephole:** a small hole with magnifying glass that allows the person in the apartment to see who is in the hallway.

(35) **(door) chain:** a weaker lock that allows the tenant to open the door slightly but still keep the door locked (on the chain).

(36) **dead-bolt lock:** a heavy lock that moves across the door frame.

(37) **smoke detector:** a safety device that gives out a loud signal when smoke is present.

Hallway

(38) **fire exit/emergency stairway:** An emergency stairway is an alternative stairway inside a building. It provides the fire exit to the outdoors. Usually these exits are only for an emergency. Otherwise an alarm will ring when someone uses them.

(39) **fire alarm:** a safety device that signals to the fire department and to building residents when there is a fire.

(40) **sprinkler system:** a water system that sprays water when there is smoke and heat from a fire.

(41) **superintendent:** the person who manages and does repairs in the apartment building. This person may also live in the building. People often refer to the superintendent as the *super*.

(42) **garbage chute/trash chute:** a pipe in multilevel buildings that carries garbage from each floor of the building to the basement.

Basement

(45) **laundry room:** a room in many apartment buildings, usually in the basement, with washers and dryers where tenants can do their laundry.

LANGUAGE & CULTURE NOTES

(A) plumber: a person who fixes pipes, toilets, and heating systems.

(1) leaking / (4) broken: *Broken* means something doesn't work any longer. *Leaking* means only that it cannot hold water. A toilet can be leaking water, but can still work.

(B) roofer: a person who fixes or installs roofs. Most roofs in the United States are asphalt or slate. In the South and West, many roofs are tile.

(C) (house) painter: a person who paints houses. Some painters paint only the insides of a house. Others do both interior and exterior painting.

(D) cable TV company: Cable TV is a commercial television service that comes through a special cable that attaches to the television from underground or from a utility pole on the street. The cable increases the number of television channels a household receives and can also provide Internet connection.

(E) appliance repairperson: a person who fixes large appliances in the home, such as refrigerators, stoves, dishwashers, washing machines, and dryers. People usually take small appliances for repair to service departments in the store where they bought the items or to stores that carry the same brand of the appliance.

(F) exterminator/pest control specialist: a person who uses chemicals or traps to kill *pests*—small animals or insects such as mice, ants, or roaches.

(11) There are _____ in the kitchen.

  (a) termites: eat wood.

  (b) fleas: have no wings and jump to move around. They bite animal or human skin and live on blood.

(f) rats: large rodents, similar to mice, with long tails and large teeth. Their bites can be dangerous to humans.

(g) mice: similar to rats, but much smaller and much less dangerous to humans. The singular form of *mice* is *mouse.*

(G) locksmith: a person who makes keys and installs and repairs locks.

(H) electrician: a person who fixes electrical systems.

(13) doesn't go on: A person *turns on* and *turns off* a light. The light itself *goes on* and *goes off.*

(15) The power is out. When the power is *out*, there is no power from the energy distributor. This usually happens when there is an interruption in the power lines in the larger neighborhood.

(I) chimneysweep: a person who cleans away the soot and creosote that collect in a chimney.

(J) home repairperson/"handyman": a person who does a wide variety of small repair jobs around the house.

(K) carpenter: a person who builds or repairs any wooden structure.

(L) heating and air conditioning service: In central heating systems, the entire house can receive heat or air conditioning through air vents. In the basement or behind the house, there is a machine that produces both the heat and the air conditioning. Older homes typically have systems that produce just heat. For cool air, people put air conditioners into their windows. These units cool air in only one or two rooms.

(A) sweep the floor: You can sweep the floor with a broom or with a carpet sweeper.

(2) dustpan: You use this with a broom or a whisk broom to collect dirt from the floor.

(3) whisk broom: any small broom that you can use with one hand while the dustpan is in the other hand.

(4) carpet sweeper: a mechanical, non-electric broom that has a pulley system of brushes inside its case.

(B) vacuum: The tool is *a vacuum*, and the verb is *to vacuum*.

(5) vacuum (cleaner): an electric appliance that sucks up dirt from wood, linoleum, and carpeted floors. Vacuums come in a variety of styles, such as a *canister* model (pictured) or an *upright* model.

(6) vacuum cleaner attachments: different shaped nozzles and brushes that you use for different types of cleaning.

(7) vacuum cleaner bag: a disposable bag that fits inside a vacuum to collect dirt.

(8) hand vacuum: a small hand-held vacuum. People often call it a *dust buster*, which is a brand name.

(C) mop the floor: You *mop* only on hard surfaces.

(9) (dust mop)/(dry) mop: You use this to collect dust from the floor and walls.

(10) (sponge) mop: a wet mop that you use to wash the floor.

(D) wash the windows: To open traditional sash windows in the United States, you move them up and down. Therefore, when you want to wash both sides of the window, someone needs to stand outside the house to wash the outer side. Newer-style windows have release latches that allow the window to swing into the room so that it's possible to wash both sides of the glass from inside the home.

(14) ammonia: a chemical that you use to clean different surfaces, including plastic, metal, and glass.

(E) dust: *Dust* (noun) is dry, powdery dirt. *To dust* is to remove the dust from the surface of furniture and walls.

(15) dust cloth: any small piece of soft fabric for cleaning. Many people call it a *rag* or a *dust rag*.

(16) feather duster: In the past, feather dusters consisted of just feathers, but today they often consist of synthetic materials.

(F) wax the floor: *Wax* (noun) is a liquid or paste that dries into a hard shiny surface. *To wax* is the verb.

(17) floor wax: liquid that you spread on a clean floor to make the surface shiny, hard, and easy to clean.

(G) polish the furniture: to clean the surfaces of furniture with a wax or liquid to make them shine.

(18) furniture polish: a liquid, cream, or pressurized spray that goes directly on wooden furniture to clean and create a shiny finish.

(H) clean the bathroom

(19) cleanser: a liquid or granular substance that you use to scrub hard surfaces such as tiles, metal sinks, and bathtubs.

(20) scrub brush: *To scrub* means to clean forcefully.

(I) take out the garbage: In the US, garbage collectors drive through neighborhoods on a regular schedule to pick up garbage that people leave in cans outside their homes.

(24) recycling bin: a container you use to collect materials that can be processed and used again (*recycled*), such as newspapers, tin cans, glass bottles, and some plastics.

LANGUAGE & CULTURE NOTES

(1) **yardstick:** a three-foot-long wooden stick you use to measure. It has lines that show 1/8", 1/4", 1/2", 3/4", and 1" increments. A yard is a little less than a meter.

(2) **fly swatter:** a hand-held implement you use to hit and kill small insects.

(3) **plunger:** a tool you use to unblock pipes in a sink or toilet by means of suction.

(4) **flashlight:** a portable light that has a bulb and batteries. Many people keep flashlights in various rooms of the home in case of power failures.

(5) **extension cord:** an electrical cord that you plug into an appliance so you can use the appliance a distance away from the electrical outlet.

(7) **step ladder:** a short folding ladder.

(8) **mousetrap:** a device that catches mice.

(9) **masking tape:** You use this on walls when you're painting to prevent paint overlap. When you take off the tape, it doesn't peel the paint away.

(10) **electrical tape:** special non-conducting rubber tape you use to wrap electrical cords that have exposed wires.

(11) **duct tape:** an all-purpose tape that is very strong. It can attach to plastic, cloth, and wood. If you first attach it to a dry surface, water can't dissolve its adhesive.

(15) **oil:** You use household oil to lubricate movable metal such as tools, hinges, and household machinery.

(17) **work gloves:** thick, padded gloves you wear to protect your hands while you work in the garden or do other heavy work.

(18) **bug spray/insect spray /** (19) **roach killer:** chemical poisons in pressurized cans you use to kill insects inside or outside the house.

(20) **sandpaper:** a special paper with fine particles of sand on one side. When you rub sandpaper on wooden surfaces, the sandpaper makes the surfaces smooth and removes paint and varnish.

(22) **paint thinner:** You use this to dilute oil-based paint and to clean it from brushes and hands.

(26) **spray gun:** You use this to paint smooth surfaces quickly and to prevent brush strokes.

TOOLS AND HARDWARE

LANGUAGE & CULTURE NOTES

(1) **hammer:** a tool you use to drive nails into wooden or plaster surfaces.

(2) **mallet:** a wooden hammer you use to pound objects such as bricks.

(3) **ax:** also spelled *axe*. This is a tool you use to cut down trees or chop wood.

(4) **saw / handsaw:** a tool to cut wood or plastic objects by means of a back-and-forth motion with the serrated edge of the blade.

(5) **hacksaw:** a saw with a replaceable, finely serrated blade. You typically use a hacksaw to cut metal.

(6) **level:** a device you use to tell if an object is on an even plane or to draw a guide line so that an object will be on an even plane.

(7) **screwdriver /** (8) **Phillips screwdriver:** tools you use to insert a *screw* (28 / 29) into material by a twisting motion. The standard slot screwdriver (7) has a flat-bladed tip that fits standard screws. The Phillips screwdriver (8) has a pointed, grooved tip that fits Phillips screws, those with *x-shaped* grooves in the head.

(9) **wrench:** a tool you use to tighten or loosen nuts (27) or bolts (30).

(10) **monkey wrench/pipe wrench:** a tool you use to screw pipes into joints or to turn large nuts or bolts.

(11) **chisel:** a tool with a narrow, sharp blade you use to cut and shape material such as wood or stone.

(12) **scraper:** a device with a wide, sharp blade that you draw or push over a surface to make it smooth or to remove paint or wallpaper.

(13) **wire stripper:** sharp blades that can tear away the insulating rubber around electrical wires.

(14) **hand drill:** This device holds a drill bit (20), which you rotate to make a hole.

(15) **vise:** a device you use to hold objects securely in place.

(16) **pliers:** a tool you use to hold an object securely so you can turn the object or keep it steady.

(18) **plane:** a tool with a sharp blade that you push across a wooden surface to make it smooth.

(19) **electric drill:** a device that holds and rotates a drill bit (20).

(20) **(drill) bit:** A grooved metal rod with a sharp point that makes holes.

(21) **circular saw/power saw:** an electrical tool you use to cut wood, metal, or plastic objects by the rotation of a serrated circular blade.

(22) **power sander:** an electrical tool you use to sand away rough surfaces, paint, or varnish.

(23) **router:** a plane (18) with two handles that you use to cut grooves.

(25) **nail:** You hit a nail with a hammer (1) to fasten two objects together.

(26) **washer:** You use a washer to improve the tightness of the fit when you fasten two objects with a bolt (30) and nut (27) and to make sure the bolt doesn't damage the material.

(27) **nut:** You use this to secure the bolt in place.

(28) **wood screw /** (29) **machine screw:** You use these to fasten two objects together with a screwdriver (7). Wood screws are for wood, and machine screws are for metal. The shaft of a screw has a spiral groove called a thread.

(30) **bolt:** You use a bolt to fasten two object together. The bolt passes completely through the material and a nut (27) holds the bolt in place. The shaft has a spiral groove called a thread.

LANGUAGE & CULTURE NOTES

(A) mow the lawn: It is also common to say "cut the grass." See *lawnmower* (1).

(B) plant vegetables: The person in this scene is placing vegetable seeds in the ground. This person is *sowing seeds*.

(C) plant flowers: When people plant flowers, they place fully grown plants into the ground.

(E) rake leaves: In the northern area of the United States, where many leaves fall off the trees in autumn, people rake the leaves and place them in compost piles so that the leaves decompose. Or they place them in special yard waste bags for trash collection.

(F) trim the hedge: Many house in the US use bushes (*hedges*) rather than walls to fence in their yards. Bushes such as privet, arborvitae, and boxwood need regular trimming. See *hedge clippers* (17) and *hedge trimmer* (18).

(G) prune the bushes: It is also common to say *cut back* the bushes. There are some bushes that people need to prune every year, and others that people don't need to prune as often.

(H) weed: *To weed* (verb) is to pull *weeds* (noun) out of the ground before they take from the soil the water and nutrients that other plants need.

(1) lawnmower: People use electric, gas, and hand lawnmowers to cut (*mow*) the grass (*lawn*). The lawnmower in the scene has a gas motor.

(2) gas can: People store gas in a can to use in gas-powered machines, such as lawnmowers, snow blowers, and chain saws.

(3) line trimmer: a gardening tool that trims areas a lawnmower can't reach.

(4) shovel: a gardening tool you use to dig large holes.

(6) hoe: a gardening tool you use to turn the earth.

(7) trowel: a hand tool you use to dig holes in a garden.

(9) fertilizer: chemical or organic matter you spread on plants to feed the plants and stimulate growth.

(11) nozzle: This hose attachment controls the force and direction of the water. You use it when you water plants and wash cars and lawn furniture.

(12) sprinkler: You attach a sprinkler to a hose to spray water onto the grass.

(13) watering can: a can you use to water plants and flowers.

(14) rake: a tool you use to gather leaves in the autumn in climates where the leaves fall off the trees.

(15) leaf blower: a power blower that pushes leaves along so that a gardener can quickly make a pile.

(16) yard waste bag: You fill this with leaves or other unwanted botanical waste. Most cities provide a special collection for this type of waste, which they recycle for public use.

(17) (hedge) clippers: a manual tool you use to trim small bushes. A hedge is a thick row of shrubs usually at the boundary of a person's property.

(18) hedge trimmer: a power tool you use to prune small bushes and trim trees.

(19) pruning shears: sharp shears that can cut through small branches.

(20) weeder: a tool you use to pull weeds from the ground. See *weed* [H].

LC35

(3) barber shop: a place where men and boys get their hair cut.

(5) bus station: a place where travelers can purchase tickets and board a commuter or long distance bus. A bus stop is a place alongside the street where a local bus stops to pick up and let off passengers.

(8) card store: a store that sells cards for special occasions such as birthdays and holidays. These stores also sell small gift items such as stuffed animals, chocolate, and candles.

(9) child-care center/day-care center: a place where care-givers keep young children during the day while their parents are at work.

(10) cleaners/dry cleaners: a place that cleans people's clothes, especially clothes that people can't wash in their washing machines. Cleaners also wash and iron men's shirts.

(11) clinic: a neighborhood facility where a person can go for routine medical care. For life-threatening emergencies or for intensive care, people go to the hospital instead.

(13) coffee shop: a small restaurant that serves coffee, pastries, and sandwiches.

(15) convenience store: a small grocery store that is usually open from early in the morning until late at night. It is a *convenient* place to buy common, everyday household or grocery items.

(16) copy center: a place that duplicates documents on copy machines.

(17) delicatessen/deli: a store that sells ready-to-eat foods such as sliced cold meats, cheeses, and salads.

(18) department store: a large store that sells a variety of goods, including clothing, jewelry, shoes, appliances, furniture, and household items.

(19) discount store: a store that sells products at discount (lower than regular) prices.

(20) donut shop: a place to buy donuts (small round pastries with a hole in the middle; see *Picture Dictionary* page 61). Donuts are extremely popular in the United States. People eat them for breakfast and for snacks.

(21) drug store/pharmacy: a place that fills doctors' prescriptions and sells a variety of personal care products.

(22) electronics store: a place that sells electronic equipment such as computers, DVD players, televisions, cameras, and electronic accessories, as well as movies, software, and music.

(23) eye-care center/optician: a place to get a vision check up and to purchase eyeglasses or contact lenses.

(24) fast-food restaurant: any of many restaurant chains that prepare portable food quickly. They most commonly serve hamburgers, pizzas, Mexican foods, salads, and sandwiches (see *Picture Dictionary* page 60).

(25) flower shop/florist: a place to buy cut flowers or plants or to order flowers to send to someone for a special occasion.

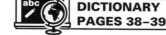
(1) **hair salon:** a place where both women and men get their hair styled.

(2) **hardware store:** a place to buy tools and home and gardening supplies. See *Picture Dictionary* pages 33 and 34 for the kinds of items people buy in hardware stores.

(3) **health club:** a place where people go to exercise and improve their physical health and condition. Health clubs usually have a variety of exercise equipment. Some have swimming pools, steam rooms, and saunas.

(8) **laundromat:** a place where people pay to use washing machines and dryers.

(10) **maternity shop:** a store that sells clothes for pregnant women.

(11) **motel:** a hotel that is usually in a suburban area or on a highway. There are normally parking spaces near the rooms in a motel for travelers to park their cars. A motel differs from a hotel (5), which is usually a large building, often downtown, and which may or may not provide parking. The word "motel" comes from the phrase "motor hotel."

(13) **music store:** a place that sells recorded music. In addition, many music stores sell sheet music and small musical instruments. Some music stores also repair instruments and offer music lessons.

(16) **pet shop/pet store:** a place that sells pet supplies and small pets such as dogs, cats, fish, hamsters, gerbils, birds, and fish.

(17) **photo shop:** a place that develops photographs and sells photographic supplies and cameras.

(23) **(shopping) mall:** a large indoor shopping area on one or two floors with a large variety of stores and places to eat.

(27) **travel agency:** a place to get information about world travel, to plan trips, to make hotel reservations, and to purchase airline tickets.

(28) **video store:** a place to rent videos and DVDs of movies.

LANGUAGE & CULTURE NOTES

(1) **courthouse:** the government building that contains the municipal court, the place where trials take place.

(2) **taxi/cab/taxicab:** Many American taxis are yellow, but they can be any color.

(3) **taxi stand:** an area for use by taxis.

(4) **taxi driver/cab driver:** Most cities require special licenses for cab drivers.

(6) **trash container:** a receptacle on city streets for garbage and trash. In most states it is illegal to litter (throw garbage or trash on the ground).

(7) **city hall:** the building with offices for departments, such as the mayor's office, the tax collector, and the city clerk.

(8) **fire alarm box:** a box that contains a lever that you pull to notify the fire station of a fire.

(13) **sidewalk:** It is customary in American cities for pedestrians to walk on the right side of the sidewalk.

(15) **street light:** a tall light that goes on automatically as the sky darkens at night and turns off when the sun comes up the next morning.

(16) **parking lot:** an outdoor facility where people pay to park their cars.

(17) **meter maid:** a person who checks to make sure that cars don't park beyond the time allowed on the parking meter, and who writes a ticket to leave on the car if they do.

(18) **parking meter:** Most American city streets have designated parking spaces. Meters show the amount of time allowed for parking and have coin slots where people pay the parking fee.

(19) **garbage truck:** U.S. cities have a private or municipal service that empties trash containers.

(20) **subway:** an underground public transportation system that may have portions that run at surface level or are elevated.

(22) **newsstand:** a shop or kiosk that sells magazines and newspapers.

(23) **traffic light/traffic signal:** a signal with red, yellow, and green lights that control traffic flow. Red means *stop*, green means *go*, and yellow means *caution —prepare to stop*.

(26) **crosswalk:** an area at a street corner where it is legal for pedestrians to cross the street. People who cross a street where there is no crosswalk are *jaywalking*, which is illegal.

(28) **ice cream truck:** a small truck that travels around the city and sells ice cream.

(30) **parking garage:** a multilevel indoor structure where people pay to park their cars.

(32) **bus stop:** an area where local buses drop off and pick up passengers.

(33) **bus / (34) bus driver:** Buses usually have a sign above the front window and on the side, which shows the number and final destination of the bus line.

(37) **street sign:** a sign at an intersection that gives the names of the streets that intersect.

(38) **manhole:** a covered hole in the street that gives workers access to sewers and utility wires.

(40) **street vendor:** a person who sells merchandise or food on the sidewalk.

(41) **drive-through window:** an area where customers can transact their business while they sit in their cars.

(2) **baby/infant:** a baby from birth up to age one. A *newborn* is a recently born child until about two months old.

(3) **toddler:** a child who is just beginning to walk, usually between the ages of one and three.

(6) **teenager:** a child between the ages of thirteen and nineteen.

(10) **senior citizen/elderly person:** a person over sixty-five years old.

(12) **middle-aged:** a person who is no longer young but not yet old, between the ages of forty and sixty.

(13) **old/elderly:** a person sixty years old or older. *Elderly* is a more polite term. *Old* has negative connotations in today's youth-oriented society.

(21) **physically challenged:** a person who has difficulty with an activity due to his or her physical condition. In the past it was common to call such a person *handicapped,* but because this term denotes a disadvantage, it is not as common today.

(22) **vision impaired:** a person who has difficulty with his or her sight. A *blind* person cannot see anything. A *legally blind* person may be able to detect shapes, colors, and lines, but still struggles to see.

(23) **hearing impaired:** a person who has difficulty hearing sounds. A *deaf* person cannot hear anything.

DESCRIBING PEOPLE AND THINGS

LANGUAGE & CULTURE NOTES

(1–2) **new–old / (3–4) young–old:** *New* and *old* describe things (a *new* car, an *old* house). *Young* and *old* describe people (a *young* girl, an *old* man).

(5–6) **tall–short:** *Tall* describes the height of both people and things (a *tall* man, a *tall* building). *Short* describes a person's height (a *short* woman).

(7–8) **long–short:** These describe the length of something (a *long* or *short* story, *long* or *short* hair).

(13–14) **heavy/fat–thin/skinny:** It is more polite to describe a person as *heavy* than *fat*. *Skinny* has the connotation of *too thin*.

(23–24) **thick–thin:** *Thick* doesn't describe people, only things (*thick* soup, a *thick* book). *Thin* describes both people and things (a *thin* boy, a *thin* line).

(27–28) **high–low:** These describe a structure's height (a *high* building, a *low* building).

(39–40) **soft–hard / (41–42) easy–difficult/hard:** *Hard* is the opposite of *soft* when it refers to something solid and firm to the touch (a *hard* piece of wood). *Hard* is the opposite of *easy* when it refers to something that is *difficult* (a *hard* English assignment).

(51–52) **pretty/beautiful–ugly / (53–54) handsome–ugly:** *Pretty* and *beautiful* are adjectives that describe women. They also describe things (a *pretty* house, a *beautiful* car). *Handsome* is an adjective that describes men. *Ugly* describes both people and things (an *ugly* man, an *ugly* painting).

(65–66) **shiny–dull / (67–68) sharp–dull:** *Dull* is the opposite of *shiny* when it means *not bright* (a *dull* day, a *dull* color). *Dull* is the opposite of *sharp* when it means *not pointed* (a *dull* knife).

DESCRIBING PHYSICAL STATES AND EMOTIONS

LANGUAGE & CULTURE NOTES

> There are cultural differences as well as individual differences in the ways people express emotions. For example, a common expression of anger in one culture may be to shout, while in another it may be to keep silent. In one culture it may be common for men to cry, and in another men do not usually cry. Also, in some cultures, people don't feel comfortable discussing their personal feelings.

(1) tired / (2) sleepy / (3) exhausted: A *tired* person is someone who possibly worked too hard or didn't sleep and needs some rest. A *sleepy* person is someone who wants to fall asleep. An *exhausted* person is someone who doesn't have any energy left for even the simplest actions.

(11) sad/unhappy / (12) miserable: A *sad* or *unhappy* person is someone who feels depressed at a particular moment. A *miserable* person feels terribly sad, uncomfortable, or in pain.

(15) upset / (16) annoyed / (17) angry/mad / (18) furious: An *upset* person is someone who feels disturbed at a particular moment. A person who is *annoyed* feels irritated but not really angry. *Angry* and *mad* have the same meanings in American English, but in British usage *mad* means insane. A *furious* person is extremely angry.

(21) surprised / (22) shocked: A *surprised* person is someone who experiences something unexpected. A *shocked* person experiences something very upsetting, usually something negative.

FRUITS

LANGUAGE & CULTURE NOTES

Fresh fruits are available year-round in the United States in supermarkets and at farm markets and fruit stands. Many fruits, such as apples, pears, and blueberries, grow during the summer months in northern climates. Other fruits, such as mangoes, papayas, pineapples, bananas, and kiwis, grow throughout the year in more tropical climates.

Americans eat fruit for breakfast in a bowl or on cereal, for dessert at lunch or dinner, or as a snack. People often cut up a mixture of different kinds of fruits and serve it as *fruit salad* for an appetizer, a light lunch, or dessert.

Fruit is normally a collective noun. People will often say, "Do you like fruit?" or "I like to eat fruit for dessert." Speakers use the plural form *fruits* when they are thinking of individual *fruits* or varieties of *fruits*.

Grammatically speaking, the following are collective nouns, usually in their singular form: *cantaloupe, honeydew (melon), pineapple, watermelon, grapefruit.* All the other fruits in this lesson are countable (two apples, four avocados, etc.)

(1) **apple:** Apples are available all year, but they are at their best in the fall. There are many varieties of red, green, and yellow apples.

(3) **pear:** There are many varieties of yellow, green, and brown pears.

(4) **banana:** Many call this the perfect fruit because it is a rich source of vitamins and fiber.

(5) **plantain:** a starchy banana that is less sweet. Most people cook plantains before they eat them.

(7) **apricot:** Dried apricots are very popular.

(8) **nectarine:** a variety of peach with a smooth skin.

(9) **kiwi:** a tropical fruit with a thin fuzzy skin and a green fruit inside.

(10) **papaya:** a large, oblong tropical fruit.

(11) **mango:** a yellowish-red tropical fruit with sweet, aromatic yellow-colored flesh.

(12) **fig:** a soft, sweet, pear-shaped fruit with many seeds that grows in warm regions.

(13) **coconut:** the large, round brown fruit of the palm tree.

(14) **avocado:** a green, pear-shaped tropical fruit that people often eat raw in salads.

(15–17): *Melon* is a general term that refers to several varieties such as cantaloupe (15), honeydew (16), and watermelon (17).

(19–23): **Grapefruit, lemons, limes, oranges,** and **tangerines** are all citrus fruits. They are a good source of Vitamin C.

(19) **grapefruit:** There are two types of grapefruit—one with a pink interior and the other with yellow.

(24) **grapes:** Grapes come in green, red, and purple varieties, with and without seeds.

(26–28): **Prunes, dates,** and **raisins** are all dried fruits.

(26) **prunes:** dried plums.

(27) **dates:** small, oblong, sweet, brown fruits that grow in hot climates.

(28) **raisins:** dried grapes.

(30) **raspberries:** delicate red or black berries that grow on dense bushes with thorns.

(31) **blueberries:** a small, round, sweet blue fruit that grows on bushes. They grow wild and also in fields.

(32) **strawberries:** small, sweet, juicy red berries that grow close to the ground. People typically eat strawberries in fruit salads, on cereal, and in a bowl with cream.

LC48

LANGUAGE & CULTURE NOTES

People cook some vegetables, they eat some raw, and they serve other vegetables either way.

People put lettuce, celery, cucumbers, tomatoes, carrots, radishes, green and red peppers, and scallions in salads, and typically cook potatoes, sweet potatoes, yams, bok choy, corn, asparagus, eggplant, acorn and butternut squash, peas, beans, brussels sprouts, beets, artichokes, and turnips. People sometimes cook the following vegetables and sometimes serve them raw: broccoli, cauliflower, spinach, onions, cabbage, zucchini, mushrooms, red and green peppers, and jalapeños.

See *Picture Dictionary* page 58 for ways in which people cook vegetables. Depending on the vegetable, people bake, boil, broil, fry, steam, stir-fry, or microwave the vegetable.

It's common to buy most vegetables by the pound. However, you buy lettuce, cabbage, and cauliflower by the *head*, and carrots, celery, broccoli, and scallions by the *bunch*.

One piece of celery is a *stalk*, one piece of asparagus is a *spear*, and one piece of corn is an *ear*.

Meat: This includes beef, lamb, and pork products.

(1) steak: a flat piece of beef that people usually broil or barbecue on a grill. Steak is a very popular American meat.

(2) ground beef: People often call this hamburger or hamburger meat. Ground beef comes in several varieties, according to how much fat is in the meat. The label on the package tells the percentage of fat.

(3) stewing beef: chunks of lower-quality beef that you usually cook slowly in liquid at low temperatures to make them tender.

(4) roast beef: a large piece of beef that you roast in the oven.

(5) ribs: several rib bones and the meat between these ribs. People usually cook them as a single piece of meat. Barbecued ribs are very popular in restaurants and at home, where it's common to grill them outdoors or bake them in the oven. Barbecue sauce is a spicy, tomato-based sauce that people put on ribs.

(6) leg of lamb: a lamb roast with or without a bone.

(7) lamb chops: A chop is a single rib bone with meat. People typically fry, broil, or bake lamb chops.

(8) tripe: the wall of a cow's stomach that people eat as food.

(10) pork: any cut of meat that comes from a pig.

(11) pork chops: A chop is a single rib bone with meat. People typically fry, broil, or bake pork chops.

(12) sausages: ground pork in a skin. Americans often eat sausages for breakfast with eggs or grill them outdoors for dinner. Other kinds of sausage (turkey and chicken) are now popular because people in the US are eating less red meat.

(13) ham: smoke- or sugar-cured pork. Americans traditionally serve ham on holidays. It's also very popular in sandwiches.

(14) bacon: a fatty cut of pork that comes in slabs or slices. Americans typically eat bacon for breakfast with eggs and in *BLT* (bacon, lettuce, and tomato) sandwiches.

Poultry: meat from any type of fowl (bird).

(15–19): Stores sell chicken (15) whole for roasting, stewing, and soups, or in packages of separate parts such as breasts (16), legs/drumsticks (17) (the lower part of the leg), wings (18), and thighs (19) (the upper part of the leg). The leg is the dark meat of the chicken. The breast and wing are the white meat.

(20) turkey: Whole turkeys and turkey parts are available both fresh and frozen. Turkey and trimmings are a traditional American meal at Thanksgiving and Christmas. Trimmings include a bread-based stuffing called dressing, potatoes, vegetables, cranberry sauce, and pumpkin pie.

(21) duck: Duck is not as popular as chicken and turkey in the United States.

LANGUAGE & CULTURE NOTES

Seafood: any edible animals from the sea, including fish and shellfish.

Fish

(22) **salmon:** a heavy fish that people usually poach or broil. Salmon is also available canned.

(23) **halibut:** a light fish that people typically broil or fry. It is one of the varieties of fish in fish sticks—fresh or frozen pieces of breaded fish.

(24) **haddock:** a light fish that people typically broil or fry. It's also common in fish sticks.

(25) **flounder:** a light, white fish that people typically broil or fry.

(26) **trout:** a freshwater light fish that people usually fry whole with its skin.

(27) **catfish:** a freshwater heavy fish that is popular in the Midwest and South.

Shellfish: any sea animal without a spine that lives in water and has a shell.

(29) **shrimp:** People generally eat shrimp cooked. *Shrimp cocktail*, a popular American appetizer, is cooked, chilled shrimp that you dip in a spicy ketchup sauce.

(30) **scallops:** People usually bake or saute scallops. The meat is white and has a delicate fish-like flavor.

(31) **crabs:** Crabs are available whole or as crabmeat, picked from the shell. It's common to put crabs in casseroles or pat them into "cakes," as well as to boil them and serve them with butter.

(32) **clams:** It's common to eat raw clams in the shell. Many people also bake them or remove them from the shell and fry them or use them in soup. Two popular soups are New England clam chowder, a milk-based soup, and Manhattan clam chowder, a tomato-based soup.

(33) **mussels:** Mussels live in freshwater and in seawater, but the seawater variety is a more popular food. Most people steam them and eat them with melted butter or in soup.

(34) **oysters:** People often eat oysters raw or bake them in the shell. Many people prefer not to eat raw oysters, which can be contaminated from pollution.

(35) **lobster:** a large crustacean that lives in the cold seawaters of the northern regions of the United States. A live lobster's shell is green, but it turns bright red after it's cooked. People usually steam, bake, or broil whole lobsters or lobster tails. Supermarkets keep live lobsters in aerated tanks.

DAIRY PRODUCTS, JUICES, AND BEVERAGES

LANGUAGE & CULTURE NOTES

Dairy Products: This department in a supermarket has products that require refrigeration, such as products from dairy cows, fresh juices, and eggs.

(1) milk / (2) low-fat milk / (3) skim milk: Milk comes in three forms—regular or whole milk; *low-fat*, which contains 1% or 2% fat; and *skim*, which is fat-free. All milk in the United States is pasteurized. Pasteurization is a heating process that kills bacteria. Most milk is homogenized. This means there is no separation of the milk and any fat content.

(4) chocolate milk: milk mixed with chocolate syrup.

(5) orange juice: Orange juice comes in cartons that need refrigeration and in frozen concentrates. Orange juice is a typical part of an American breakfast.

(7) butter: processed fat that comes from cream. Most Americans spread butter or margarine (8) on bread.

(8) margarine: processed fat that comes from milk or vegetable oils.

(9) sour cream: cream with an acidic or sour taste. It is common to serve sour cream as a topping for baked potatoes.

(10) cream cheese: a rich soft cheese from whole milk and cream.

(11) cottage cheese: soft, unripened cheese that comes from milk curds. People on a diet often eat cottage cheese that is low in fat.

(12) yogurt: milk with fermented bacteria cultures. Fruit-flavored yogurts are popular snacks with American dieters.

(13) tofu: a curd that comes from mashed soybeans.

(14) eggs: Eggs come in cartons of a dozen or half-dozen. The common sizes of eggs are jumbo, extra large, large, and medium.

Juices: Juice is very popular in the US. It comes in cans or bottles or in frozen concentrates that need water.

(20) fruit punch: a mixture of several juices.

(21) juice paks: small single-serving cartons of juice that are popular snacks for children and drinks for people who carry their lunches to work or school.

(22) powdered drink mix: flavored powder to which you add water to make a flavored drink.

Beverages: These drinks are carbonated soft drinks and bottled water.

(23) soda: a carbonated beverage that comes in many flavors, including cola, ginger ale, raspberry, orange, and lemon-lime.

(24) diet soda: soda that has artificial sweeteners instead of sugar.

(25) bottled water: mineral spring water. Many people feel that bottled water tastes better and is purer and healthier than water from city reservoirs.

Coffee and Tea: Coffee is an extremely popular beverage in the US. People commonly drink it during breakfast and after lunch or dinner.

(27) decaffeinated coffee/decaf: coffee that doesn't contain any caffeine, which is a stimulant.

(28) instant coffee: freeze-dried coffee that dissolves in hot water.

(30) herbal tea: Many prefer to drink tea that comes from herbs because of its flavor, medicinal benefits, and lack of caffeine.

(31) cocoa/hot chocolate mix: a hot drink of powdered chocolate and milk or water.

LANGUAGE & CULTURE NOTES

Deli: an abbreviated form of *delicatessen*. This section of the supermarket has a wide variety of pre-made salads that come in pints and quarts, and sliced meats and cheeses that people buy by the pound.

(2) **bologna:** processed meat from beef, pork, and/or veal. Bologna sandwiches are popular with children.

(3) **salami:** a hard, spicy beef sausage.

(4) **ham:** cooked, cured pork. A ham and Swiss cheese sandwich is a popular American sandwich.

(6) **corned beef:** cured, cooked beef.

(7) **pastrami:** smoked beef.

(8) **Swiss cheese:** the popular name of *Ementhaler cheese*, a hard cheese that has distinctive holes that form during the aging process.

(9) **provolone:** a hard Italian cheese with a mild taste.

(10) **American cheese:** yellow or white processed cheese.

(11) **mozzarella:** The low-moisture variety in the illustration is a semi-hard Italian cheese with a mild taste. People often use mozzarella cheese in sandwiches and as a topping on pizza and in Italian pasta casseroles.

(12) **cheddar cheese:** a hard yellow cheese with a sharp flavor. Cheddars range in sharpness from mild to extra-sharp.

(13) **potato salad:** a cold (or sometimes warm) salad that consists of cooked potatoes with mayonnaise or an oil-based salad dressing or sauce. It is a popular side dish at restaurants, summer picnics, and home barbecues.

(14) **cole slaw:** a cold salad of thinly sliced cabbage and mayonnaise. It is a popular side dish at restaurants, summer picnics, and home barbecues.

(15) **macaroni salad:** a cold salad of macaroni and mayonnaise. It is a popular side dish at restaurants, summer picnics, and home barbecues.

(17) **seafood salad:** a cold salad of white fish and mayonnaise. It is popular with dieters in a salad or in a sandwich.

Frozen Foods: Since many Americans shop only once a week, frozen foods are very popular. All refrigerators in the US have a freezer unit, and many Americans also have a separate freezer appliance.

(20) **frozen dinners:** a wide variety of prepared meals that contain an entree, vegetable, potato or rice or pasta, and sometimes a dessert. People cook them in a microwave or oven.

(21) **frozen lemonade/** (22) **frozen orange juice:** frozen juice concentrates that you have to defrost and dilute before you serve them.

Snack Foods: Americans are fond of *snack foods*—foods that people eat between meals as snacks. These foods don't provide much nutrition. They include a wide variety of chips, pretzels, crackers, and nuts.

(23) **potato chips:** very thin slices of fried or baked potatoes. They are a popular snack. People also serve them with sandwiches.

(24) **tortilla chips:** fried corn-based chips that are usually triangular in shape. People often dip them in a spicy tomato salsa (see *Picture Dictionary* page 53, word 27).

(25) **pretzels:** twisted bread dough in the shape of a bow with salt on top.

(26) **nuts:** This category includes peanuts, cashews, almonds, pecans, and Brazil nuts, among others.

(27) **popcorn:** kernels of corn that pop with heat.

GROCERIES

LANGUAGE & CULTURE NOTES

Packaged Goods: This section of the supermarket typically stocks pasta and rice products, cookies and crackers, and cereals.

(4) **macaroni:** small pasta tubes in the shape of an elbow.

(5) **noodles:** long, wide pasta.

(6) **spaghetti:** long, thin pasta.

(7) **rice:** a grain that is either brown (unprocessed) or white (processed to remove the bran and germ).

Canned Goods: This department has canned fruit, vegetables, meat, and fish.

(8) **soup:** Some soups are available ready to serve or concentrated. Soups are also available as dry mixes.

(9) **tuna (fish):** Tuna fish sandwiches (tuna mixed with mayonnaise and celery) are very popular in the US.

Jams and Jellies: fruit- and nut-based spreads that you put on a variety of bread products.

(12) **jam** / (13) **jelly:** Jam is a cooked fruit spread that includes pieces of fruit and the seeds of the fruit. Jelly is a clear, strained fruit spread that has no seeds.

(14) **peanut butter:** a spread of ground peanuts that comes in two varieties—chunky, with small pieces of nuts in the spread, and creamy, without pieces of ground nuts.

Condiments: a general term for a wide variety of items that people commonly use in cooking or serve with a food to add flavor.

(15) **ketchup:** a thick, sweetened, tomato-based sauce that people use in cooking and often serve on hamburgers.

(16) **mustard:** a yellow, mayonnaise-based sauce with mustard spice and other ingredients.

(17) **relish:** a sweet or zesty sauce of pickles and other ingredients.

(18) **pickles:** cucumbers preserved in vinegar.

Stores sell pickles whole, in wedges, or in slices.

(19) **olives:** Olives are either green or black (ripe) and come pitted or whole.

(21) **pepper:** the ground powder from the berry of an East Indian plant. Americans often have salt and pepper on their dinner table.

(22) **spices:** a variety of herbs and vegetables that are fresh, dried, or in powdered form.

(23) **soy sauce:** a brown sauce of fermented soybeans. It's common in Asian cooking.

(24) **mayonnaise:** a sauce of egg yolks, oil, and vinegar. People commonly use it on sandwiches.

(25) **(cooking) oil:** liquid vegetable fat from corn, safflower, canola seeds, or sunflower seeds, peanuts, and soybeans.

(26) **olive oil:** cooking oil that comes from olives.

(27) **salsa:** a tomato-based sauce with peppers, onions, and jalapeños.

(28) **vinegar:** a sour, acidic liquid of fermented fruit juice. You mix vinegar with oil to make salad dressing.

(29) **salad dressing:** a sauce that you put on green, leafy vegetables.

Baked Goods: This department in a supermarket includes breads, muffins, cookies, cakes, pies, and donuts.

(32) **English muffins:** small round breads that people split in half and toast in the toaster.

(33) **pita bread:** flat, round Middle Eastern bread with a pouch for sandwich fillings.

Baking Products: ingredients that you use to bake cakes and breads.

(37) **cake mix:** a packaged mixture of flour, baking powder, and other dried ingredients that you use when you make cakes.

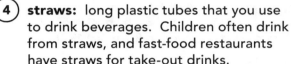
HOUSEHOLD SUPPLIES, BABY PRODUCTS, AND PET FOOD

LANGUAGE & CULTURE NOTES

Paper Products: Many Americans use paper products for their convenience. There are napkins (1) and paper towels (6) in almost every kitchen, and people commonly use paper cups (2) and paper plates (5) for picnics and for informal parties.

(4) straws: long plastic tubes that you use to drink beverages. Children often drink from straws, and fast-food restaurants have straws for take-out drinks.

Household Items: Besides the items on *Picture Dictionary* page 54, this department may also have such things as party goods, greeting cards, candles, flashlights, batteries, and various household cleaning products. (See *Picture Dictionary* page 32 for household cleaning products.)

(8) sandwich bags: plastic bags in the shape and size of a sandwich for people who make their lunch at home and take it to school or work. There are also larger plastic bags that you use to store food.

(9) trash bags: plastic bags that come in a variety of sizes that you use to collect household trash and yard debris.

(10) soap / (11) liquid soap: Soap comes in units called bars. Liquid soap comes in a dispenser.

(12) aluminum foil: a very thin sheet of metal paper that comes in a roll. You use it to wrap food to preserve its freshness.

(13) plastic wrap: a very thin sheet of plastic that comes in a roll that you use to cover food to preserve its freshness.

(14) waxed paper: a sheet of paper that has wax on it and comes in a roll. You use it to cover food to preserve its freshness.

Baby Products: See *Picture Dictionary* page 25 for more vocabulary for baby products.

(15) baby cereal: dry flakes of a variety of cereal grains that you mix with warm water to feed to infants.

(16) baby food: prepared fruits, vegetables, meats, and meals that come in different consistencies for babies of different ages.

(17) formula: a milk- or soybean-based drink for babies who are not nursing.

(18) wipes: disposable soft tissues with a mild lotion for cleaning a baby.

(19) (disposable) diapers: soft, absorbent, plastic-lined diapers that many people prefer to use for their convenience instead of cloth diapers, which you need to wash.

Pet Food: Dogs and cats in America live and eat well. Stores sell many varieties of wet and dry food, even special kinds for the gourmet, aged, or overweight dog.

THE SUPERMARKET

LANGUAGE & CULTURE NOTES

Besides food, many supermarkets sell personal care products (such as those on *Picture Dictionary* pages 98–99); flowers and plants; small hardware items such as lightbulbs, batteries, and extension cords; party goods, including wrapping paper, ribbon, greeting cards, and candles; and small automotive items such as oil, windshield washer fluid, and car polish. A popular section of the Produce Department is the *salad bar,* where people select various pre-cut salad ingredients and make their own salads.

After shoppers choose the items they want, they pay at the checkout area. Some supermarkets also have a customer service desk where people can cash checks, get film developed, or use an ATM machine (see *Picture Dictionary* page 80, word 12).

(1) **aisle:** any open space between two objects where people walk, such as the space between grocery shelves. (There are also aisles in a theater, in an airplane, and in a church.)

(3) **shopping basket**/(8) **shopping cart:** Customers who plan to buy several items push a shopping cart around the store to collect the items they wish to buy. People who plan to buy just a few items may choose to put them in a shopping basket instead.

(4) **checkout line**/(5) **checkout counter**/ (6) **conveyor belt:** When shoppers have everything they need, they move to the checkout counter. Often there is a checkout line where the customers wait to purchase their items. When their turn comes, shoppers put their items on a conveyor belt that moves the items toward the cashier (12).

(7) **cash register**/(12) **cashier:** The cashier enters (rings up) prices into the cash register. To do this, the cashier punches in the code number and price of the product or drags its bar code across the scanner.

(9) **(chewing) gum:** a soft, sweetened, flavored plastic substance that you chew, but don't swallow. It comes in packs of flat sticks or squares.

(10) **candy:** any of a class of sugary sweets that include hard candies, chocolate, and chewy sweets.

(11) **coupons:** rebates on products. Each coupon states the amount of money that will come off the price of the product when the cashier rings up the item on the cash register.

(13) **paper bag**/(19) **plastic bag:** At checkout, cashiers ask customers whether they prefer their items in plastic or paper bags. Some people prefer plastic bags because they are recyclable and conserve paper, and some prefer paper because they are larger.

(14) **bagger/packer:** the person who loads groceries into the bags. In some stores the bagger also takes the bags to the customer's car.

(15) **express checkout (line):** a special checkout counter for people who are buying only a few items.

(16) **tabloid (newspaper):** a newspaper that carries sensational stories.

(18) **scanner:** Most products have a bar code on the label. The scanner and cash register are computerized so that when a scanner reads a bar code, the cash register automatically shows the item and its price.

(20) **produce:** all fresh vegetables and fruits.

(22) **clerk:** an employee of a store.

(24) **can-return machine**/(25) **bottle-return machine:** a machine that receives and crushes bottles or cans for their recycling.

LC55

CONTAINERS AND QUANTITIES

LANGUAGE & CULTURE NOTES

(1) bag: Flour and sugar come in paper bags, snacks such as potato chips and cookies come in cellophane bags, and bakery items come in plastic bags.

(2) bottle: has a narrow mouth (top), whereas a jar (10) has a wide mouth.

(4) bunch: a number of things of the same kind that grow together, such as bananas and grapes. Stores also sell carrots in bunches, although they don't grow together.

(6) carton: the container for items such as milk, orange juice, ice cream, and eggs. It's more common to refer to these items by weight (a quart of orange juice, a gallon of milk, a half-gallon of ice cream) or number (a dozen eggs). See (8) and (18)–(21).

(7) container: a general term for items such as yogurt, cottage cheese, or packaged fruits (blueberries, strawberries).

(8) dozen: There are twelve items in a dozen. We say a *dozen* eggs, not a *dozen of eggs*. The plural is *two dozen eggs*, not *two dozens eggs*. The most common item that people buy by the dozen is eggs. It is also possible to refer to twelve of any fruit or vegetable as a dozen—for example, a dozen cucumbers, a dozen apples, a dozen oranges.

(9) head: refers to the shape of a whole lettuce or cabbage.

(10) jar: See *bottle* (2).

(12) pack / (13) package: Both of these refer to things that are wrapped together.

(14) roll: Paper products and household goods that *roll out* as you use them come in a roll.

(15) six-pack: six cans or bottles together in one package. Soda often comes in a six-pack.

(16) stick: a quarter-pound of butter or margarine. A piece of chewing gum is a *stick of gum*.

(18–21), (23): Also see *Picture Dictionary* page 57.

(18) pint: 16 fluid ounces. It's common to buy ice cream, sour cream, and cold deli salads by the *pint*.

(19) quart: 32 fluid ounces.

(20) half-gallon: 64 fluid ounces.

(21) gallon: 128 fluid ounces.

Soda, milk, orange juice, and ice cream frequently come in these amounts.

(22) liter: a liquid measure equal to about one and three-quarter pints. In the US, soda often comes in one- and two-liter bottles.

(23) pound: a standard measure of weight equal to 16 ounces. Stores commonly sell cheese, butter, poultry, meat, seafood, deli, and baking products by the pound.

Liquid Measure: The top portion of the page depicts units of liquid measure:

measurement	abbreviation	equivalent
1 teaspoon	1 tsp.	
1 tablespoon	1 Tbsp.	= 3 teaspoons
1 fluid ounce	1 fl. oz.	= 2 tablespoons
1 cup	1 c.	= 8 fluid ounces
1 pint	1 pt.	= 16 fluid ounces/ 2 cups
1 quart	1 qt.	= 32 fluid ounces/ 4 cups
1 gallon	1 gal.	= 128 fluid ounces/ 16 cups/4 quarts

Dry Measure: The bottom portion of the page depicts units of dry measure:

measurement	abbreviation	equivalent
1 ounce	1 oz.	
1 pound	1 lb.	16 ounces
1/4 pound		4 ounces
1/2 pound		8 ounces
3/4 pound		12 ounces

There are two kinds of utensils that you use to measure things—one for liquids such as milk and water, and the other for dry ingredients such as flour and sugar. The utensil for measuring liquids is usually glass and comes in one-cup, two-cup, and four-cup sizes. These cups are marked off in ounces as well. The cups for dry measures are plastic or aluminum and come in a set of five in graded sizes: one-quarter cup, one-third cup, one-half cup, three-quarter cup, and one-cup.

In addition to the cups, there is a set of spoons that you use to measure both liquid and dry ingredients. These spoons are in different sizes and usually come as a five-spoon set: one-eighth teaspoon, one-quarter teaspoon, one-half teaspoon, one teaspoon, and one tablespoon.

FOOD PREPARATION AND RECIPES

LANGUAGE & CULTURE NOTES

1. **cut (up):** to cut into pieces of about 1/2 to 1 inch. The particle *up* adds the feeling of *cut completely*.

2. **chop (up):** to cut into pieces about the size of a pea.

3. **slice:** to cut something large into thin, flat pieces.

4. **grate:** to shred into fine pieces when you rub against a rough-surfaced utensil called a *grater* (see *Picture Dictionary* page 59, word 17).

5. **peel:** to remove the skin or outer covering of fruits, vegetables, or hard-cooked eggs.

6. **break:** to crack open raw eggs.

7. **beat:** to stir or mix thoroughly.

8. **stir:** to mix something when you move it around in a circular motion with a spoon.

9. **pour:** to cause a liquid to flow out of a container.

15. **bake:** to cook by dry heat in the oven.

16. **boil:** to cook in hot water.

17. **broil:** to cook under the direct flame of an oven.

18. **steam:** to cook over hot boiling water, but not in it.

19. **fry:** to cook in hot fat.

20. **saute:** to cook quickly in a small amount of hot oil.

21. **simmer:** to cook liquid slowly at a temperature just below boiling.

22. **roast:** to bake in an oven and occasionally pour fat or oil over the food.

23. **barbecue/grill:** to cook over hot coals.

24. **stir-fry:** to cook and stir very quickly over high heat. People often do this with a combination of several vegetables and meats.

25. **microwave:** to cook in a microwave oven, a type of oven that uses electric waves that cook food more quickly than a conventional oven.

KITCHEN UTENSILS AND COOKWARE

LANGUAGE & CULTURE NOTES

> *Utensil* is a general term for a tool or implement. A *gadget* is a small tool or implement that you use for a specialized purpose, such as an ice cream scoop (1), a vegetable peeler (4), an egg beater (5), a garlic press (16), a cookie cutter (29), and a whisk (31).
>
> *Pan* is a general term for a container you use to cook foods. Pans may be copper, aluminum, stainless steel, or iron. Many of the words for pans describe their use—for example, frying pan (8), roasting pan (19), saucepan (22), and cake pan (34).

(4) **(vegetable) peeler:** a gadget you use to remove the outer skin (the peel or rind) from vegetables and fruit.

(7) **pot:** a pan with deep sides with or without a lid and with single or double handles.

(9) **double boiler:** a pan with a second pan that fits inside it. You put the food you want to cook in the upper pan and heat the water in the lower pan. As a result, delicate foods such as sauces don't burn.

(10) **wok:** a pan you use to stir-fry food on a burner (see *Picture Dictionary* page 58, word 24).

(11) **ladle:** a spoon with a long handle you use to serve liquids such as soup and punch.

(12) **strainer:** a metal mesh bowl with a handle and with or without legs that you use to rinse and drain food.

(13) **spatula:** an implement you use to lift and turn flat food items such as pancakes and hamburgers as they cook.

(14) **steamer:** a metal implement you put in a pot over a small amount of boiling water. Food in the steamer cooks by the intense heat of the steam and retains its food value that might leak into boiled water.

(17) **grater:** a gadget you use to cut foods such as cheese, citrus fruit peels, and nuts into small pieces.

(18) **casserole dish:** a ceramic, glass, or metal pan with or without a lid that you use to bake food in the oven. The term *casserole* also refers to the mixture of several foods that you bake and serve in a casserole dish.

(19) **roasting pan:** an oval or rectangular pan with or without a lid. Meat roasts in the oven in the roasting pan.

(21) **carving knife:** a large knife you use to cut large pieces of meat.

(23) **colander:** a metal bowl with holes or a wire mesh bowl on legs. You use it to rinse or drain food.

(29) **cookie cutter:** a gadget that comes in a variety of shapes and you use to cut cookies from cookie dough.

(31) **whisk:** an implement you use to mix things such as eggs and sauces.

(32) **measuring cup/** (33) **measuring spoon:** Sets of measuring spoons include 1/8 teaspoon, 1/4 teaspoon, 1/2 teaspoon, 1 teaspoon, and 1 tablespoon (see *Picture Dictionary* page 57).

(35) **wooden spoon:** a spoon you use to stir food as it cooks on a hot stove. Wooden spoons don't conduct heat and don't scratch treated surfaces of non-stick pans.

LANGUAGE & CULTURE NOTES

The typical American is busy and in a hurry and frequently eats rapidly (*on the run*). Therefore, fast food is very appealing because you don't have to wait for it, you can usually eat it by hand, and you can take it anywhere to eat. (People often refer to it as *take-out* food.) It's very common to see people walk down the street with a hamburger in their hands, or perhaps eat a donut or drink a cup of coffee while they ride to work on a bus or train. McDonalds, Burger King, Wendy's, Kentucky Fried Chicken, Pizza Hut, and Dunkin' Donuts are some of the restaurant chains that serve fast food.

(1) **hamburger:** a flat cake of ground beef that is broiled, grilled, or fried and comes on a roll. Popular accompaniments are ketchup, mustard, lettuce, tomato, onion, and relish.

(2) **cheeseburger:** a hamburger with melted cheese on top, under the roll.

(3) **hot dog:** a long, thin sausage of beef, pork, or poultry. Hot dogs usually come on a long roll with mustard and relish.

(8) **nachos:** corn chips with a melted cheese topping. It's typical to serve nachos with sour cream and guacamole (an avocado-based dip).

(9) **taco:** a rolled, fried tortilla with seasoned meat, cheese, and lettuce inside.

(10) **burrito:** beans, rice, and sometimes meat inside a soft flour tortilla.

(11) **slice of pizza:** A pizza is a flat baked crust that has tomato sauce, cheese, and a variety of toppings such as ground beef, onions, green and red peppers, olives, sausage, and mushrooms. You can buy pizza whole or by the slice in fast-food restaurants.

(12) **bowl of chili:** a dish of cooked meat, beans, and hot, spicy chili powder.

(15) **frozen yogurt:** a dessert similar to ice cream, but with yogurt instead of cream. It can be either hard or soft.

(16) **milkshake:** a cold drink with ice cream, milk, and a sweet syrup that you mix together in a blender.

(17) **soda:** a fizzy sweet drink. The most popular brands are Coca Cola and Pepsi, but there are many possible flavors of soda including orange, lemon, and berry. The most popular sodas come in both regular and light (sugarless) varieties. In many regions of the US, people call soda *pop*. In fast-food restaurants, soda normally comes in disposable cups with lids.

(23) **ketchup:** a thick, sweetened, tomato-based sauce that people commonly put on hamburgers and sometimes french fries. (Another way to spell *ketchup* is *catsup*.)

(24) **mustard:** a yellow, mayonnaise-based sauce with mustard spice and other ingredients. People commonly put it on hot dogs and on ham sandwiches.

(26) **relish:** a sweet or zesty sauce of pickles and other ingredients. People often put relish on hamburgers and hot dogs or mix it into various sandwich fillings.

THE COFFEE SHOP
AND SANDWICHES

LANGUAGE & CULTURE NOTES

Some coffee shops in the US serve just coffee and pastry snacks. Others, like the one on *Picture Dictionary* page 61, also serve sandwiches.

Drinks normally come in several different sizes: small, medium-size, large, and extra-large. (See Model 1 at the bottom of *Picture Dictionary* page 61.) The sizes of each of these differ depending on the restaurant.

(1) **donut:** (also spelled *doughnut*) a sweet, round, fried yeast cake usually with a hole in the middle. There are many kinds of donuts, including plain, chocolate, sugared, coconut, jelly-filled, chocolate-filled, and honey-dipped.

(2) **muffin:** a small individual bread that looks like a little cake.

(3) **bagel:** a donut-shaped roll. People usually eat bagels with cream cheese.

(4) **bun:** a sweet yeast roll.

(5) **danish/pastry:** a small, sweet cake that sometimes contains cinnamon, nuts, or fruit. Some people call it a *danish*, some call it a *pastry*, and others call it a *danish pastry*.

(6) **biscuit:** a small, round soft bread that people often eat with butter and jam or serve with meat gravy.

(7) **croissant:** a flaky, buttery French pastry in the shape of a crescent.

(8) **eggs:** In the United States, people very often eat a large breakfast with eggs, meat, and bread.

(9) **pancakes/**(10) **waffles:** Both of these griddle cakes have a similar batter of flour, milk, and eggs. You cook waffles in waffle irons that have a grid pattern.

(14) **home fries:** fried cut-up potatoes, sometimes with chopped onions.

(16) **decaf coffee (decaffeinated coffee):** coffee without caffeine.

(22–28) **sandwich:** two pieces of bread with meat, cheese, or some other food between them. Sandwiches are a popular lunch meal in the US.

(22) **tuna fish sandwich:** canned flaked tuna with mayonnaise and sometimes celery and/or onion.

(23) **egg salad sandwich:** a sandwich with chopped-up hard-boiled eggs.

(24) **chicken salad sandwich:** a sandwich with cut-up cooked chicken.

(31) **pita bread:** a round flat bread with a pouch in the middle. Various kinds of fillings can fill the pouch.

(32) **pumpernickel:** a type of heavy dark brown bread.

(35) **a submarine roll:** a long round bread that gets its name from the warship of the same shape. People sometimes call it a *sub* or *sub roll*.

THE RESTAURANT

LANGUAGE & CULTURE NOTES

There are many types of restaurants in the US—fast-food restaurants (see *Picture Dictionary* page 60); cafeterias where people serve themselves; coffee shops (see *Picture Dictionary* page 61) that serve breakfasts and light lunches; restaurants that serve ethnic foods such as Chinese, Thai, Mexican, French, Hungarian, Russian, Japanese, Middle Eastern, and Greek; delicatessens (see *deli* on *Dictionary* page 52) that offer many varieties of cheese, salads, and sandwiches of cold meats; diners, which are small, informal restaurants that offer traditional hearty meals of meat and potatoes at reasonable prices; and typical American restaurants such as the one in this lesson.

(1) **hostess**/(2) **host:** The host or hostess greets the diners, seats them and arranges any special seating needs (*booster seat* or *high chair*), and gives the diners their menus. *Hostess* is for women and *host* is for men.

(4) **booth**/(5) **table:** A booth is an enclosed dining space with a fixed table and benches for seats. A table is a free-standing table with chairs around it.

(6) **high chair**/(7) **booster seat:** A high chair is for a baby, and a booster seat is for a toddler or young child.

(11) **waitress**/(12) **waiter:** *Waitress* refers to a female, and *waiter* refers to a male. *Server* is a neutral term for both males and females.

(16) **chef:** A chef is a highly trained cook who studied cooking in culinary school.

(20) **dessert cart:** Some restaurants present their desserts on a dessert cart from which the diners choose their desserts.

(22) **tip:** In the US, it is customary to leave a tip for the waiters, buspersons, and hosts. The average tip is 15% of the total check. However, many people leave 20%.

China is a general term that includes plates, bowls, cups, saucers, and serving pieces (see *Picture Dictionary* page 22). People call it *china* because historically it was fine porcelain dishware that came from China.

Silverware (also called *flatware*) is a general term that includes knives, forks, spoons, and serving utensils. Silverware was originally silver, but today it is usually stainless steel.

In general, people use more china and silverware for formal meals than they do for informal meals. An informal place setting normally consists of a plate, glass, knife, fork, spoon, and napkin. The place setting on *Picture Dictionary* page 63 is a more formal one and therefore includes more china and silverware.

The location of the flatware depends on when people use it during the meal. The diner uses the flatware on the outside in the early dishes and uses the flatware closer to the main plate for the later dishes. The usual order of dishes for a meal in the U.S. is first salad or soup with bread on the side and then the main dish of meat and vegetables.

(23) **salad plate:** It's very common in the US to serve a salad either before or along with the main dinner course.

(24) **bread-and-butter plate:** It's very common to serve rolls or bread and butter with dinner.

(27) **water glass:** The water glass is generally larger than a wine glass.

(28) **wine glass:** Wine connoisseurs and formal restaurants use different-shaped glasses for different wines.

An *appetizer* is a small portion of food that people eat at the beginning of a meal. A *salad* usually comes before (and sometimes during) the main course. The *main course* is the principal part of the meal, which is usually meat, fish, or pasta. *Side dishes* are the accompaniments to the main course. There is usually a choice between potatoes, rice, and several vegetables. Americans like to finish their meals with a sweet *dessert*—usually pie, cake, ice cream or pudding, and sometimes fresh fruit.

(1) **fruit cup/fruit cocktail:** a combination of small pieces of fresh fruit.

(3) **shrimp cocktail:** several cold cooked shrimp on lettuce with a chili and horseradish sauce.

(4) **chicken wings:** chicken wings in a special sauce.

(5) **nachos:** corn chips with a melted cheese topping. Restaurants usually serve them with sour cream and guacamole (an avocado-based dip).

(6) **potato skins:** just the skin (without the potato itself). The baked potato skins come with melted cheese and a variety of toppings.

(7) **tossed salad/garden salad:** a salad with a variety of greens and raw vegetables, such as lettuce, tomato, cucumber, peppers, and onions. People usually eat salads with a choice of toppings or *dressings*. Some popular ones are French dressing, Russian dressing, Italian dressing, blue cheese dressing, or just oil and vinegar.

(8) **Greek salad:** a salad with greens, onions, sometimes cucumber and tomato, a special dressing, and feta cheese.

(9) **spinach salad:** a salad with spinach leaves, crumbled pieces of bacon, and a special dressing.

(10) **antipasto (plate):** a combination of Italian meats and cheeses, often with mushrooms and olives.

(11) **Caesar salad:** a salad with romaine lettuce and a special dressing of a raw egg, Parmesan cheese, anchovy fillets, and croutons (seasoned bread cubes).

(12) **meatloaf:** a combination of ground beef, eggs, onions, tomato sauce, and seasonings.

(18) **a baked potato:** a potato that you bake in the oven at a high temperature in its skin. People commonly eat baked potatoes with butter or sour cream.

(19) **mashed potatoes:** potatoes that you peel, boil, and crush to make a soft, smooth consistency, and then mix with milk and butter.

(20) **french fries:** fried cut potato strips. People also call them *fries* or *french fried potatoes.*

(23) **mixed vegetables:** a combination of cooked vegetables.

(25) **apple pie:** a pastry with a top and bottom crust and apple filling.

(27) **jello:** a fruit-flavored gelatin dessert. *Jello* is actually the brand name of a very popular gelatin dessert that is so popular that the brand name is now the name for the dessert itself.

(28) **pudding:** a milk-based creamy dessert that comes in various flavors, such as chocolate, vanilla, and butterscotch.

(29) **ice cream sundae:** a combination of ice cream, sauce (usually fudge, strawberry, or butterscotch), and whipped cream.

LANGUAGE & CULTURE NOTES

(2) **pink:** In American culture, pink is traditionally a feminine color. Baby girls often have pink things and wear pink clothes.

(7) **blue:** In American culture, blue is traditionally a masculine color. Baby boys often have blue things and wear blue clothes.

(8) **navy blue:** a dark blue color, the same as that of U.S. Navy uniforms.

(11) **light green** / (12) **dark green:** Most colors have shades of light and dark—for example, light/dark blue, light/dark brown, light/dark yellow, light/dark purple, light/dark gray.

(14) **black:** In American culture, black is the color that people often associate with death and dying. People often wear black to a funeral.

(15) **white:** In American culture, white is the color that people often associate with purity. It is traditional for a bride to wear white at her wedding.

LANGUAGE & CULTURE NOTES

People in the United States always want to wear the appropriate clothing. However, what is appropriate is always changing. Every season there are new fashions in the stores as popular styles and colors change.

Most people have a variety of clothes and dress according to where they are going and what they are doing. Casual dress is *in*. Dress codes (statements of required dress) are *out*, and freedom of expression in clothing is *in*. In the past, people thought of jeans as work pants. These days, however, people of all ages wear jeans everywhere, even to parties and to the office.

In most offices, men typically wear a suit or a sports coat. Women typically wear a dress, a suit, or a skirt or pants with a blouse. Both men and women usually have several outfits. They do not wear the same outfit two days in a row and often not even twice in the same week.

(1) **blouse:** Women typically wear a blouse with a skirt, suit, or sweater.

(4) **pants/slacks:** Both men and women wear these with sweaters, jackets, or shirts and blouses.

(5) **sport shirt:** This is a man's shirt that is usually checked, plaid, or multi-colored. It may be long- or short-sleeved.

(6) **jeans:** casual pants of denim material that males and females of all ages wear.

(7) **knit shirt/jersey:** Both men and women wear this. It can be either short- or long-sleeved and is usually soft cotton.

(10) **jacket:** Men wear this with slacks. Women wear this with slacks or a skirt.

(11) **sport coat/sport jacket/jacket:** Men wear this with dress slacks.

(12) **suit:** a matching jacket and pants for a man, or a matching jacket and skirt or pants for a woman.

(13) **three-piece suit:** a suit with a vest.

(15) **uniform:** a required outfit of clothing that all members of a group wear—for example, a police uniform, a flight attendant's uniform, a security guard's uniform.

(16) **T-shirt:** a knit cotton top that has short sleeves and no collar or buttons. Both

men and women wear T-shirts.

(18) **maternity dress:** a dress with space around the waist for pregnant women.

(19) **jumpsuit:** a one-piece casual outfit. It is common for people who do manual labor to wear a jumpsuit.

(21) **jumper:** a simple sleeveless dress that women wear over a blouse or shirt.

(22) **blazer:** a casual jacket for men and women, usually a solid color. Blazers often have brass buttons.

(23) **tunic:** a long plain blouse, with or without sleeves, that comes in many different lengths. Some come to the knees.

(24) **leggings:** tight-fitting knit pants. Women wear these under a short skirt or a loose top such as a tunic.

(25) **overalls:** loose-fitting trousers, usually of strong fabric, with a bib front and shoulder straps. People who do manual labor sometimes wear these over their regular clothes to protect them from dirt.

(26) **turtleneck:** a soft cotton jersey with a high neck for both men and women.

(27) **tuxedo:** a formal suit for men.

(29) **(evening) gown:** a formal dress, usually floor-length.

LANGUAGE & CULTURE NOTES

1 **coat:** the general term for a man's or woman's warm outer garment that comes down to a person's knees or below.

2 **overcoat:** a long dressy coat that a man wears over a suit. Another word for overcoat is *topcoat*.

3 **hat:** the general term for men's and women's headgear. The piece of material that surrounds the middle part of the hat is the *brim*.

4 **jacket:** the general term for a man's or woman's outer garment that comes down to the waist or hips. Also see *jacket* (10) and *sport jacket/jacket* (11) on *Picture Dictionary* page 66.

5 **scarf/muffler:** an article of clothing that keeps the neck warm during cold weather. The plural form of scarf is *scarves*.

6 **sweater jacket:** a warm sweater in the style and length of a jacket.

7 **tights:** long, thick knit socks that pull on like pants. Tights are not *panty hose* (see *Picture Dictionary* page 68, word 20). Tights are common outerwear for young girls and women in casual dress.

8 **cap:** a man's hat with a small brim.

10 **baseball cap:** a cap with a baseball team's logo on the front and a protruding front brim. Baseball caps are extremely popular with adolescents. In fact, many youngsters wear them all the time, both outdoors and inside the house. It's common to wear baseball caps in the opposite direction, with the brim facing backwards.

11 **windbreaker:** a short coat that closes tightly at the wrists and neck for protection against the wind. Both men and women wear windbreakers.

13 **rain hat:** a waterproof man's or woman's hat that people wear during rainy weather.

14 **trench coat:** a man's or woman's raincoat with a removable lining. A trench coat usually has epaulets, ornamental pieces of material on the shoulders and sleeves.

16 **poncho:** a man's or woman's armless rain garment that goes on over the head.

19 **ski hat:** a hat that's usually wool and brightly colored that men and women wear in cold weather or while they ski. Many people also wear ski hats as a casual winter hat. The protruding ball of yarn on the top is a *pom pom*.

20 **ski jacket:** a nylon jacket that has a filling of down or other insulating material. Ski jackets are lightweight, but give a great deal of warmth. Both men and women wear them in cold weather and while they ski and ice skate.

22 **ski mask:** a hat with holes for the eyes and mouth. Both men and women wear them in cold weather and while they ski.

23 **down jacket:** a man's or woman's jacket that has a filling of goose down (small feathers) for warmth.

25 **parka:** a heavy jacket for men and women that people wear in very cold temperatures.

27 **ear muffs:** Both men and women wear these to protect their ears in cold weather.

28 **down vest:** a man's or woman's sleeveless jacket with a goose down lining.

SLEEPWEAR AND UNDERWEAR

LANGUAGE & CULTURE NOTES

Sleepwear and underwear come in a variety of styles, patterns, colors, fabrics, and textures for both men and women. People select articles of underwear and sleepwear with as much thought as they select other types of clothing.

Socks, stockings, and pantyhose also come in many styles, patterns, and colors. Many people consider them an important part of their whole *look*.

The general term for women's underwear is *lingerie*, and the term for women's stockings and pantyhose is *hosiery*. Socks, stockings, pantyhose, and underwear come in pairs—for example, *a pair of socks, a pair of underpants, a pair of pantyhose, a pair of stockings*.

(1–6): These are sleepwear items.

(1) pajamas: two-piece sleepwear for both men and women.

(3) nightshirt: one-piece sleepwear that resembles a long shirt. Both men and women wear nightshirts.

(4) bathrobe/robe: Both men and women wear bathrobes over sleepwear.

(5) slippers: comfortable footwear with soft soles that people wear indoors.

(6) blanket sleeper: one-piece sleepwear of thick cloth for a young child. A child who kicks off his or her covers may wear a blanket sleeper.

(7–12): These are underwear garments for men.

(7) undershirt/T-shirt: Many men wear T-shirts under their dress shirts. T-shirts are also popular casual outerwear for both men and women. They may be either V-necked or rounded *crewneck* style.

(10) athletic supporter/jockstrap: Many men wear this when they play sports.

(11) long underwear/long johns: Both men and women wear this under their clothing to help them keep warm in cold weather, especially for winter sports.

(13–23): These items are underwear garments for women.

(13) (bikini) panties: low-cut underwear for women. Men also have bikini style underwear. Both come in a variety of patterns and colors.

(14) briefs/underpants: more practical underwear for women.

(15) bra: a common abbreviation for *brassiere*.

(16) camisole: a short undergarment that women usually wear with a half-slip.

(17) half slip / (18) (full) slip: A half slip is an undergarment that women wear under skirts. A full slip is an undergarment that women wear under dresses. Slips come in various lengths.

(20) pantyhose: stockings and panties all in one garment. The word *pantyhose* is plural.

(21) tights: heavier weight stockings that come in a variety of colors.

(22) knee socks: wool or cotton socks that come up to the mid-calf region.

(23) knee-highs: nylon stockings that come up to the knee. Women wear them under their pants.

EXERCISE CLOTHING AND FOOTWEAR

LANGUAGE & CULTURE NOTES

> The goal for many Americans is to be slim and physically fit. As a result, companies manufacture a wide variety of exercise clothing in many different styles and fabrics. There is also a wide variety of footwear for both men and women in casual and dress styles to complement different types of clothing. Footwear comes in pairs—for example, *a pair of shoes, a pair of boots.*
>
> Sneakers are one of the most popular footwear items. Many people, especially adolescents, think it's important to have the *right kind* of sneaker. There are many sneaker styles to choose from as well as a variety of uses for sneakers. People of all ages also wear sneakers for casual everyday use.

(1) **tank top:** a sleeveless garment for both men and women.

(2) **running shorts:** lightweight shorts of cotton or nylon that are comfortable for recreational running.

(3) **sweatband:** a soft cotton band that many people wear around their heads.

(4) **jogging suit/running suit/warm-up suit:** a two-piece suit of durable lightweight fabric—usually nylon, cotton, or polyester.

(5) **T-shirt:** a cotton garment for both men and women. People wear T-shirts not only when they exercise but also for casual dress in warm weather.

(6) **lycra shorts/bike shorts:** body-hugging shorts of firm stretchy nylon.

(7) **sweatshirt:** a heavyweight cotton pullover that both men and women wear.

(8) **sweatpants:** heavyweight cotton pants that often match the sweatshirt.

(9) **cover-up:** a top that women wear over their bathing suits.

(10) **swimsuit/bathing suit** and (11) **swimming trunks/swimsuit/bathing suit:** Both men and women call their swimwear a *swimsuit* or *bathing suit.* Men can also call their swimwear *a pair of swimming trunks* if the swimwear is a bit long and baggy like men's shorts.

(12) **leotard:** a one-piece exercise garment of stretchy material for women.

(13) **shoes:** the general term for items 13–27. People use this word when they aren't referring to specific types of shoes.

(15) **pumps:** low-heeled shoes for women.

(16) **loafers:** casual leather shoes without laces for both men and women.

(17) **sneakers/athletic shoes:** casual canvas or leather shoes with rubber soles for both men and women.

(18) **tennis shoes:** sneakers people wear when they play tennis.

(19) **running shoes:** athletic shoes especially for running.

(20) **high-tops/high-top sneakers:** Although people traditionally wore these to play basketball, high-tops are now popular daily footwear for adolescents.

(21) **sandals:** casual summer footwear for both men and women.

(22) **thongs/flip-flops:** rubber sandals for both men and women.

(23) **boots:** waterproof high-top shoes that both men and women wear in the winter.

(25) **hiking boots:** rugged shoes with a great deal of ankle support for long walks and mountain climbing.

(26) **cowboy boots:** western-style boots.

(27) **moccasins:** comfortable casual shoes of soft leather.

Jewelry is any adornment a person wears on the body. *Costume jewelry* is inexpensive jewelry that copies precious metals and gems. Accessories include clothing such as ties, belts, and gloves as well as things that people use to carry their belongings. People commonly give jewelry and accessories as gifts.

(1) **ring:** Both men and women wear rings in the United States.

(2) **engagement ring:** the ring that a man gives to a woman when they decide to get married. The traditional engagement ring is a diamond. In the US, women wear the engagement ring on the third finger of the left hand.

(3) **wedding ring/wedding band:** the ring that the bride and groom exchange during the wedding ceremony. In the US, people wear them on the third finger of the left hand.

(4) **earrings:** There are two types of earrings—earrings for *pierced* ears and those for *non-pierced* ears. For someone with pierced ears, the earring goes into a tiny hole in the ear lobe. For someone with non-pieced ears, the earring clips onto the earlobe.

(5) **necklace:** a general term that includes a necklace such as the item (5) *necklace*, a pearl necklace (6), and a chain (7).

(6) **pearl necklace/pearls/string of pearls:** either a necklace of authentic pearls from wild oysters, or a less expensive one of farmed pearls, or even synthetic pearls.

(8) **beads:** a string of small pieces of gems, glass, wood, or plastic.

(9) **pin/brooch:** an ornamental piece of jewelry that women wear on dresses, sweaters, coats, blazers, and scarves.

(10) **locket:** A locket is usually metal and may have the shape of a flower or animal, or may be a religious symbol or other design.

(11) **bracelet:** It is common for women in the US to wear bracelets around their wrists. Some also wear thin, narrow *ankle bracelets* or *anklets* around their ankles.

(12) **barrette:** a clip for women's hair.

(13) **cuff links:** Instead of buttons, some shirts have narrow slits in the cuffs. *Cuff links* go through these slits and hold together the shirt's cuffs. Men typically wear cuff links on formal occasions.

(14) **suspenders:** elastic shoulder straps that hold up a man's pants.

(15) **watch/wrist watch:** There are *sport watches* for leisure and informal wear and *dress watches* for more formal occasions. Some watches indicate the day and even the month and year.

(18) **change purse:** a small purse women use to carry change.

(19) **wallet:** People commonly put cash, credit cards, forms of identification, small family pictures, and other paper items in their wallets.

(21) **purse/handbag/pocketbook:** In the US, virtually all women carry one. It is uncommon for a man to carry one.

(22) **shoulder bag:** a large purse with long straps that a woman wears over one shoulder.

(23) **tote bag:** an all-purpose bag of leather, canvas, or plastic.

(24) **book bag:** a canvas or leather bag with straps that someone carries on his or her back or shoulders.

(25) **backpack:** an all-purpose bag with many pockets that someone carries on his or her back by means of shoulder straps.

(26) **makeup bag:** a special small bag for a women's makeup.

(27) **briefcase:** a leather case that professional people use to carry their business papers.

Types of Clothing

1 **long-sleeved shirt:** *Shirt* is the generic name for items 1–4, the general term people use when they aren't referring to a specific type of shirt. Both men and women wear long-sleeved shirts.

2 **short-sleeved shirt:** Short sleeves are more casual than long-sleeved shirts. People wear them when the weather is warm.

6 **cardigan sweater:** a sweater with buttons that opens in the front.

9 **knee-high socks:** socks that come up to the knee. They are usually a heavier weave.

10 **ankle socks:** socks that cover the ankles. They are usually sports socks.

11 **crew socks:** socks with a cuff that come over the ankle. They are usually sports socks.

12 **pierced earrings:** earrings that go through a hole in the person's ear.

13 **clip-on earrings:** earrings that clip on to a person's earlobe and do not require the person to have pierced ears.

Types of Material

14 **corduroy *pants*:** Corduroy is a heavy cotton material with ribs. Corduroy is a popular material for pants, jackets, and heavy shirts because it is washable.

18 **denim *jacket*:** Denim is a heavy cotton material. One of the most common uses of denim is in jeans and casual jackets.

19 **flannel *shirt*:** Flannel is a brushed cotton material that is soft and warm. Winter sheets are sometimes flannel.

20 **polyester *blouse*:** Polyester is any fabric that comes from polymers. It is popular because it doesn't wrinkle or shrink.

21 **linen *dress*:** a natural material that comes from flax. Linen is common in summer wear such as shirts, pants, dresses and jackets. It is a fabric that wrinkles easily, but is cool and comfortable in warm or hot weather.

Patterns

27 **plaid:** This is fabric that has both horizontal and vertical colored lines.

28 **polka-dotted:** Fabrics with large circles have *big polka dots* and fabrics with small circles have *little polka dots*.

29 **patterned/print:** A fabric design that has a design or pattern that is not specifically striped, checked, plaid, polka dotted, flowered, or paisley. Print patterns usually have some sort of geometric design.

31 **paisley:** a paisley design with abstract colorful figures. Depending on the particular fabric, the size of the figures may vary, but the distinctive paisley shape remains.

32 **solid *blue*:** Any design that is all of one color—solid *blue*, solid *green*, etc.

Sizes

33–37: These size names are for both children's and adults' clothes. For children, *small* is usually for ages 5–7, *medium* is usually for ages 8–10, *large* is usually for ages 10–12, and *extra large* is usually for ages 14–16. For adults, these sizes are for less tailored clothes, such as T-shirts, jerseys, and pajamas. Number sizes are typical for more tailored clothes, such as pants, blouses, long-sleeved shirts, and jackets.

CLOTHING PROBLEMS AND ALTERATIONS

LANGUAGE & CULTURE NOTES

(1–2) long–short: These describe the length of clothing, usually the length of the sleeves, the hem (the bottom of a skirt or dress), and the cuff (the bottom of pants).

(3–4) tight–loose/baggy: These describe how clothing fits. *Tight* and *loose/baggy* may have a negative connotation (the clothing doesn't fit right), or a neutral one (the style of the particular piece of clothing may be a tight or loose/baggy style).

(7–8) high–low: These typically refer to the height of shoes, a waistline, or a neckline.

(9–10) fancy–plain: *Fancy* describes clothing that is highly decorated, ornamental, or brightly colored. *Plain* clothing is without decoration.

(11–12) heavy–light: These refer to the weight of fabrics. People wear heavy clothing in colder weather and light clothing in warmer weather.

(13–14) dark–light: These refer to shades of color.

(15–16) wide–narrow: These refer to width, typically of shoes, a collar, a lapel, a striped design (see *Picture Dictionary* page 71, word *25*), or a tie.

(18) ripped/torn *pocket*: When a piece of clothing is pulled apart, it is *ripped* or *torn*.

(20) missing *button*: when a part of the clothing is lost, it is *missing*.

(23) take in the *jacket*: To *take in* a piece of clothing means to alter the size of the garment to make it smaller. When a jacket is too loose or baggy, the owner will ask a tailor to *take in* the jacket.

(24) let out the *pants*: To *let out* a piece of clothing means to alter the size of the garment to make it larger. When pants are too tight, the owner will ask a tailor to *let out* the pants.

LANGUAGE & CULTURE NOTES

Laundry refers to clothing and household items such as sheets, blankets, and towels that people need to wash.

People who don't have washers and dryers in their homes or apartment buildings typically go to a laundromat, a place where they deposit money in coin-operated washers and dryers.

Most clothing in the United States has a tag that gives instructions for how to clean the item, either in words or symbols. Some items must go to a professional cleaner, who *dry cleans* the item. *Dry cleaning* is a process that uses chemicals instead of water to clean fabric materials. There are many items that people can wash in water. Permanent press material is very popular because you wash and dry it, but you don't have to iron it.

A **sort the laundry:** Before someone washes clothes, it is common to sort the clothes into groups according to their color—*light clothing* (2) and *dark clothing* (3)—in case the dark colors *run* during the washing and stain the light-colored clothes.

B **load the washer /** **C** **unload the washer:** *To load* the washer means to fill the washer with water, set the water temperature, select the wash cycle, and add the laundry detergent (7) and other cleaning agents such as fabric softener (8) to soften the fabric and reduce its static electricity and bleach (9) to whiten clothes, then the dirty laundry. To *unload* means to empty the washer after the washing.

D **load the dryer:** *To load* the dryer means to fill the dryer, as well as to set the temperature and select the length of the cycle. Many people like to put a sheet of static cling remover (13) in the dryer along with the clothes. Static cling remover is a small foam sheet with a chemical that eliminates static electricity so the fabric, particularly synthetics, hangs freely and doesn't cling.

E **hang clothes on the clothesline:** You hang clothes on a clothesline (14) with clothespins (15). Some homes in the US have private backyards where homeowners hang their wet laundry to dry in the sun. Some apartments also have clotheslines for tenants to use.

F **iron:** Many contemporary fabrics are wrinkle-resistant so you don't have to iron them. Also, with the common use of clothes dryers, it's not necessary to iron many clothing items. Still, many people continue to iron their wrinkled clothing (18) with an electric iron (16) on an ironing board (17). If someone wants a shirt to be stiffer in order to hold its shape, that person sprays some spray starch (20) onto the clothes before he or she irons them.

H **hang up clothing:** You hang shirts, jackets, dresses, pants, and suits on hangers (23). A typical U.S. bedroom has a closet (22) where you can hang clothing.

I **put things away:** When a person *tidies up* around the house, he or she *puts things away*. This verb also means to *put clothes away* in drawers (24) and on shelves (25).

THE DEPARTMENT STORE

LANGUAGE & CULTURE NOTES

> A department store offers a variety of merchandise in separate sections or *departments*. Historically, department stores developed from the general store, which was an important store on the main street of U.S. towns and urban centers. When more and more people moved from cities to the suburbs, many department stores relocated to suburban shopping malls. City department stores typically have several floors. Mall department stores are usually two or three stories.

(1) (store) directory: Most U.S. department stores have a directory on the first floor that gives the locations of the store's departments and facilities.

(3) Perfume Counter: Some department stores also have makeup products in this area.

(6) Men's Clothing Department: This department typically sells men's coats, suits, jackets, pants, shirts, jerseys, underwear, hats, and ties.

(7) customer pickup area: This is a place where customers can park their cars to pick up heavy or large purchases.

(8) Women's Clothing Department: This department typically sells women's coats, suits, dresses, skirts, blouses, jerseys, and underwear. Sometimes it includes women's shoes.

(9) Children's Clothing Department: This department typically sells clothing for infants, toddlers, and young children. Many also sell stuffed animals and other small playthings for babies and young children.

(10) Housewares Department: This department typically sells pots and pans, dishes, glassware, and small appliances such as irons, toasters, and hair dryers.

(11) Furniture Department/Home Furnishings Department: This department typically sells upholstered and wooden furniture for all rooms in the house. Many stores also sell lamps, rugs, and curtains.

(12) Household Appliances Department: This department typically sells large items such as microwave ovens, dishwashers, washing machines, dryers, and vacuum cleaners.

(13) Electronics Department: This department typically sells the type of video and audio equipment depicted on *Picture Dictionary* pages 76 and 77.

(14) Customer Assistance Counter/ Customer Service Counter: Here customers can return merchandise that is damaged or that they don't wish to keep, order special items, or complain about defective items and store service.

(15) men's room / (16) ladies' room: These are the terms for men's and women's public bathrooms. *Restrooms* is a general term for both facilities. The words *Men* or *Women* or stick figures of a man or of a woman are typically on the door.

(18) snack bar: Many U.S. department stores have snack bars that serve items such as sandwiches, salads, soft drinks, coffee, cookies, cakes, pies, and ice cream.

(19) Gift Wrap Counter: This is the place where customers can bring an item they purchased in the store to be gift wrapped.

LANGUAGE & CULTURE NOTES

(A) buy / (E) pay for: *To buy* something means to look for something, choose the right item, and then *to pay for* it. *To pay for* something describes only the money transaction.

(B) return / (C) exchange: When a shopper *returns* an item, he or she doesn't want the item, and gets money back or store credit. When a shopper *exchanges* an item, he or she wants the item, but has a problem with its size, color, or performance. The shopper returns the problematic item and gets another one in *exchange*.

(D) try on: In department stores in the United States there are fitting rooms where customers can try on the clothes before they buy them.

(6) size: see the Language and Culture Notes for *Picture Dictionary* page 71 for a description of sizes.

(7) material: see *Picture Dictionary* page 71 for a list of materials.

(8) care instructions: This label describes how to wash the garment. If the garment is delicate, the label may indicate *cold water only*, *lay flat to dry*, *no bleach*, *professional dry clean only*, or *cool iron*. If the garment has a sturdy fabric, the label may indicate *warm water wash*, *tumble dry warm*. For further vocabulary about washing clothes, see *Picture Dictionary* page 73.

(12) sales tax: In the United States, each individual state has its own sales tax. Some states have no sales tax or a very low one (New Hampshire, for example). Other states have high sales taxes (New York). Some states don't tax clothing (Massachusetts), and other states do (New Jersey). Some cities impose additional sales taxes on all purchases or just on restaurant purchases.

The video and audio items in this lesson that are not portable are called home entertainment equipment. You can find them in the home entertainment department of department stores or in stores that specialize in this electronic equipment.

(1) **TV/television:** Television sets come in many models (see items 2–5) and range in size from miniature sets small enough to carry in the palm of your hand to sets with giant wall-size screens. Many U.S. households have more than one TV.

(2) **plasma TV:** a high-definition TV that uses high-speed digital processing to give extremely clear images on the screen. Plasma TVs are flat screen TVs and usually measure only a few inches thick. Plasma televisions are very expensive.

(3) **LCD TV:** another flat-screen television with high definition. LCD screens are usually smaller than the plasma or projection televisions (see 2 and 4).

(4) **projection TV:** a large screen TV that is more affordable (less expensive) than a plasma TV. It works either by rear projection, in which case it functions like a very large conventional television, or by front projection, where it is possible for a laptop computer to project an image on the screen.

(5) **portable TV:** a battery-operated TV that people can carry from one place to another.

(6) **remote (control):** a device that allows the viewer to change the channel and the volume of a TV, DVD, or VCR from a distance.

(7) **DVD:** stands for *digital video disk.*

(8) **DVD player:** plays movies and any recorded material on a compact disc (CD).

(9) **video/videocassette/videotape:** It's possible to record on a blank video or to record over a previously recorded program.

(10) **VCR/videocassette recorder:** a device that plays recorded videotapes and that allows a person to record television programs. VCRs are available with a wide range of features. Most have a pause button that allows the viewer to freeze the action of the tape, as well as a timer to record programs when the viewer is not at home.

(11) **camcorder/video camera:** a camera that records home movies on videotape, which someone can then insert into a VCR and view on a television screen.

(12) **battery pack:** a bundle of rechargeable batteries that inserts into and provides power for portable telephones, cameras, and other electronic devices.

(13) **battery charger:** Most portable electronic equipment requires special batteries. When the batteries wear out, they need to be charged again. To charge the battery, you connect the battery to the charger and plug the charger into an electrical outlet.

(14) **radio:** a piece of equipment that receives AM (*amplitude modulation*) or FM (*frequency modulation*) radio signals and locks in on the channel or frequency the listener selects. Each radio station has an assigned frequency. It's common to refer to stations by their names and frequencies, such as WBRT 1190 AM.

(15) **clock radio:** a radio with an alarm clock. People set the alarm to turn on at a certain hour (usually to wake them up in the morning). At that time, the radio begins to play.

LANGUAGE & CULTURE NOTES

(16) shortwave radio: a radio that receives radio signals from around the world.

(17) tape recorder/cassette recorder: a device that plays and records audio tapes.

(18) microphone: a device that picks up sound. When it attaches it to recording equipment, it sends sound into the recorder. When it attaches it to an amplifier, it makes a person's voice or music louder.

(19) stereo system/sound system: the group of audio components that includes the turntable, CD player, tape deck, radio, one or more speakers, and tuner and amplifier (together called the *receiver*). Many people buy the components as a complete system. Others buy them separately. The individual components include some or all of items 20–27 below.

(20) record: a plastic disc that contains recorded sound (music or speech). You play a record on a stereo system turntable (21) or on a record player.

(21) turntable: the component of a stereo system that plays records (20).

(22) CD/compact disc: a plastic or plastic-coated metal disc that contains recorded sound (music or words). You play CDs on a CD player (23).

(23) CD player: the component of a stereo system that plays CDs (24). Some CD players hold several discs, and it's possible to switch instantaneously from one disc to another and from one song to another.

(24) tuner: the radio component of a stereo system. It receives AM and FM radio signals and locks in on the frequency or radio station the listener selects.

(25) (audio)tape/(audio)cassette: a tape/cassette with recorded sound (music or speech). People use audiotapes in

tape recorders (17), tape decks (26), boomboxes (28), and personal cassette players (30).

(26) tape deck/cassette deck: the component of a stereo system that plays and records audio cassette tapes. Some tape decks (such as the one in this lesson) accommodate two tapes, so it's possible to copy from one tape to the other. Other tape decks have just one.

(27) speakers: the component of a stereo system that produces the sound. Speakers are available in a wide variety of sizes and sound qualities.

(28) portable stereo system/boombox: a large portable cassette player and radio with two side speakers that usually detach. When the speakers are apart, they produce stereophonic sound. The name *boombox* refers to the *booming* sound of loud rock music that teenagers often listen to on this type of equipment.

(29) portable/personal CD player: a small, lightweight portable CD player with headphones.

(30) portable/personal cassette player: a small, lightweight portable cassette player with headphones.

(31) headphones: a device that allows people to listen to audio equipment so others don't hear the sound.

(33) video game system: a device that attaches to a TV. It presents a visual game that one or two players can play.

(34) video game: The video game inserts into the video game system (33).

(35) hand-held video game: a portable device that displays a video game on a small screen.

(1) **telephone/phone:** Most homes in the United States have more than one telephone. Some people buy their telephones, and others rent them from the telephone company for a monthly fee.

(2) **cordless phone:** a cordless telephone that you don't have to plug in. This makes it possible to carry it from room to room, or even outside.

(3) **cell phone/cellular phone:** a cordless telephone that communicates by wireless technology.

(4) **battery** / (5) **battery charger:** Cell phones come with a battery that over time loses its energy. To charge the battery, plug it into a charger, which plugs into an electrical outlet.

(6) **answering machine:** a device that attaches to a telephone and answers incoming calls.

(7) **pager:** a small, portable device that picks up a signal to indicate someone is calling. The person's number shows on the small screen.

(8) **PDA/electronic personal organizer:** PDA is an abbreviation for *personal digital assistant*. It is also called a *Palm Pilot*. This device serves as an agenda, notebook, and phone book.

(9) **fax machine:** a device that sends copies of printed material over telephone lines. *Fax* is an abbreviation of *facsimile machine*.

(10) **(pocket) calculator:** a hand-held device that people use for mathematical and scientific calculations.

(11) **adding machine:** a machine that automatically performs mathematical functions such as addition, subtraction, multiplication, and division.

(12) **voltage regulator:** a device that converts electrical current from one voltage to another. Many electrical devices come with a voltage regulator.

(13) **adapter:** a device that changes or *adapts* the plug of a small appliance to a different style of electrical outlet. For example, many travelers carry adapters when they visit a foreign country so they can use a hair dryer or electric razor. Adapters may or may not have converters that also allow for a difference in voltage, such as between the standard 110 in the United States and 220/240 in many other countries.

(14) **(35 millimeter) camera:** a camera with controls for focus, speed, and light. These cameras have detachable equipment such as a lens (15), zoom lens (17), and flash (21).

(16) **film:** There are many types of film for different types of light, different kinds of cameras, and for different uses such as photographs (*prints*) or slides.

(17) **zoom lens:** an attachment for a camera that makes distant objects appear closer.

(18) **digital camera:** a camera that records its images digitally so you can send the images directly to a computer.

(19) **memory disk:** a small computer disk that increases the memory of a digital camera so it can store more data.

(20) **tripod:** a three-legged stand that holds a camera on top.

(21) **flash (attachment):** a camera attachment people use when there isn't enough light.

(22) **camera case:** a case with pockets that holds the camera, film, and various camera attachments.

(23) **slide projector:** a machine that passes light through slides (small color films with cardboard frames) and projects them onto the screen.

(24) **(movie) screen:** a portable screen on which you show slides and movies.

LANGUAGE & CULTURE NOTES

Computer software programs are sets of instructions that make a computer perform different activities such as word-processing, spreadsheets, graphics, and educational and video games. The programs allow the computer to receive, store, manipulate, and print information. Most computer software comes with user manuals that tell how to use the program.

(1) **(desktop) computer:** a computer that has separate components: the keyboard, the monitor, the mouse, the disk drive, and the central processing unit (2).

(2) **CPU:** stands for *central processing unit.* The CPU is the brain of the computer system.

(3) **monitor/screen:** The monitor is the whole unit. The screen is the part you look at.

(4) **CD-ROM drive:** the slot where you insert a CD-ROM (5) into the computer.

(5) **CD-ROM:** a round plastic disc that stores large quantities of data.

(6) **disk drive:** the slot where you insert a floppy disk (7) into the computer.

(7) **(floppy) disk:** a thin square disk with a magnetic surface. The term *floppy* refers to the fact that the disks are lightweight and somewhat bendable.

(8) **keyboard:** the main device that provides input to the computer to tell the computer what to do. It consists of a typical typewriter keyboard plus special function keys.

(9) **mouse:** a device people use to provide input to the computer. It controls and moves a pointer around the screen. The device is called a *mouse* because of its shape with a long wire *tail.*

(10) **flat panel screen/ LCD screen:** a very thin screen that originally was for notebook computers (11), but is now also a common component of desktop computers. LCD is an abbreviation for *liquid crystal display.*

(11) **notebook computer:** a personal computer that can operate with batteries and is small enough to carry in a briefcase.

(12) **joystick:** a device that provides input to the computer when someone is playing computer games.

(13) **track ball:** Just like the mouse (9), this device provides input to the computer. It controls and moves a pointer around the screen. You click it to give different commands.

(14) **modem:** a device that receives information from the computer it is connected to and transmits the information over telephone lines to a modem and computer at another location.

(16) **printer:** a device that makes a printed copy of whatever the user creates.

(17) **scanner:** a type of copy machine that reads a text or photographic image and digitally stores it in a computer.

(18) **cable:** a plastic-coated wire that connects external devices, such as a monitor, mouse, keyboard, or scanner, to the computer.

(19) **word-processing program:** a software program that people use to type documents or write newsletters.

(20) **spreadsheet program:** a software program that people use to work with data and develop statistics.

(21) **educational software program:** a software program that helps children or adults learn.

LANGUAGE & CULTURE NOTES

1. **board game:** a game you play with plastic playing pieces on a heavy cardboard playing area. Some popular board games are *Monopoly* and *Scrabble.* (See *Picture Dictionary* pages 134–135.)

2. **(jigsaw) puzzle:** cardboard or wooden pieces that interlock to make a picture.

3. **construction set:** metal or wooden pieces that lock together to create a variety of structures.

4. **(building) blocks:** wooden or plastic cubes, squares, rectangles, and other geometric shapes that stack or interlock so it's possible to build things.

6. **beach ball:** a lightweight inflatable plastic ball to use at the beach.

7. **pail and shovel:** popular toys that children use to scoop sand in a sandbox or at the beach.

9. **doll clothing:** Stores sell whole wardrobes of miniature clothing for dolls.

10. **doll house:** a miniature house complete with wallpaper and curtains.

11. **doll house furniture:** miniature furniture that children put in a doll house.

12. **action figure:** a doll-version of a TV or movie hero that children use when they play action games.

14. **matchbox car:** one of a large variety of miniature cars about two inches in length. Children frequently collect these.

17. **train set:** People often refer to this as *electric trains*. Train sets are popular with both children and adults. A train set often fills a very large table.

18. **model kit:** pieces of an airplane, ship, car, or other item that you assemble and paint.

19. **science kit:** a kit with a variety of equipment and supplies for science experiments.

20. **walkie-talkie (set):** a portable two-way radio that allows one person to *walk* a distance from another person and *talk* to that person through the built-in microphone.

21. **hula hoop:** a circular plastic ring that you attempt to keep around your hips while you move your hips in a circular motion.

22. **jump rope:** a rope with handles that you swing over your head and under your feet as you jump.

23. **bubble soap:** a soap and water mixture that you blow through a wand to make bubbles.

24. **trading cards:** It's very common for young people to collect trading cards of sports figures as well as movie and television action heroes. Youngsters often *trade* one card for another as they build their collections.

28. **construction paper:** a package of paper of different colors.

30. **(modeling) clay:** a soft substance that you can mold into shapes.

31. **stickers:** colorful stick-on pieces of paper in many shapes, colors, and designs. Children collect and trade them.

33. **tricycle:** a bicycle with three wheels.

35. **skateboard:** a board with four wheels on which a person stands, pushes off with one foot, and then stands on with both feet and glides along.

36. **swing set:** Many people have a swing set in their yard. Swing sets are also standard equipment for school and park playgrounds.

37. **play house:** a one-room structure that looks like the exterior of a house. Young children use this structure to *play house*, where they pretend to live.

38. **kiddie pool/inflatable pool:** a shallow circular pool that people put in their yards and fill with water for children to play in during the summer.

LANGUAGE & CULTURE NOTES

Banks in the United States offer a variety of services, including checking accounts, savings accounts, investment services, and life insurance. A bank is the best place to keep money safe. There are many different types of checking and savings accounts for this purpose, and a choice is made depending on the customer's needs and financial situation. As the name implies, a savings account is for money people want to save, while a checking account is for money that people use to pay expenses.

(A) make a deposit: put money in a bank account.

(B) make a withdrawal: take money out of a bank account.

(C) cash a check: exchange a check for its cash value. In order to cash a check at a bank, a person usually must have an account at that bank and must endorse the check (write one's signature on the back of the check).

(D) get traveler's checks: Banks sell traveler's checks for a small fee.

(E) open an account: start a new account at a bank. The account may be a checking or savings account.

(F) apply for a loan: Bank customers and anyone else in the public may apply for a loan from a bank. Banks give home equity loans (loans against the value of a person's house), home mortgages, car loans, as well as other business loans.

(G) exchange currency: Travelers can exchange currencies at some banks for a small fee.

(1) deposit slip: a piece of paper you fill out when you make a deposit into an account.

(2) withdrawal slip: a piece of paper you fill out when you withdraw money from your account.

(3) check: When most people pay their bills, they write a check against the money they have in their checking account. Each check has a number and includes the person's name and address in the upper left corner.

(4) traveler's check: People commonly use traveler's checks instead of cash when they don't want to carry a lot of money.

(5) bankbook/passbook: a book with a record of savings account deposits and withdrawals.

(6) ATM card: the card someone uses in an ATM machine (see word 12).

(7) credit card: a plastic card that people use to purchase many goods and services.

(8) (bank) vault: a special room where the bank securely stores people's money and other important documents.

(9) safe deposit box: Many people rent one in which to keep their valuables and important documents.

(10) teller: the person at the bank who helps with transactions.

(11) security guard: an armed, uniformed guard who stands near the entrance of a bank to help maintain order and security.

(12) ATM (machine)/cash machine: a computerized machine outside a bank's entrance where a person can withdraw money, deposit money, obtain account balances, and make transfers from one account to another.

(13) bank officer: the person who helps with transactions other than deposits and withdrawals—for example, new accounts, loans and mortgages, and investments.

Forms of Payment: This section introduces various forms of payment for purchases in stores as well as for household bills.

(2) **check** / (a) **check number** / (b) **account number:** Many stores no longer accept payment by check, but checks are still the most popular way for people to pay household bills. Every check has a serial check number in the upper right corner. The account number is the number of the person's account from which the bank takes the money.

(3) **credit card** / (a) **credit card number:** Most stores accept payment by credit card, as do all phone and Internet retailers. When someone gives the credit card information over the phone or the Internet, the retailer will ask for the sixteen digit *credit card number* as well as the expiration date of the card. Many

people now prefer to use a debit card. This is a card that draws money directly from someone's checking account to pay for a purchase.

(4) **money order:** a check that can you can buy from a bank for any amount plus a small service charge. People who don't have checking accounts often buy money orders to pay their bills. Others use them when a store or other vendor won't accept a personal check.

(5) **traveler's check:** People commonly use traveler's checks instead of cash when they don't want to carry a lot of money. Traveler's checks are available at a bank for the face value plus a small service charge. The advantage of traveler's checks is that if they are lost, the issuing company will replace them.

Household Bills

Most household bills in the United States are due within thirty days of the billing date. If someone doesn't pay within thirty days, that person might need to pay an additional interest fee. Some companies offer special rates for senior citizens (those over the age of 65), as well as billing plans that equalize charges over the year or provide installment payment plans.

People pay their bills in a variety of ways. Most people use checks or money orders and mail payments directly to companies. Some companies have arrangements with banks in which the bank deducts money directly from a person's checking account. It's also possible to pay cash in person at a company's place of business. It's never a good idea to send cash through the mail.

---

(6) **rent:** the monthly bill a tenant pays a landlord. It's common for a landlord to ask a tenant to pay a security deposit equivalent to one or two months rent at the beginning of a lease. The landlord returns the security deposit at the end of the lease if there is no damage to the property.

(7) **mortgage payment:** the monthly payment a homeowner pays to a bank

for a home loan. A mortgage payment has two parts—the *principal*, which goes toward the ownership of the home, and the *interest*, which goes toward the cost of the loan.

(8) **electric bill:** Every home in the US receives an electric bill for the amount of electricity that household used in a given month.

LANGUAGE & CULTURE NOTES

(9) telephone bill: U.S. telephone companies provide either local or long-distance service. People may receive separate local and long-distance bills, or the two charges might be together on a single bill.

(10) gas bill: Homes that get their heat from natural gas receive monthly bills for the estimated quantity of gas that the house used. Every two or three months, a person from the company visits the home to read the meter and check the actual amount that the house used.

(11) oil bill/heating bill: Homeowners who heat their homes with oil can pay for the oil when the heating company delivers it, or they can pay for the purchase over several months.

(12) water bill: When a home is connected to the town or city water system, the homeowner pays for the water service. In most states, people who rent don't have to pay these bills.

(13) cable TV bill: Cable TV is a commercial television service that comes through a special cable that attaches to the television and links either underground or to a utility pole on the street. The cable expands the number of television channels that television can receive. The price for such service depends on the number of extra channels that the customer chooses. Often consumers can also rent Internet cable access for their computers.

(14) car payment: If a consumer chooses to buy a car over several years, he or she can make monthly car payments which include a servicing fee.

(15) credit card bill: A credit card holder can choose to pay the bill in full or to make the minimum monthly payment. The credit card company charges interest on any unpaid portion of the bill.

(16) balance the checkbook: It is extremely important to balance the payment amounts and deposit amounts in a checkbook so that there is sufficient money for every check that someone writes from the account. If a checkbook is not balanced and a check is for more money than is in the checking account, the check will *bounce*, and the account holder will have to pay fees to the bank and the recipient of the check.

(17) write a check: To write a check, you must write the date, the name of the person or company who is going to receive the check, the amount of money both in numbers and words, and your signature. It is optional to also write information about the payment in the *memo* section of the check.

(18) bank online: to use banking services on the Internet in order to pay bills and balance the checkbook.

(19) checkbook: a small booklet that contains numbered checks (see word 2) and a check register (see word 20). There are different styles of checkbooks.

(20) check register: the portion of a checkbook where you enter the number of the check, the amount, the date, and the recipient. When a person writes a check, he or she enters the amount in the check register and subtracts this amount from the previous balance.

(21) monthly statement: a record of all monthly transactions on a person's bank account. The statement includes the deposits and withdrawals, the amount of each check, the check number, the date, any interest that the account earned, and the final balance in the account.

(24) select a transaction: this may be *to* make a deposit, to get cash, to request account balance, or transfer funds.

(25) make a deposit: In order to make a deposit, you must put your money or check in a deposit envelope and enter the amount on the screen.

THE POST OFFICE

LANGUAGE & CULTURE NOTES

The post office is a branch of the United States government. It's the place where people mail letters and packages. It also offers other useful services and sells many postal-related items. People can apply for a passport at the post office; they can buy envelopes, boxes, and mailing tubes; and they can purchase money orders.

(5) first class: First-class mail receives preferential attention. Most first-class personal and business letters travel by plane within the continental United States.

(6) priority mail: For a small extra fee, this mail receives faster service and arrives at its destination within two to three days.

(7) express mail/overnight mail: guaranteed overnight delivery in the continental United States.

(8) parcel post: Parcel post packages are cheaper than first class and take longer to get to their destinations.

(9) certified mail: People do this when the sender wants proof that the recipient actually received the piece of mail. The sender fills out a special form and the recipient must sign it when he or she receives it.

(10) stamp: the postage that is necessary to send a letter or package. The rate depends on the weight of the item.

(11) / (12) / (13): Stamps come in perforated sheets, rolls of one hundred, or books of twenty.

(14) money order: People use this instead of a personal check.

(15) change-of-address form: People need to fill this out when they move to a new address.

(16) selective service registration form: This is the form people use to register for the

U.S. armed services. All eighteen-year-old males are required by law to register.

(19) return address: the address of the person who is sending the letter. It is normally at the top left front corner or on the top back portion of an envelope.

(20) mailing address: The standard format for writing an address is as follows:

first name/last name
street address/apartment number
city/state/zip code

(21) zip code: The United States is divided into five-digit postal zones to make it more efficient for post offices to sort the mail. There are an additional four digits that further define the location of an address, but the "+4" digits are not a required part of an address.

(22) postmark: stamped by the post office across the postage. This indicates the date and city of origination.

(23) stamp/postage: put in the top right corner of the envelope.

(26) scale: Most post offices have a computerized system that weighs and computes postage amounts.

(27) stamp machine: a coin-operated machine that sells stamps.

(29) mail truck: Mail carriers use this when they collect letters from mailboxes and deliver mail to homes and businesses.

(30) mailbox: located outside all post offices and on many street corners.

LANGUAGE & CULTURE NOTES

Most American communities have a public library, a lending library for the public's use. Libraries provide a wide range of services beyond the basic lending of books, magazines, and newspapers. Libraries may offer English classes, Internet classes, and special book groups for adults. Libraries also open their facilities to the community. It's common for libraries to provide meeting space for clubs and for discussion of city or town issues.

It's acceptable to talk quietly in libraries. Some have a special reading room where nobody is allowed to talk.

(1) **online catalog:** a computerized card catalog. Like the card catalog, book information is accessible by author, by title, by subject, and also by keyword.

(2) **card catalog:** a card-based system that people use to locate books in the library. Every book that the library owns has three call cards with identical information. The card catalog arranges the cards into three sectors, alphabetically by author, by title, and by subject.

(5) **library card:** a card that allows a person to borrow materials from the library.

(7) **shelves:** Books are on library shelves according to their classification as fiction or non-fiction. Fiction books are on shelves alphabetically by the author's last name. Non-fiction books are on shelves by topic based on the Dewey Decimal System.

(8) **children's section:** a special area with children's books and media.

(10) **periodical section:** a special area that contains current journals (11), magazines (12), and newspapers (13). It isn't possible to check materials in this section out of the library.

(11) **journals:** a special term for publications by special-interest, professional groups. Such publications generally appear on a monthly, bi-monthly, semi-annual, or annual basis.

(14) **media section:** a special area that contains books on tape (15), audiotapes (16), CDs (17), videotapes (18), computer software (19), and DVDs (20) for education and entertainment.

(21) **foreign language section:** a special area that only contains books in foreign languages.

(23) **reference section:** a special resource area of the library that has dictionaries (26), encyclopedias (27), and atlases (28). Books in the reference section must remain in the library.

(24) **microfilm** / (25) **microfilm reader:** a photographic record of printed matter (typically newspapers and academic journals) on a roll of film. You view microfilm on a special machine called a *microfilm reader* (25).

(29) **reference desk:** the place where someone goes to locate a book, get information, or ask questions about library services.

(30) **(reference) librarian:** a specially-trained librarian who provides information and helps people locate books.

(31) **checkout desk:** the area where people take out books after they present a library card (5).

(D) town hall/city hall: the building that contains most of the official city or town offices—for example, the office of the mayor or city manager, the city council, the office of the city or town clerk, the office of assessment and taxation, and office of town planning.

(E) recreation center: Some towns, cities, or neighborhoods have recreation centers with sports facilities where children and adults can gather for sports and games.

(F) dump: a place to leave garbage. Some small communities do not have a dump, but rather a transfer station, where people leave their garbage and then trucks move the garbage to a larger dump area. Most dumps only accept garbage that people have sorted into recyclables (glass, plastic, and newspaper), toxic waste (old paint cans, car batteries, etc.), large items (sofas, tables), AV equipment (televisions, monitors), and garbage.

(H) senior center: These community centers offer activities to seniors such as exercise classes, art classes, information sessions, luncheons, and excursions. Some centers are open every day, all day, and provide day-care for seniors who are in need of company and assistance. Other centers just open a few hours a day for specific activities.

(I) church: a place where Christians worship.

(J) synagogue: a place where Jews worship.

(K) mosque: a place where Muslims worship.

(L) temple: a place where Buddhists or Hindus worship. Jews also sometimes refer to a synagogue as a *temple.*

(1) emergency operator: the person who answers 911 emergency calls and contacts the appropriate emergency

responders, such as police (2) EMTs (7), or firefighters (5).

(3) police car: People often refer to a police car as a *cruiser* because it *cruises* (moves) through the neighborhood to see what's happening.

(4) fire engine: There are two kinds of fire engines that firefighters use to fight fires—a *pumper,* which pumps water from the fire hydrant (see *Picture Dictionary* page 40, word 5) and a *hook and ladder,* which carries the large ladders that firefighters use to scale tall buildings.

(6) emergency room: The area of a hospital that admits patients at any hour of the day or night. People often refer to it as the *ER.* Its purpose is to attend people in medical emergencies. Many people with no health insurance also use the Emergency Room for sick care because they don't have regular doctors and usually the ER does not require medical insurance for treatment.

(7) EMT/paramedic: EMT stands for Emergency Medical Team. EMTs work in ambulances.

(9) mayor/city manager: The person who manages or runs the city.

(11) gym: an abbreviation for *gymnasium.*

(12) activities director: The person in a recreation center (E) or senior center (H) who develops and coordinates the activities.

(15) sanitation worker: a person who collects garbage in a garbage truck or manages garbage in a *dump* (F).

(18) nursery: the room in a child-care center where the babies stay.

(20) eldercare worker/senior care worker: a person who takes care of elderly people in a *senior center* (H) or nursing home facility.

1. **car accident:** After any accident, the drivers must stop and exchange contact and car insurance information. They should also call the police so that they may fill out an accident report.

2. **fire:** If you witness a fire, you should immediately dial *911*. The emergency operator will ask you for your location and your name and phone number.

4. **robbery:** when a person steals something from someone.

5. **burglary:** when a person *breaks and enters* a place and steals something.

6. **mugging:** when someone attacks and robs you.

7. **kidnapping:** the abduction of someone. Sometimes criminals kidnap a person in order to get a ransom (money) from the person's family.

8. **lost child:** when a child wanders away and gets lost. If the child disappears for several days, the child is *missing*.

9. **car jacking:** when a person attacks a driver while he or she is driving, throws the person out of the car, and then drives the car away, thus stealing the car.

11. **assault:** when someone attacks another person. *Assault and battery* is a term police use to describe what happens when one person attacks and hurts another person.

12. **murder:** when someone kills another person.

13. **blackout/power outage:** when the electrical power goes out. In a blackout, residents should call their electrical company to report it.

14. **gas leak:** when there is a leak in an underground gas line. Since gas is explosive, a gas leak is very dangerous.

15. **water main break:** Town and city homes are connected to a public water system. If a water pipe breaks, it is called a *water main break*. The city or town attempts to repair the break as quickly as possible.

16. **downed power line:** In a storm, utility poles which carry electrical, telephone, and cable lines may fall down. The result is a power outage (13). A downed power line is very dangerous because if the live electricity line touches water, a person who touches that water can be electrocuted.

17. **chemical spill:** Occasionally a truck, train, or ship with dangerous chemicals can have an accident or mishap. This results in a chemical spill. Depending on the type of chemical, specialist emergency response workers will come to isolate the chemical and clean it up.

18. **train derailment:** when a train runs off its tracks.

19. **vandalism:** the destruction of other people's property.

21. **drunk driving:** The "legal limit" for blood alcohol ranges from 0.07% to 0.10%, depending upon the state law. Drunk driving is responsible for many car accidents and deaths every year so the laws, although they vary from state to state, are quite strict. All drunk-driving offenses carry possible jail sentences. However, most first offenders receive lesser punishments, such as restrictions on their driver's license, a fine, alcohol counseling, or community service. Habitual drunk drivers face more severe punishments. They might lose their driver's license, go to jail, or pay very large fines. It's common for people to go to jail for a second drunk-driving conviction.

22. **drug dealing:** a *(drug) dealer* buys large quantities of illegal drugs and sells the drugs in smaller quantities to individual users. Although state laws vary, generally the laws are very strict on drug dealers and less strict on people who own small amounts of a drug.

LANGUAGE & CULTURE NOTES

The body consists of eight systems of internal organs. The *respiratory system* functions in the breathing process (the inhaling of oxygen and the exhaling of carbon dioxide). *The digestive system* processes food into nutrients and waste products. *The urinary system* processes waste products. *The nervous system* carries signals necessary for body functioning along the nerves. *The circulatory system* is a closed system that carries oxygen, nutrients, and wastes in the blood throughout the body. *The muscular system,* which includes the muscles, is involved in the movement of the body. *The endocrine system* consists of glands that produce the enzymes and hormones necessary for body functioning. *The skeletal system* or skeleton is the frame of the body.

(2) **hair:** People usually describe hair by *color*, such as black, brown, red, auburn (reddish-brown), or blond and by *shades of color*, such as light, medium, or dark. It is also common to describe hair by *texture*, such as straight, wavy, or curly.

(3) **forehead:** Another word for forehead is *brow*.

(9) **iris:** the colored part of the eye.

(10) **pupil:** the dark center of the eye that admits light and images.

(11) **cornea:** a transparent covering over the iris and pupil.

(15) **jaw:** The upper and lower jawbones hold the teeth.

(17) **lip:** The plural *lips* is most common, except when someone is referring to only one *lip*.

(24) **chest:** This term is for both men and women.

(25) **abdomen:** the main part of the body between the chest and the legs. People sometimes refer to this external part of the body as the *stomach*, even though the stomach is an internal organ.

(26) **breast:** The milk-secreting organs that women have. A woman's breasts are also sometimes called her *bust*.

(28) **arm:** The shoulder, elbow, hand, and wrist are all part of the arm.

(33) **leg:** The hip, thigh, knee, calf, shin, foot, and ankle are all part of the leg.

(36) **calf:** The plural of *calf* is *calves*.

(37) **shin:** the front part of the calf.

(39) **wrist:** You can feel the pulse, or heartbeat, at the wrist.

(42) **palm:** Some people believe you can *read* a person's future from the lines in the palm.

(47) **foot:** The plural of *foot* is *feet*.

(53) **throat:** a general term for the internal part of the neck. The passageway in the throat is divided into the *windpipe* for breathing and the *esophagus* for passing food to the stomach.

(69) **skull:** refers specifically to the bone that surrounds the brain, but generally can indicate the connected bones of the head, including the jaw bone and the teeth.

(71) **pelvis:** The pelvis is a bone. The hip (31) is a joint that is located in the cavity of the pelvis bone.

(72) **spinal column/spinal cord:** The spinal column is a series of vertebrae that go from the head to the bottom of the back.

LANGUAGE & CULTURE NOTES

Ailment is a general term for diseases and major and minor illnesses. *Injury* is a general term for medical problems related to bones, such as twists, sprains, dislocations, and breaks. *Sore* is a general term for problems related to the skin, such as rashes, scratches, scrapes, bruises, burns, and cuts.

Some ailments and symptoms use *a/an*, such as a headache, an earache, a toothache. A few ailments and symptoms use *the*, as in the flu, the hiccups, the chills. Some ailments and symptoms don't use *a/an* or *the*—for example, cramps, diarrhea, chest pain.

(1–5) **headache/earache/toothache/ stomachache/backache:** These are common ailments that affect internal organs of the body. People say, "I have a headache" or "My head aches."

(6) **sore throat:** a common symptom of a cold (8) or laryngitis (26).

(7) **fever/temperature:** A person has a *fever* or *temperature* when the body temperature goes above 98.6 degrees Fahrenheit.

(8) **cold:** a common ailment that comes from a virus. Cold symptoms may include a headache, runny nose or congestion, a sore throat, and a cough. It's common to treat a cold with rest, liquids, and over-the-counter medications to relieve the discomfort.

(10) **infection:** a general term for ailments that come from germs—either bacterial, which respond to antibiotics, or viral, which do not. A term with the suffix *-itis* indicates which organ is infected. For example, pancreatitis is infection of the pancreas, and bronchitis is infection of the bronchial tubes leading to the lungs.

(11) **rash:** itchy red spots on the body. A rash may be the result of an allergy or may be a symptom of a disease.

(12) **insect bite:** Insect bites typically cause swelling and itching. These symptoms are usually of short duration, but may be severe if there are multiple bites or if a person has an allergic reaction.

(13) **sunburn:** redness of the skin from overexposure to the sun. A suntan is bronzing from exposure to the sun. This normally has a positive connotation, as opposed to the negative connotation of a sunburn.

(14) **stiff neck:** sore muscles in the neck.

(16) **bloody nose:** Bleeding happens when blood vessels in the nose break. It may occur when a person blows his or her nose frequently or when something hits the nose.

(17) **cavity:** an area of decay in the tooth.

(18) **blister:** Where there is rubbing or a burn, a blister will form. It is a thin swelling of liquid under the skin.

(19) **wart:** a small hard growth on the skin from a virus.

(20) **(the) hiccups:** a repetitive and uncontrollable quick intake and catching of the breath. When people have the hiccups, they usually make the sound *hic!* A popular home remedy for hiccups is to take small rapid sips of water or to breathe into a paper bag.

(21) **(the) chills:** a coldness and shaking of the body when a person's temperature goes up rapidly in a fever, a common symptom of a virus.

AILMENTS, SYMPTOMS, AND INJURIES
(continued)

LANGUAGE & CULTURE NOTES

(22) **cramps:** severe pain from the sudden tightening of a muscle in the abdomen or legs.

(23) **diarrhea:** loose, frequent bowel movements that are a symptom of gastrointestinal ailments or a virus.

(24) **chest pain:** may be a symptom of a heart attack.

(25) **shortness of breath:** difficulty in breathing.

(26) **laryngitis:** an infection of the larynx, the upper part of the windpipe near the vocal cords. It causes a person to temporarily lose his or her voice.

(27) **faint:** *To feel faint* is to feel light-headed. *To faint* is to collapse when you feel light-headed.

(28) **dizzy:** to feel a loss of balance, as if the surroundings were going around and around.

(30) **bloated:** swollen, usually in the face and neck area and the abdomen. People who have too much to drink often feel bloated afterwards.

(31) **congested:** a condition that occurs when mucus (phlegm) blocks the nose or lungs.

(32) **exhausted:** very tired with little energy.

(33) **cough:** (verb) as opposed to the noun *cough*, as in "I have a cough." It is polite in the US to cover your mouth when you cough.

(35) **wheeze:** to make a whistling sound when a person is having difficulty breathing.

(36) **burp:** to get rid of stomach gas through the mouth. In U.S. culture, people think it's impolite to burp.

(37) **vomit/throw up:** to uncontrollably expel food.

(39) **twist:** to turn sharply and cause minor pain usually to the leg, ankle, foot, knee, or wrist.

(40) **scratch:** to get a single small cut.

(41) **scrape:** to get multiple small cuts, as when the skin rubs against a rough, hard surface.

(42) **bruise:** to bump sharply and cause discoloration of the skin.

(46) **sprain:** to damage a joint (commonly the wrist, knee, or ankle) when you twist sharply and suddenly.

(47) **dislocate:** to move a bone (commonly the shoulder, elbow, knee, or hip bone) out of its socket.

(49) **swollen:** an adjective. The verb is *to swell*, as in "His finger started to swell."

(50) **itchy:** an adjective. The verb is *to itch*, as in "His skin itched so he scratched it."

Keys to 39-50:

39 I twisted my ankle.
40 I scratched my eye.
41 I scraped my knees.
42 I bruised my arm.
43 I burned my hand.
44 I hurt my back.
45 I cut my finger.
46 I sprained my wrist.
47 I dislocated my shoulder.
48 I broke my leg.
49 My finger is swollen.
50 My foot is itchy.

LANGUAGE & CULTURE NOTES

1. **first-aid manual:** a booklet that gives care instructions for various injuries.

2. **first-aid kit:** a small box with all the essential materials for first aid.

3. **(adhesive) bandage/Band-Aid™:** a cotton bandage with tape. *Band-Aid* is the most popular brand of this product in the United States and has become synonymous with adhesive bandages.

4. **antiseptic cleansing wipe:** a disposable piece of cloth soaked in antiseptic cleanser. You use this to clean a wound.

5. **sterile (dressing) pad:** a cotton bandage that hasn't had contact with germs or bacteria.

6. **hydrogen peroxide:** a clear liquid that kills bacteria.

7. **antibiotic ointment:** You put on antibiotic ointment after you clean the wound. This helps the body fight off infection and also keeps the wound moist.

8. **gauze:** cotton bandage material that is not sterile. You apply gauze to larger cuts and scrapes when there aren't any sterile pads are available or when the wound has already developed a scab and the risk of infection is lower.

9. **adhesive tape:** You use this to attach gauze (8) or a sterile pad (5) to the skin.

10. **tweezers:** You use tweezers to pull out splinters (thin pieces of wood stuck under the skin) or other debris in a wound.

11. **antihistamine cream:** You use this to soothe a rash or swelling due to an insect bite or allergic reaction.

12. **elastic bandage/Ace™ bandage:** a thick elastic piece of cloth that provides support to strained, twisted, or sprained joints such as wrists, ankles, elbows, and knees. *Ace bandage* is the most popular brand of this product in the United States and has become synonymous with elastic bandage.

14. **non-aspirin pain reliever:** *Acetaminophen* is a popular non-aspirin pain reliever. It relieves pain and reduces fever and is more popular than aspirin because it doesn't upset the stomach. It's also safer than aspirin for people with special medical conditions.

15. **CPR (cardiopulmonary resuscitation / (a) has no pulse:** You use CPR when someone has suffered a terrible trauma and his or her heart has stopped, in other words, when there is no pulse.

16. **rescue breathing / (b) isn't breathing:** When a person isn't breathing, you pinch the person's nose tightly, cover the mouth with yours, and blow until you see the chest rise. Give 2 breaths. Each breath should take 2 seconds.

17. **the Heimlich maneuver / (c) is choking:** When a person is choking on a piece of food and is unable to speak or breathe, you wrap your arms around the person from behind. You place your arms over the person's abdomen, hold one hand with your other arm, and pull hard very fast.

18. **splint / (d) broke a finger:** A splint attached to the broken bone can help stabilize the area and make it safer to move the person.

19. **tourniquet / (e) is bleeding:** To apply a tourniquet, you wrap a bandage just above the wound (closer to the heart) and then use a stick to tighten the bandage to reduce the flow of blood.

LANGUAGE & CULTURE NOTES

(2) **in shock:** After a trauma, a person may go into shock. A person in shock has extremely low blood pressure. Depending on the specific cause and type of shock, symptoms will include one or more of the following: anxiety, confusion, pale and cool skin, and rapid but weak pulse. When someone is in shock, you lay the person on the back and elevate their legs about 12 inches. Keep the person warm.

(3) **unconscious:** not responsive. Being asleep is not the same thing as being unconscious. A sleeping person will respond to loud noises or gentle shaking. However, an unconscious person will not. An unconscious person cannot cough or clear his or her throat. This can lead to death if the airway becomes obstructed.

(4) **heatstroke:** If a person is exposed to excessive heat and does not drink enough fluids, the person will first get heat exhaustion (the result of dehydration) and then heatstroke. Heatstroke can cause shock, brain damage, organ failure, and even death. The symptoms of heatstroke include fever; confusion; dry, hot, and red skin; rapid breathing; weak pulse; and unconsciousness.

(5) **frostbite:** Skin can be damaged when it is exposed to extreme cold. The term for this damage is frostbite. The first symptom of frostbite is numbness. If the frostbite is severe, the skin turns white and hard.

(7) **allergic reaction:** Some people have mild allergic reactions to mold, pollen, and animal hair that result in congestion, irritated eyes and throat, and hives. Some people, especially those with food allergies, can have severe allergies that can result in anaphylaxis—a potentially fatal reaction. These people need to

carry the medication epinephrine in case they have contact with the food by accident.

(8) **swallow poison:** If someone swallows poison, you should immediately contact a poison control center or a poison hotline. The emergency operator will give instructions for what to do.

(9) **overdose on drugs:** Every year many people die because they have taken too large a dose of a drug or medication.

(12) **the flu/influenza:** The flu, or influenza virus, usually begins abruptly, with a fever between 102 to 106 degrees Fahrenheit, body aches, and exhaustion. Each year tens of millions of people in the United States get the flu.

(13) **an ear infection:** When external bacteria (for example, from a swimming pool), infects the ear, it is a middle ear infection. When internal congestion (for example, congestion from a head cold) infects the ear, it is an inner ear infection.

(14) **strep throat:** a common infection of the throat that comes from Streptococcus bacteria. The illness usually begins suddenly with a fever and sore throat, and often other symtoms such as a headache, stomachache, nausea, or the chills.

(15) **measles:** Measles is a highly contagious viral illness with symptoms of a fever, cough, conjunctivitis (redness and irritation in membranes of the eyes), and rash. It's possible to relieve the symptoms with bed rest, acetaminophen, and humidified air.

(16) **mumps:** Mumps is a contagious, viral disease that causes painful swelling of the salivary glands between the ear and the jaw. It's possible to relieve the painful symptoms with ice and acetaminophen.

LANGUAGE & CULTURE NOTES

(17) **chicken pox:** Chicken pox is the result of a virus. Most children with chicken pox have symptoms such as a fever, headache, stomachache, or loss of appetite for a day or two before the classic pox rash breaks out. The average child develops 250 to 500 small, itchy blisters or red spots on the skin. The symptoms last about five days. There now is a chicken pox vaccine for children and adults who never had the disease.

(18) **asthma:** Asthma is a disease in which a sudden inflammation of the windpipe restricts a person's breathing. Characteristic symptoms of an asthma attack are wheezing, shortness of breath, chest tightness, and coughing.

(19) **cancer:** Cancer involves the uncontrolled growth of abnormal cells that have mutated from normal tissues. This growth can kill when these cells prevent normal function of vital organs or spread throughout the body and damage essential systems. The three most common cancers in men in the US are prostate cancer, lung cancer, and colon cancer. In women, the three most frequently occurring cancers are breast cancer, lung cancer, and colon cancer. Treatment of cancer includes surgery to remove the tumors, chemotherapy, and radiation.

(20) **depression:** Depression is a feeling of extreme sadness. Symptoms include trouble sleeping or excessive sleeping, weight gain or loss, lack of energy, difficulty concentrating, and thoughts of death or suicide. Depression is a disorder in which feelings of sadness, loss, anger, or frustration interfere with everyday life for an extended time. The most common treatments for depression are talk therapy and anti-depressant medications.

(21) **diabetes:** Diabetes is a life-long disease in which there are high levels of sugar in the blood. It may be the result of too little insulin (a hormone the pancreas produces to regulate blood sugar), resistance to insulin, or both. The symptoms include frequent urination, thirst, hunger, fatigue, weight loss, and blurry vision. The most common treatment for diabetes is for the person to take insulin, control his or her diet, and consistently measure sugar levels.

(22) **heart disease:** Heart disease is any disorder that affects the heart's ability to function normally. The most common cause of heart disease is blockage of the coronary arteries, which supply blood to the heart.

(23) **high blood pressure/hypertension:** High blood pressure is when a person's blood pressure frequently goes over 140/90. It is more common in men than in women. A person with high blood pressure should eat a low salt diet, exercise, quit smoking, lose weight, and avoid alcohol.

(24) **TB (tuberculosis):** TB is a contagious infection that results from bacteria. The lungs are primarily involved, but the infection can spread to other organs, too. The symptoms include fatigue, weight loss, coughing up blood, and fever.

(25) **AIDS:** HIV (human immunodeficiency virus) causes the disease AIDS (acquired immunodeficiency syndrome). The virus attacks the immune system and leaves the body vulnerable to a variety of life-threatening infections and cancers. AIDS is the fifth leading cause of death among persons between ages 25 and 44 in the United States. About 47 million people worldwide have been infected with HIV since the start of the epidemic.

(A) measure *your* height and weight: A nurse, or nurse assistant, first measures the height and weight of the patient and records it in the patient's medical *chart.* If the patient is a child, the nurse records the measurements on a *growth chart* to compare the child's growth to the average growth of children of the same age. The nurse measures weight on a scale (1).

(B) take *your* temperature: The nurse, or nurse assistant, takes the patient's temperature with a thermometer (2). Body temperature in the United States is in Fahrenheit. A normal temperature is 98.6 degrees (37 degrees Centigrade).

(C) check *your* blood pressure: The nurse, or nurse assistant, checks the patient's blood pressure with a blood pressure gauge (3) and a stethoscope (8). Normal blood pressure is 110/70.

(D) draw some blood: the nurse, or a lab technician, takes a sample of the patient's blood to send to a lab for blood work (page 94, word 15). The lab tests the blood to measure the internal functions of the body.

(E) ask *you* some questions about *your* health: This is when the doctor asks the patient about any chronic conditions and how the patient is feeling in general. This is also the opportunity for the patient to tell the doctor about any concerns.

(F) examine *your* eyes, ears, nose, and throat: A nurse, or nurse assistant, administers the eyesight test. The patient covers one eye and reads from a distance letters on a chart. If there are any problems, the doctor refers the patient to an eye doctor (*ophthalmologist,* page 96, word 7). During the physical exam, the doctor also looks inside the eyes, nose, and throat with a bright light.

(G) listen to *your* heart: The doctor listens to the patient's heart and lungs with a stethoscope (8).

(H) take a chest X-ray: The doctor may require the patient to get an X-ray of the chest. Since X-rays carry some radiation, the patient usually wears a lead apron over any part of the body the doctor isn't x-raying in order to prevent radiation from penetrating the body.

(2) thermometer: The thermometer may be an old-style *mercury thermometer* or the more current *digital thermometer.* Digital thermometers can measure a patient's temperature from the ear or the mouth.

(4) needle/syringe: You use this when you give a person an injection or shot (page 93, word 14).

A **clean the wound:** It's most common to clean a wound with cotton balls (9) and alcohol (10) or hydrogen peroxide (page 90, word 6).

B **close the wound:** If the wound is a deep or serious cut, the doctor may decide to stitch the wound (11) with a needle and thread so that the skin heals together faster.

C **dress the wound:** This means to cover the wound with gauze (12) or a bandage (page 90, word 3).

D **clean *your* teeth:** To clean a patient's teeth, the dental hygienist scrapes away the tartar (calcified plaque), flosses between the teeth with dental floss (page 98, word 3), and then polishes the teeth with an electric brush.

E **examine *your* teeth:** During a dental examination, the dentist or dental hygienist counts the patient's teeth, looks at the patient's gums to make sure they are healthy, and looks for any cavities that may be evident to the eye.

F **give you a shot of anesthetic/ Novocaine™:** If the dentist needs to drill a cavity or do any dental work that may be painful for the patient, he or she first gives the patient a local anesthetic that deadens the nerves.

G **drill the cavity:** If decay (a cavity) is evident in a tooth, the dentist will drill the decay out before he or she fills the tooth.

H **fill the tooth:** First the dentist drills the decay out of the tooth, then cements a piece of silver in the hole to fill the tooth.

2 **receptionist:** the person who greets the patients when they enter the waiting room, arranges appointments, and gathers billing information.

3 **insurance card:** In general, medical care in the United States is expensive. Most people join health insurance programs, often through their place of employment. This helps pay for the high costs of medical care. Very poor people or elderly people can receive some government supported medical care through programs such as Medicaid and Medicare, or state-funded programs. When a patient registers for an appointment, he or she must show an insurance card before treatment.

4 **medical history form:** a form a patient must fill out the first time he or she sees a new doctor. The questions on the form ask general health questions and also whether the patient has had any major diseases.

6 **doctor/physician:** There are two categories of doctors in the United States—primary care physicians and specialists (see *Picture Dictionary* page 96). A primary care physician, sometimes called a *family practice specialist* or *general practitioner*, is someone who examines and treats all members of the family for routine illnesses and injuries. If necessary, a primary care physician will refer a patient to a specialist, someone who treats one particular part of the body.

Many doctors form medical groups, with specialists in different areas, in order to meet all the medical needs of patients at one location.

Doctors in the United States like to practice preventive medicine. Doctors stress the importance of annual physical examinations even if a person feels healthy in order to maintain a healthy body. The reason is to detect problems early before they become serious.

8 **nurse:** In the United States, nurses are highly-trained and skilled health

MEDICAL AND DENTAL PROCEDURES
(continued)

LANGUAGE & CULTURE NOTES

professionals who work in doctors' offices and hospitals. In a doctor's office, they perform many of the routine parts of an examination. For example, they do blood and urine tests, take blood pressure, give injections, and administer medicine. In the hospital, the nurse serves as a liaison between the doctor and the patient and has a great responsibility for the patient's care.

A *nurse practitioner* is a specially trained nurse who, in addition to the responsibilities above, can perform an entire physical examination, diagnose certain minor illnesses, and recommend treatment.

A *nurse-aide* is a trained assistant who helps with the care of the patient.

(9) **cotton balls:** small pieces of cotton you use to apply alcohol. During a dental procedure, a dental hygienist uses cotton balls to absorb saliva.

(10) **alcohol:** an antiseptic you use to sterilize an area of the body before a medical procedure.

(11) **stitches:** A doctor uses stitches to close an incision after surgery or to close a serious cut.

(14) **injection/shot:** Doctors give a patient an injection as prevention against disease (such as a vaccine) and as a treatment for an existing condition.

(16) **ice pack:** You put an ice pack in the freezer and then apply it to an area of the body to relieve swelling or pain.

(17) **prescription:** an order for medication that a doctor writes. It's necessary to take the prescription to a pharmacy in order to fill it.

(19) **cast:** A cast stabilizes a bone as it heals. Traditional casts were plaster. Now there are casts of many different materials including fiberglass and plastic.

(20) **brace:** This holds a part of the body stable as it heals. A brace may be removable at night for the patient's comfort while he or she is sleeping.

(21) **dental hygienist:** a person who cleans teeth and checks the mouth for oral hygiene. Dentists and hygienists recommend a cleaning and dental check-up every six months.

(22) **mask:** All practitioners wear masks when they are in close contact with patients in order to prevent contagious contact.

(23) **gloves:** thin, flexible plastic gloves that all health care professionals wear to protect both the health care worker and the patient from infection.

(24) **dentist:** a doctor who specializes in the care of the teeth and gums and diseases related to both.

(25) **dental assistant:** The person who assists the dentist. The hygienist passes instruments to the dentist and prepares materials for the dental procedures.

(26) **drill:** a dental instrument a dentist uses to remove decay from a tooth.

(2) **drink fluids:** For medical purposes, to drink fluids usually means clear fluids such as water and/or juice.

(3) **gargle:** usually with warm water and salt for a sore throat or mouth abrasions.

(4) **go on a diet:** an eating plan for losing weight. A doctor gives a patient a diet; a person then *goes on a diet* to lose weight.

(5) **exercise:** Physical exercise is important for people of all ages in order to maintain a healthy body. Many people do some form of exercise several days a week. For example, they run, jog, walk, play tennis, or do some other activity. The person in the scene in the *Picture Dictionary* is doing calisthenic exercises at home.

(6) **take vitamins:** Although a balanced diet should provide all the vitamins a person needs, many Americans take a daily multi-vitamin supplement. These vitamin pills follow government-recommended daily dosages. Some people use specific vitamins for specific problems: Vitamin A and D to promote calcium absorption for strong bones and teeth, Vitamin B1 for gastrointestinal problems, Vitamin B5 for fatigue and headaches, Vitamin C for colds and flu symptoms, and Vitamin E creams for burns. (See also page 95, word 3.)

(7) **see a specialist:** A general practitioner or family doctor may tell the patient to see a specialist who has more specific knowledge of a medical problem. (See *Picture Dictionary* page 96 for a list and description of medical specialists.)

(8) **get acupuncture:** Acupuncture is an ancient Chinese medical practice that is becoming more common in the United States, though most insurance companies do not pay for acupuncturist visits.

(9) **heating pad:** a flat pad with heat that comes from electricity. You place it on a part of the body to relieve pain.

(10) **humidifier:** There are two kinds of humidifiers—steam and cool mist. Steam humidifiers heat water to produce hot steam, which can burn to the touch. Cold mist humidifiers produce cool mist so there is no danger of getting burned.

(11) **air purifier:** As more and more people suffer from allergies and asthma, air purifiers have become more popular. Air purifiers clean dust and pollen from the air.

(15) **blood work/blood tests:** the nurse, or a lab technician, draws some blood (see page 92 D) to send to a lab for blood work. The lab tests the blood to measure the internal functions of the body and the patient's cholesterol and iron levels.

(16) **tests:** The medical procedures depicted are an electrocardiogram (EKG), a test that measures heart functioning, and an ultrasound, a test that uses ultrasonic waves to diagnose a medical problem.

(17) **physical therapy:** special exercises for rehabilitation of injured parts of the body. The scene in the *Picture Dictionary* shows a physical therapist (page 96, word 10) who is doing physical therapy on a patient's knee.

(19) **counseling:** An individual, a couple, or a family may get counseling (therapy) if they are depressed or are having other emotional and social problems. They go to a counselor or therapist (see page 96, word 11).

(20) **braces:** When a person's teeth are not straight, the person might visit an orthodontist (see page 96, word 16) to get braces to force the teeth into a better position. The best time to get braces is in early puberty, although adults also can get braces.

LANGUAGE & CULTURE NOTES

There are two types of medicines, prescription and non-prescription (over-the-counter) medicines. Prescription medicines require a doctor's written order (a prescription) and are for serious illnesses and injuries. A prescription is required because of the strength of the medicine or because the medicine contains government-controlled narcotic substances. Prescription medicines are available only through the pharmacy department of a drug store.

Non-prescription or over-the-counter medicines do not require a doctor's written order. They are available for minor illnesses and injuries, such as headaches, colds, coughs, sore throats, insect bites, digestive problems (upset stomach, indigestion, and diarrhea), burns, and cuts. Such medicines are available at drug stores, convenience stores, and in the personal care or health products department of groceries and discount department stores.

1. **aspirin:** a very common medicine for head, tooth, and muscular aches. It is available in varying strengths and forms for children and adults.

2. **cold tablets:** very common medicines that relieve the symptoms of colds. They are available in a variety of combinations for different symptoms, such as congestion or a runny nose, and may include expectorants or cough suppressors.

3. **vitamins:** See the Language & Culture Notes for *take vitamins* (page 94, word 6).

4. **cough syrup:** a liquid that suppresses coughing. It can also serve as an expectorant to bring out the mucous that settles in the lungs.

5. **non-aspirin pain reliever:** (See the Language & Culture Notes for *Picture Dictionary* page 90, word 14.)

6. **cough drops:** small, hard or semi-soft drops that you place and dissolve in the mouth.

7. **throat lozenges:** small round flat disks that dissolve in the mouth to relieve the discomfort of a sore throat.

8. **antacid tablets:** for the relief of stomach indigestion.

9. **decongestant spray/nasal spray:** You spray this in the nose to relieve blocked nasal passages.

10. **eye drops:** for the relief of tired or sore eyes. You use an eye dropper to dispense the liquid medicine.

11. **ointment** / 12. **cream/creme:** You rub these into the skin to relieve the pain of muscular and joint aches and to promote the healing of rashes, cuts, and burns.

13. **lotion:** a more liquid form of an ointment or cream.

14. **pill** / 15. **tablet** / 17. **caplet:** small, round solid pieces of medicine.

16. **capsule:** a measured amount of medicine inside a dissolvable covering. *Time-released* products allow the medicine to be absorbed into the body gradually over time—typically six or twelve hours.

18. **teaspoon** / 19. **tablespoon:** typical dosages of liquid medicine in the United States. A teaspoon is 5 milliliters and a tablespoon is 10 milliliters.

MEDICAL SPECIALISTS

LANGUAGE & CULTURE NOTES

> In the United States, doctors fall into two general categories—primary care physicians and specialists. A primary care physician, sometimes called a *family practice specialist* or *general practitioner,* is someone who examines and treats all members of the family for routine illnesses and injuries. If necessary, a primary care physician will refer a patient to a specialist, someone who treats one particular part of the body.
>
> Many doctors form medical groups, with specialists in different areas, in order to meet all the medical needs of patients at one location. Some of these medical groups are part of a hospital.

(1) **cardiologist:** a doctor who specializes in the heart, its function, defects, and diseases.

(2) **gynecologist:** a doctor who specializes in women's reproductive health.

(3) **pediatrician:** a doctor who specializes in the treatment of children.

(4) **gerontologist:** a doctor who specializes in the treatment of elderly patients.

(5) **allergist:** a doctor who specializes in the treatment of allergies.

(6) **orthopedist:** a doctor who specializes in the treatment of the bones.

(7) **ophthalmologist:** a doctor who specializes in the treatment of the eyes.

(8) **ear, nose, and throat (ENT) specialist:** a doctor who specializes in the treatment of the ears, nose, and throat.

(9) **audiologist:** a doctor who specializes in the treatment of ears and the hearing sense.

(10) **physical therapist:** a medical specialist who supervises patients as they recuperate strength and mobility in an injured body part.

(11) **counselor/therapist:** a specialist in mental health who provides talk therapy for patients, but not medications.

(12) **psychiatrist:** a medical doctor who specializes in the treatment of mental health patients. A psychiatrist may provide talk therapy, but is also authorized to prescribe medications.

(13) **gastroenterologist:** a doctor who specializes in stomach and digestive health problems.

(14) **chiropractor:** a specialist who manipulates muscles to correct spinal problems.

(15) **acupuncturist:** a specialist in the ancient Chinese medical practice of acupuncture. An acupuncturist inserts small needles into the patient's skin and tissue to activate autoimmune responses.

(16) **orthodontist:** a dental specialist who corrects the placement of teeth with braces and other devices.

A person must be very sick to be admitted to a hospital. More often patients visit a hospital day clinic to receive treatments, such as chemotherapy. Hospitals also have medical specialists' offices for daytime visits.

Hospitals provide other services, such as health screening clinics for specific conditions, informational talks by healthcare specialists, exercise and fitness programs, weightloss clinics, support groups for family members who have seriously ill relatives, support groups for patients after they leave the hospital, newsletters that discuss health issues and hospital services, and referral networks to help people find physicians.

Hospital care in the United States is very expensive. Most people subscribe to private health insurance plans to cover their medical expenses, often through the company where they are employed. Some states in the US. offer free medical care to people who are very poor.

(A) patient's room: the room on *Picture Dictionary* page 97 is a private room for a single patient. These rooms are less common and more expensive than the double room, which has two beds.

(2) hospital gown: This is sometimes called a *johnny*. This is the garment that all patients in the hospital must wear. It is loose-fitting and fastens at the neck and ties at the waist.

(3) hospital bed: a special bed that adjusts electrically to several different positions. To do this, the patient pushes the bed control (4).

(4) bed control: A patient uses this to raise or lower the position of the bed.

(5) call button: A patient pushes this button to call for a nurse.

(6) I.V.: the common abbreviated form of *intravenous*, a needle that inserts into a patient's vein in order to inject fluids and/or medication.

(8) bed table: an adjustable table that patients use for eating.

(9) bed pan: patients who are unable to get to a bathroom use this.

(10) medical chart: a careful detailed record of a patient's medications and condition.

(11) doctor/physician: In this scene the doctor is making his rounds and visiting patients to find out about their progress.

(B) nurse's station: In each wing of a hospital there is a nurse's station where nurses organize their care of the admitted patients.

(12) nurse: Traditionally nursing was a woman's occupation. In recent years, some men have also become nurses. They are usually called *male nurses*. To become a registered nurse (RN), a person must have at least a bachelor's degree in nursing. There are other personnel who can assist as nurse, such as a licensed practical nurse (LPN) who has one year of hospital training, or a nurse's aide who has a shorter course of training.

(13) dietician: a specialist in diets who makes sure that each patient follows the appropriate diet.

(14) orderly: a person who takes care of patient transportation, delivery of meals, and other non-medical matters.

LANGUAGE & CULTURE NOTES

(C) **operating room:** also called an *OR*.

(15) **surgeon:** a doctor who has received special training to perform surgeries or operations.

(16) **surgical nurse:** a nurse who has special training to assist doctors in surgeries.

(17) **anesthesiologist:** a doctor who administers anesthesia so the patient doesn't experience pain during an operation. Sometimes a patient must go under (be unconscious) during an operation. Sometimes it is better for the patient to be conscious during the operation.

(D) **waiting room:** a room where friends and family can wait until they are allowed to see a patient.

(18) **volunteer:** Most hospitals have many volunteers who help patients and their families in non-medical ways. Volunteers may visit patients to keep them company or give information at reception. The volunteer in this illustration is helping by playing with a child.

(E) **birthing room/delivery room:** a hospital room where women give birth. In the United States, there has been a trend to make childbirth less medical and more natural. Hospitals have started providing birthing rooms that feel more like a room in a home than in a hospital. These are private rooms with space for a family member to stay.

(19) **obstetrician:** a medical doctor with special training for delivering babies.

(20) **midwife/nurse-midwife:** A midwife is the traditional practitioner who helps a woman give birth in her home. Some hospitals allow midwives to take care of patients as long as the midwives allow doctors to intervene if there is an emergency. A nurse-midwife is a midwife with a nursing degree as well. Many hospitals allow nurse-midwives to deliver babies.

(F) **emergency room (ER):** the place where people with emergency medical conditions go. This is not just one room, but usually a whole wing of a hospital with a waiting room, a triage room, and many examination rooms. Doctors send patients to other parts of the hospital if they need specific care (for example: an operating room or an X-ray).

Most patients walk into an emergency room, but seriously ill or injured patients go to the emergency room in an ambulance.

(21) **emergency medical technician (EMT):** a person who has the training to administer emergency medical procedures to stabilize a patient before they reach a hospital. EMTs travel in ambulances.

(G) **radiology department:** Every hospital has a radiology department where patients can get X-rays, ultrasound sonograms, MRIs, and CAT scans.

(23) **X-ray technician:** a person who takes X-rays.

(24) **radiologist:** a doctor with special training to interpret images from radiology.

(H) **laboratory/lab:** the area of a hospital where lab technicians (25) examine and diagnose blood, urine, and tissue samples.

(A) **brush *my* teeth:** Dentists recommend that people brush their teeth two times a day.

(1) **toothbrush:** The toothbrush depicted is a traditional one. Nowadays, many people also use electric toothbrushes.

(2) **toothpaste:** Toothpaste comes in two varieties—paste (opaque) and gel (clear). Toothpastes can have many properties. For example, they whiten teeth; freshen breath, and reduce tartar (a calcified substance that collects on teeth).

(B) **floss *my* teeth:** Dentists recommend that people floss their teeth after they brush them.

(3) **dental floss:** a string you use to remove pieces of food and plaque from between the teeth.

(C) **gargle:** (See *Picture Dictionary* page 94, word 3.)

(4) **mouthwash:** a liquid you use after you brush your teeth to kill germs and freshen breath.

(D) **whiten my teeth:** Over the years teeth get stained by coffee, tea, and dark fruit juice. People use a whitener (5) to remove those food stains.

(5) **teeth whitener:** a gel you place on your teeth every day over a period of weeks to remove stains.

(E) **bathe/take a bath:** *Bathe* is a transitive verb. For example, "A mother bathes her child." *Take a bath* is intransitive. For example, "A mother takes a bath (herself)."

(7) **bubble bath:** a scented liquid that you add to bath water to make many bubbles in the bath.

(8) **shower cap:** a plastic hat you wear to keep your hair dry during a shower.

(9) **shampoo:** There are many shampoos for varying hair types—oily, normal, and dry.

(10) **conditioner/rinse:** a lotion you use after you shampoo to give the hair more body (shape) or to decrease tangles (make it easier to comb).

(K) **style *my* hair:** After you wash your hair, you can style it to make it take a shape. People use products 14–19 to style their hair.

(14) **hot comb/curling iron:** a hairstyler that makes curls in the hair. Women who want straight hair may use a straightening iron.

(15) **hairspray:** a liquid you spray on dry hair to keep it in place.

(16) **hair gel:** a gel you apply to wet hair in order to style and shape the hair. Both men and women use this product.

(17) **bobby pin / (18) barrette / (19) hairclip:** Women use these to pin or clip their hair.

(21) **razor / (22) razor blade / (23) electric shaver:** Both men and women in the US use razors and electric shavers. American women customarily shave the hair on their legs and under their arms. Men only shave their faces.

(24) **styptic pencil:** a stick of an astringent material that stops the bleeding of small cuts.

(25) **aftershave (lotion):** an alcohol-based aromatic liquid that men put on their faces after they shave.

(26) **nail file:** a metal file that shapes fingernails.

(27) **emery board:** a wooden file that shapes fingernails.

(28) **nail clipper:** These come in two sizes: *small* for the smaller hand nails, and *large* for the larger toe nails.

(29) **nail brush:** People use this to brush dirt from under the nails.

(30) **scissors:** also called *nail scissors.*

LANGUAGE & CULTURE NOTES

(31) nail polish: a varnish some women put on their nails to color them or make them shiny. There are three possible types of nail polish—base coat, nail polish, and top coat. When a woman puts on nail polish, she polishes her nails. Some people go to a manicurist to have their nails *done* by a trained person.

(32) nail polish remover: a strong solvent that dissolves the nail polish and any other varnish.

(33) deodorant: Most American men and women wear underarm deodorant in order to eliminate odor. The deodorant on *Picture Dictionary* page 99 is a stick deodorant that the person puts on. Spray deodorants are also very common.

(34) hand lotion: You use this so your hands don't become dry and chapped.

(35) body lotion: similar to hand lotion, but usually a thinner consistency to put on a larger skin surface.

(36) powder: You use this to absorb extra perspiration.

(37) cologne/perfume: *Perfume* is synthetic or natural fragrance that has a pleasant aroma. *Cologne* is fragrance mixed with alcohol. *Eau de cologne* or *toilet water* is diluted cologne. Women wear perfume. Both men and women wear cologne.

(38) sunscreen: a lotion or gel you put on the skin to reduce the damage of the sun. There are many different kinds of sunscreen with different active ingredients and different levels of effectiveness. A sunscreen with an SPF of 4 is the weakest sunscreen available and SPF 45 is the maximum.

(39) blush/rouge: red toned powder women put on their cheeks to add color to the face.

(40) foundation/base: skin-tone cream that eliminates uneven tones in the skin.

(41) moisturizer: People use this to prevent dry skin. This is usually a product specifically for the face.

(42) face powder: skin-tone powder that absorbs perspiration on the face.

(43) eyeliner: Women use this to draw lines around the eyes to make them more defined.

(44) eye shadow: colored powder that women put on their eyelids.

(45) mascara: brown or black liquid that women put on their eyelashes to make them appear longer and thicker.

(46) eyebrow pencil: This makes the eyebrows darker and more defined.

(47) lipstick: color that women put on their lips to make them more colorful or shiny.

(48) shoe polish: This adds color and shine to smooth leather shoes and boots.

(49) shoelaces: The length of the shoelaces depends on the number of eyelets the shoes have.

BABY CARE

LANGUAGE & CULTURE NOTES

Baby or *infant* is the general term people use for children under one year old.

(A) feed: To *feed* is to give food to another person or animal who cannot eat without help.

(1) baby food: commercially-prepared meats, fruits, and vegetables that come in jars.

(2) bib: a piece of material that a baby wears around his or her neck to protect the clothing when eating.

(4) nipple: a piece of rubber with a small hole in the tip that allows the baby to suck milk or formula from a bottle.

(5) formula: a milk- or soy-based liquid food for babies who are not nursing (drinking breast milk).

(6) (liquid) vitamins: Some doctors advise parents to give these liquid vitamin supplements to their infants.

(B) change the baby's diaper: It's common to change a baby's diaper on a changing table (see page 25, word 7).

(7) disposable diaper: diapers with a plastic covering, an inner layer of absorbent material, and adhesive tape fasteners. You throw them away after one use.

(8) cloth diaper: a diaper of absorbent cloth that you fasten with diaper pins (9). People launder and reuse cloth diapers. Many families who use cloth diapers use laundering services that pick up soiled diapers and deliver clean ones two times a week.

(9) diaper pin: a large pin that you use to fasten cloth diapers.

(10) (baby) wipes: soft wet paper cloths that you use to clean the baby's skin after you remove a diaper.

(11) baby powder: Some people like to put baby powder on the baby after they change a diaper to keep the skin dry and prevent rashes.

(12) training pants: These are meant to be less comfortable than diapers so the baby is aware that he or she has just soiled the pants. You use these when a child is ready to stop using diapers and start toilet training. In the United States this is usually between the child's second and third birthday.

(13) ointment: a cream or salve that prevents rashes.

(14) baby shampoo: a special shampoo that does not irritate the eyes.

(15) cotton swab: a cotton-tipped wooden or plastic stick that you use to clean a baby's ears and nose.

(16) baby lotion: a semi-liquid cream that you use to soften and protect the skin from wetness and to prevent rashes.

(17) pacifier: a nipple that a baby sucks on. *To pacify* is to calm or quiet.

(18) teething ring: a plastic or rubber ring that babies chew on to ease the pain when teeth are coming in.

(E) nurse: When a baby nurses, the baby drinks the mother's breast milk. This is also called *breast-feeding*.

(19) child-care center: a place where parents can leave their young children for the day while they go to work.

(20) child-care worker: a person who takes care of young children in a child-care center.

(21) rocking chair: a chair that rocks back and forth.

(22) cubby: the place where children store their belongings during the school day.

(I) play with: In this scene, the child-care worker is playing with the child. A person can also play with toys alone.

(23) toys: Many parents want to encourage their children to learn and develop quickly, so they buy developmental toys that encourage children to learn.

TYPES OF SCHOOLS

LANGUAGE & CULTURE NOTES

Schools in the United States are either public or private. Public schools receive government funding, and as a result they are free for students who attend them. Private schools charge tuition since they don't receive funding from the government. Children enter school in kindergarten at approximately age 5 and continue through twelfth grade. School is compulsory until age 16–18, depending on the state.

1. **preschool/nursery school:** Most preschools are private schools for children from age two years and nine months to five years old. They are usually half-day programs that teach their young students music, art, and how to get along with others.

2. **elementary school:** All elementary schools begin with kindergarten. Some go up to fifth grade or sixth grade. Many new schools now have elementary programs and middle school programs in the same building.

3. **middle school/junior high school:** This serves children in grades 5–9, depending on the school. In middle school, students move from classroom to classroom to take more specialized classes with specialized teachers.

4. **high school:** In the United States, high schools are very large institutions that serve all the students in the school district. They offer many different types and levels of classes. Some students may study college-preparatory classes so they are prepared to go to a four-year college. Others may take standard classes so they can go to a two-year college after graduation.

5. **adult school:** Students who don't finish high school or need to study more to get into a community college can attend an adult school.

6. **vocational school/trade school:** an educational program for high-school-age students who want to learn a trade such as car mechanics, hair dressing, heating and air conditioning, or printing.

7. **community college:** These colleges offer many two-year degree programs and occasionally four-year degree programs. Because they usually receive public funding, they are more affordable.

8. **college:** a four-year degree program. Upon completion, a student receives a bachelor of arts degree (B.A.) or a bachelor of science degree (B.S.). Most colleges are private schools with competitive admissions and expensive tuition.

9. **university:** a higher education institution that has both a college and graduate school. State universities receive public funding, but many others are private.

10. **graduate school:** any school that offers a post-bachelor's degree, either a master's degree (two year degree after a four-year college) or a doctorate degree (4–7 year program after a master's degree).

11. **law school:** To get into law school in the United States, a student must first have a bachelor's degree from a college. Law school is a three-year program.

12. **medical school:** To get into medical school in the United States, a student must first have a bachelor's degree from a college. Medical school training can go from four years to twelve years, depending on the extent of specialization.

THE SCHOOL

LANGUAGE & CULTURE NOTES

Children enter school in kindergarten at approximately age 5 and continue through twelfth grade. School is compulsory until age 16–18, depending on the state. There are usually three grade divisions: *elementary* (kindergarten through grade 6), *middle school* (grades 7–8), and *high school* (grades 9–12).

(A) **(main) office:** the place where the business of the school takes place.

(C) **nurse's office:** a room for private consultations with the (school) nurse (3).

(D) **guidance office:** the office of the (guidance) counselor (4).

(E) **classroom:** In U.S. high schools, students go to different classrooms for each subject. The homeroom is the classroom where students go at the beginning and end of the school day.

(F) **hallway / (a) locker:** Students move between classrooms. They each have a locker in one of the school hallways where they can go between classes to get books and other personal belongings.

(G) **science lab:** a special room with large tables, sinks, gas lines for heating instruments, and other equipment for scientific experiments.

(H) **gym/gymnasium / (a) locker room:** The gym is the area for indoor athletic activities, such as basketball and calisthenic exercises. Gym class is required in all U.S. schools. The locker room is the area where students change into their gym clothes— the outfits they wear for gym activities.

(I) **track / (a) bleachers:** The track is an outdoor running path. Bleachers are the benches where sports spectators sit.

(J) **field:** the area where outdoor athletic activities, such as football, baseball, and soccer, take place.

(K) **auditorium:** the place where school assemblies (gatherings), concerts, and drama productions take place.

(L) **cafeteria:** Most U.S. high schools have a cafeteria that sells hot and cold breakfasts and lunches.

(M) **library:** Every school has a library where students can take out books and do research.

(1) **clerk/(school) secretary:** This person checks in all school visitors and students who arrive late.

(2) **principal:** the director of the school.

(3) **(school) nurse:** The school nurse treats minor health needs of students and administers medications to students with chronic conditions, such as asthma.

(4) **(guidance) counselor:** the person who helps students with course selection as well as any personal problems students wish to discuss.

(6) **assistant principal/vice-principal:** the person who assists the principal in the day-to-day running of the school.

(7) **security officer:** This person makes sure that students who enter the school aren't carrying any dangerous weapons.

(9) **P.E. teacher:** the person who teaches gym. P.E. stands for *Physical Education*.

(10) **coach:** a person in charge of an athletic team.

(11) **custodian:** a person who cleans and does repair work in the school building.

(12) **cafeteria worker:** a person who serves food in the cafeteria.

(13) **lunchroom monitor:** a teacher who oversees the lunch periods in order to maintain order in the cafeteria.

(14) **(school) librarian:** a trained librarian who runs the school library and teaches students how to do research.

LC102

This lesson depicts subjects that high school students commonly study.

(1) **math/mathematics:** a general term that includes algebra, geometry, trigonometry, and calculus.

(2) **English:** includes English grammar, literature, composition, and critical thinking.

(3) **history:** includes both United States and world history.

(5) **government:** Students study the systems and organization of the United States government and ways to be participatory citizens.

(6) **science:** a general term that includes biology (7), chemistry (8), and physics (9).

(10) **health:** This includes nutrition, drug and alcohol awareness, and information about sexually transmitted diseases (STDs).

(11) **computer science:** includes instruction in how to use software as well as computer programming.

(12) **Spanish** / (13) **French:** These are the two most common foreign languages that students study in U.S. high schools. Some high schools also offer Latin, Chinese, Italian, German, and Japanese.

(14) **home economics:** includes food preparation and sewing, with an increasing emphasis on child growth and development and the issues of family life.

(15) **industrial arts/shop:** This includes woodworking, metalworking, and technical drawing.

(16) **business education:** includes how to run a small business.

(17) **physical education/P.E.:** It's common to refer to this as *gym class*.

(18) **driver's education/driver's ed:** Depending on the state laws, a teenager as young as 16 can get a driver's license, so many high schools offer driver's education after school hours. Instruction is both in the classroom and on the road.

(19) **art:** can include drawing, painting, graphics, photography, pottery, sculpture, jewelry making, stained glass making, and weaving.

(20) **music:** general instruction to all students about rhythm, notation, and music theory. For students who are learning to play an instrument, there are extracurricular activities such as band and orchestra (see Language & Culture Notes for *Picture Dictionary* page 104).

EXTRACURRICULAR ACTIVITIES

LANGUAGE & CULTURE NOTES

This lesson depicts activities that many high schools in the United Sates offer their students. These are not required activities. Schools encourage students to become involved in one or more extracurricular activities. It is not necessary for the student to excel or to have talent in the area he or she chooses. The availability of these offerings gives all students an opportunity to try something they might not otherwise have a chance to do.

(1) **band:** instrumental popular music. There are both standing bands that perform on stage and marching bands that perform in parades and at school sports events. The band on *Picture Dictionary* page 104 is a marching band.

(2) **orchestra:** classical orchestral music.

(3) **choir/chorus:** vocal music.

(4) **drama:** a club that usually produces a school play.

(5) **football:** one of the many competitive sports that schools offer after regular school hours. Football games typically take place on Saturdays in the fall. They are usually very popular school events for students and their families. Other very popular school sports are basketball, soccer, swimming, lacrosse, and track.

(6) **cheerleading/pep squad:** Both male and female students with good gymnastic abilities work together to perform gymnastic stunts and cheer on the school team at athletic events.

(7) **student government:** a group that students elect to organize student activities and represent students' needs to school officials.

(8) **community service:** For community service, students perform some voluntary service in the community. For example, they might help in a nursing home, pick up trash, or work in a homeless shelter.

(9) **school newspaper:** a newspaper that students write and publish about school-related issues.

(10) **yearbook:** a book that students create and publish at the end of the year, which has many photographs and gives an overview of the activities of the entire school year, with an emphasis on graduating seniors.

(11) **literary magazine:** a publication with original student poems and stories.

(12) **A.V. crew:** Students volunteer to manage, repair, and run the high school's audiovisual equipment, such as video cameras, digital cameras, and music systems.

(13) **debate club:** Students develop debate skills and then compete against debate teams from other schools.

(14) **computer club:** Students meet to share computer knowledge and learn more about computers.

(15) **international club:** Students share cultural traditions and sponsor events that celebrate the culture of various foreign countries.

(16) **chess club:** Students meet to play chess and develop their ability. They also compete against other school teams in chess tournaments.

The short form of mathematics is math. It is a singular noun.

The four arithmetic operations are addition, subtraction, multiplication, and division.

You say fractions with a combination of cardinal and ordinal numbers. For example: 3/5 is three fifths, 5/8 is five eighths, and 7/16 is seven sixteenths.

MEASUREMENTS AND GEOMETRIC SHAPES

LANGUAGE & CULTURE NOTES

Measurements: There are two systems of units used for measuring—the *metric* and the *customary* systems. The metric system is the standard measuring system in most countries around the world, except for the United States and Canada, which use the customary system. The US passed the *Metric Conversion Act* in 1975, which required voluntary conversion to the metric system. However, at this time, the customary system is still predominant.

Customary ←→ Metric Conversions:

1 inch = 2.54 centimeters

1 foot = 30.5 centimeters/.305 meters

1 yard = .914 meters

1 mile = 1.6 kilometers

1 centimeter = .4 inches

1 meter = 39 inches/3 feet 3 inches/1.1 yards

1 kilometer = .6 mile

To go from . . .	to . . .	multiply by . . .
inches	centimeters	2.5
centimeters	inches	.4
feet	meters	.3
meters	feet	3.25
yards	meters	.9
meters	yards	1.1
miles	kilometers	1.6
kilometers	miles	.6

(1) **height:** a measurement from the base or bottom of an object to its top. (The height of an airplane or a mountain is called *altitude*.)

(2) **width:** a measurement from one side of an object to the other.

(3) **depth:** a measurement from the front to the back of an object.

(4) **length:** the space between two points— for example, the size of a building, a room, or a box. (The term *distance* is for units longer than a mile. See word 10 below.)

(5) **inch:** The equivalent of 2.54 centimeters. The symbol " stands for inches.

(6) **foot–feet:** the basic unit of the customary system. There are twelve inches in a foot. The symbol ' after a number stands for feet. Thus, 5'10" means *five feet ten inches*.

MEASUREMENTS AND GEOMETRIC SHAPES
(continued)

LANGUAGE & CULTURE NOTES

(7) **yard:** 3 feet or 36 inches.

(8) **centimeter:** a metric unit that equals one one-hundredth of a meter.

(9) **meter:** the basic unit of the metric system.

(10) **distance:** the space between two points that are apart by more than a mile—for example, the distance between two cities. (See word 4 above.)

(11) **mile:** 5,280 feet.

(12) **kilometer:** a metric unit that equals 1,000 meters.

(15) **parallel lines:** two lines that are an equal distance from each other at all points.

(16) **perpendicular lines:** two lines that intersect at a right angle, 90 degrees.

Geometric Shapes: flat figures that have length and width.

---

(17) **square:** a figure with four equal *sides* (a) and four right angles (see 19b below).

(18) **rectangle:** a four-sided figure with four right angles and opposing sides of equal length.

> (a) **length:** the longer opposing sides.
>
> (b) **width:** the shorter opposing sides.
>
> (c) **diagonal:** a line that joins opposite corners. This creates two right triangles (see 19 below) of equal size.

(19) **right triangle:** a three-sided figure with one right angle.

> (a) **apex:** the highest point from the base.
>
> (b) **right angle:** an angle that equals 90 degrees.
>
> (c) **base:** the bottom side of the triangle.
>
> (d) **hypotenuse:** the side opposite the right angle.

(20) **isosceles triangle:** a three-sided figure that has two equal sides.

> (a) **acute angle:** an angle less than 90 degrees.
>
> (b) **obtuse angle:** an angle larger than 90 degrees.

(21) **circle:** a continuous curved line, all points of which are equal distance from the *center* (a).

> (b) **radius:** a line that goes from the center to any point in the circle.
>
> (c) **diameter:** a line that goes from one side of the circle to the other side and passes through the center.
>
> (d) **circumference:** the distance around the circle.

(22) **ellipse/oval:** a continuous curved line with a symmetrical shape when you cut it in half.

Solid Figures: three-dimensional figures that have length, width, and height.

---

(23) **cube:** a solid figure with six sides that are equal squares.

(25) **sphere:** The earth is a sphere.

(27) **pyramid:** a figure with a square base and four triangular sides. The most famous man-made pyramids are in Egypt.

Word by Word Picture Dictionary
Page 106 Language & Culture Notes

LC106a

ENGLISH LANGUAGE ARTS AND COMPOSITION

LANGUAGE & CULTURE NOTES

Types of Sentences

(A) **declarative:** a sentence that makes a statement.

(B) **interrogative:** a sentence that asks a question.

(C) **imperative:** a sentence that gives a command or makes a request.

(D) **exclamatory:** a sentence that expresses strong feeling

Parts of Speech

(1) **noun:** a person, place, or thing. There are proper nouns (*Jennifer*) and common nouns (*woman*).

(2) **verb:** a word that expresses actions or otherwise helps make a statement.

(3) **preposition:** a word that shows the relation of a noun to another word.

(4) **article:** the word that precedes a noun. The definite article (*the*) indicates that the speaker has already identified and knows the noun. An indefinite article (*a, an, some*) makes the noun more general and not specific.

(5) **adjective:** a word that describes a noun. For example: *happy* child, *big* man, *cold* day.

(6) **pronoun:** You use this in place of one or more nouns.

(7) **adverb:** a word that describes a verb. For example: spoke *loudly*.

Punctuation Marks

(8) **period:** This comes at the end of a (declarative) statement.

(9) **question mark:** These come at the end of question (an interrogative sentence).

(10) **exclamation point:** This comes at the end of an exclamatory sentence.

(11) **comma:** You use a comma to separate and set off items in a list, clauses, and phrases in a sentence.

(12) **apostrophe:** You use this with an *s* to indicate possession by a person. For example: *John's watch* or *Judy's desk.*

(13) **quotation marks:** You use these to mark the beginning and end of a person's exact spoken words.

(14) **colon:** You use this within a sentence to indicate that something immediately follows.

(15) **semi-colon:** You use this between independent clauses (sentences) to indicate that the sentences are closely related.

The Writing Process

(16) **brainstorm ideas:** The writer writes out all possible ideas related to a topic and doesn't worry if all the ideas fit.

(17) **organize *my* ideas:** When the writer has finished brainstorming, he or she reads through the ideas and organizes them.

(18) **write a first draft:** After the writer has organized the ideas, he or she can write out a first draft to try out the ideas in full written form.

(19) **make corrections/revise/edit:** These all mean the same thing—to improve the writing.

(20) **get feedback:** The writer can ask another student or a teacher to read the piece to get that person's feedback.

(21) **write a final copy/rewrite:** The writer writes out the final copy and adds the final revisions.

(1) **fiction:** a piece of writing that describes imaginary people and events. Fiction can have different lengths. A *novel* (2) is a book length piece of fiction. A *short story* (3) is a shorter piece of fiction.

(4) **poetry/poems:** Poetry is the *genre,* and poems are the poetry compositions.

(5) **non-fiction:** a piece of writing that describes real people and events.

(6) **biography:** a written account of another person's life.

(7) **autobiography:** a written account of one's own life.

(8) **essay:** a short composition on any subject. An essay is often a reflective and interpretive piece of writing that strongly indicates the author's point of view.

(9) **report:** a composition that presents research on a subject (non-fiction). A report should not indicate the author's point of view.

(12) **editorial:** an article that expresses an opinion about an issue in the news. The *Op-ed* section of the newspaper features editorials that the newspaper's editors write, as well as *opinion* pieces that people in the community write and send in to newspapers.

(15) **note:** a short letter.

(16) **invitation:** People usually send written invitations to large events, such as birthday parties, anniversary parties, or wedding parties. For smaller events, such as a dinner party with friends, a verbal invitation on the phone or in person is more common.

(17) **thank-you note:** a short letter that expresses thanks for a gift or effort someone has made. It is customary to write a thank-you note after you receive a gift from someone, especially when the giver wasn't present when you received the gift.

(18) **memo:** a piece of writing for internal communication in a business. A memo is a letter to employees about company policy or events.

(19) **e-mail:** an abbreviation of *electronic mail.* E-mail is both the Internet communication system and the *messages* people write.

(20) **instant message:** also known as *IM. IM* is both a noun and a verb. To *IM* is to communicate in real time via the Internet with other Internet users. Many people can join in the IM conversation at the same time.

LANGUAGE & CULTURE NOTES

(1) **forest/woods:** Forests may be broadleaf, coniferous, or mixed (see *Picture Dictionary* pages 156–157).

(2) **hill:** an area of higher ground, but smaller than a mountain.

(3) **mountain range:** a line of mountains connected by high ground.

(4) **mountain peak:** the highest point of a mountain.

(5) **valley:** low land between hills or mountains.

(6) **lake:** usually a freshwater inland body of water.

(7) **plains:** flat treeless country.

(8) **meadow:** low grassland often near a stream or lake.

(9) **stream/brook:** a small river.

(10) **pond:** a small lake, either natural or man-made.

(11) **plateau:** a flat-topped mountain.

(12) **canyon:** a steep-sided narrow valley.

(13) **dune/sand dune:** a hill of sand caused by the action of the wind.

(14) **desert:** a hot arid region of san d.

(15) **jungle:** a forest with thick, viney undergrowth in a tropical area of high heat and humidity.

(16) **seashore/shore:** the beach area along ocean coasts.

(17) **bay:** an inlet of the coastline that results from the erosive action of the surf.

(18) **ocean:** a large body of salt water. Oceans cover 70% of the earth's surface.

(19) **island:** a piece of land with water all around it.

(20) **peninsula:** a piece of land that projects into a sea or lake.

(21) **rainforest:** a tropical forest with heavy rainfall.

(23) **waterfall:** when water passes from a higher to a lower point of land.

(3) **slide:** a flat piece of clear glass on which you place a sample of material to view under a microscope.

(4) **Petri dish:** a shallow dish with a cover that you use to grow bacteria.

(5) **flask:** a bottle with a narrow neck. Science flasks can withstand high heat.

(7) **beaker:** a jar with an open mouth and pour spout that you use to pour liquids.

(8) **test tube:** a narrow glass tube that you use for experiments.

(9) **forceps:** You use these to pull something out of a narrow place (such as a test tube).

(10) **crucible tongs:** You use these to pick up very hot objects.

(11) **Bunsen burner:** a gas-powered heating device to heat materials in science experiments.

(12) **graduated cylinder:** You use this to measure liquids and occasionally solids by their displacement of water.

(14) **prism:** a piece of cut glass that refracts light.

(15) **dropper:** You use this to add very small portions of a liquid in an experiment.

(16) **chemicals:** any of many different substances that you use in scientific experiments.

(18) **scale** / (17) **balance:** two different kinds of scales. A balance is a scale with two sides and compares the weight of two objects. A science scale measures the weight of an object in kilograms.

The Scientific Method
In school, students learn this approach to scientific inquiry and follow it when they do experiments.

(A) **state the problem:** The student identifies a problem or question that he or she wants to investigate in an experiment.

(B) **form a hypothesis:** This is a statement that predicts what will happen in an experiment.

(C) **plan a procedure:** This is the experiment plan.

(D) **do the procedure:** This procedure must follow the above plan.

(E) **make/record observations:** At regular intervals, the student writes down what is happening in the experiment.

(F) **draw conclusions:** The student compares the experiment observations to the hypothesis and develops an explanation.

The Universe: This encompasses all things that exist. It is made up of billions of galaxies.

1. **galaxy:** a collection of stars. The earth is a planet in a solar (star) system that is part of the Milky Way galaxy.

2. **star:** a burning, gaseous mass.

3. **constellation:** a designation of a group of stars. People in different cultures call star groupings by different names. Western cultures use the designation of the Greeks, the names of mythological heroes, heroines, and beasts. Scientists have designated 88 different constellations.

3a. **The Big Dipper:** part of the Ursa Major/Big Bear constellation.

3b. **The Little Dipper:** part of the Ursa Minor/Little Bear constellation.

The Solar System: a star system that includes nine planets and their moons, as well as smaller objects called *comets* (10) and asteroids (11), all of which orbit around the sun.

4. **sun:** The sun is a star. It is part of the Milky Way galaxy and has its own system of orbiting planets.

5. **moon:** a natural satellite, a solid or gaseous object that orbits around a planet. The number of moons a planet has varies.

6. **planet:** a large object that orbits around the sun and rotates on its own axis.

7. **solar eclipse:** This occurs when the moon passes between Earth and the sun, and Earth's shadow obscures the sun.

8. **lunar eclipse:** This occurs when Earth passes between the moon and the sun, and Earth's shadow obscures the moon.

9. **meteor:** a chunk of rock or metal that results from the collision of asteroids or the breaking up of a comet.

10. **comet:** a body of dust, ice, and frozen gases that orbits around the sun. Halley's Comet is a well-known comet that is visible every 77 years.

11. **asteroid:** a small planet that orbits around the sun.

12. **Mercury:** the planet nearest the sun (36,000,000 miles away). Mercury is 2/5 the size of Earth. It has no moons.

13. **Venus:** the second planet from the sun (67,000,000 miles away). Venus is about the same size as Earth. It has no moons.

14. **Earth:** the third planet from the sun (93,000,000 miles away). Earth is the fifth-largest planet, with a diameter of 8,000 miles. It has one moon.

15. **Mars:** the fourth planet from the sun (141,700,000 miles away). Mars is half the size of Earth, with two moons.

16. **Jupiter:** the fifth planet from the sun (483,000,000 miles away). Jupiter is the largest planet, 11 times the size of Earth. It has two moons.

17. **Saturn:** the sixth planet from the sun (885,200,000 miles away). Saturn is half the size of Earth. It has 23 moons and 7 rings.

18. **Uranus:** the seventh planet from the sun (1,781,000,000 miles away). Uranus is four times the size of Earth. It has 5 moons and 9 rings of dust and ice.

19. **Neptune:** the eighth planet from the sun (2,788,000,000 miles away). Neptune is about the same size as Uranus and is four times the size of Earth. It has two moons.

20. **Pluto:** the ninth and farthest planet from the sun (3,660,000,000 miles away). Pluto is one quarter the size of Earth. It has one moon.

21. **new moon:** when we see no moon in the sky because it is between the earth and the sun and its sunlit side is facing the sun.

LANGUAGE & CULTURE NOTES

(22) crescent moon: when we can only see the smallest part of the sunlit side of the moon in the first and last part of its cycle. A *waxing crescent moon* is when the moon is beginning its cycle and is growing. A *waning crescent moon* is when the moon is nearing the end of its cycle and is shrinking.

(23) quarter moon: when we see a half moon because the moon in its first or third quarter of its cycle. From the earth we can only see half of the sunlit side.

(24) full moon: the moon at half its cycle around the earth when from the earth we can fully see the sunlit side.

Astronomy: the study of the stars and the celestial bodies.

(25) observatory: a room or a building with telescopes (26) for the observation of astronomical and meteorological phenomenon. The best observatories are in remote areas where artificial light at night doesn't obscure a view of the sky.

(26) telescope: a combination of lens and mirrors that makes distant objects appear nearer and larger.

(27) astronomer: a person that studies astronomy.

Space Exploration: Probes and manned crafts have explored Mercury, Venus, Mars, Jupiter, and Saturn.

(28) satellite: an object that orbits around another object. It may be natural, like the moon, or man-made. Man-made satellites go into orbit around Earth, the moon, and other planets for military purposes, scientific research, weather reporting, and/or for telecommunication and navigational purposes.

(29) space station: a manned orbiting laboratory for scientific research, such as the International Space Station.

(30) astronaut: the American name for a person who goes on a spacecraft. The Russian name is *cosmonaut*. A group of astronauts is a *crew*.

(31) U.F.O./Unidentified Flying Object/ flying saucer: any object in the sky or hovering near Earth's surface that scientists aren't able to explain. Some people believe these are spacecraft for visitors (aliens) from outer space. In science fiction literature, UFOs are typically spacecraft with an elliptical shape and a raised center—hence *flying saucers*.

Word by Word Picture Dictionary
Page 111 Language & Culture Notes

LC111a

(1) accountant: a person who records the financial transactions of businesses or individuals.

(2) actor / (3) actress: a person who performs in theater, television, or movies.

(4) architect: a person who designs buildings.

(6) assembler: a person who assembles parts of a product on an assembly line.

(7) babysitter: a person who takes care of children when the parents are away from the home.

(8) baker: a person who prepares bread and cookies.

(9) barber: the term for a person who works on men's hair. See hairdresser (34) below.

(10) bricklayer/mason: A bricklayer strictly lays bricks, but a mason also lays stones in the ground or in walls.

(11) businessman / (12) businesswoman: a salaried employee of a company.

(13) butcher: a person who prepares meat.

(16) chef/cook: A *chef* is a highly trained cook who prepares food and also plans the restaurant's menu. A *cook* prepares food in a restaurant or institutional kitchen.

(18) computer software engineer: a person who writes computer programs.

(19) construction worker: a person who builds buildings, roads, and bridges.

(20) custodian/janitor: a person who provides cleaning services.

(21) customer service representative: a person who speaks to customers and helps them buy, use, or return a product.

(22) data entry clerk: a person who enters information into a computer database.

(23) delivery person: a person who delivers items to a person's home from a store or from a take-out restaurant.

(24) dockworker: a person who helps load and unload containers on ships.

(25) engineer: a person who designs buildings, machines, bridges, or roads.

(26) factory worker: a person who works alongside the machinery to manufacture goods.

(28) firefighter: a city employee who puts out fires.

(29) fisher: The traditional term for this occupation is *fisherman*. However, since both men and women do this work, the term *fisher* is more appropriate.

(30) food-service worker: a person who prepares or serves food in large institutional kitchens.

(31) foreman: the supervisor on a factory assembly line or a construction site.

(32) gardener/landscaper: a person who plants and maintains outdoor lawns, gardens, and other planted areas.

(33) garment worker: a person who sews clothes in a clothing factory.

(34) hairdresser: a person who works on both women's and men's hair.

(35) health-care aide/attendant: a person who feeds and bathes patients, especially those in around-the-clock care such as a nursing home.

(36) home health aide/home attendant: someone who feeds, bathes, and attends to the needs of a sick person in his or her home.

(37) homemaker: a parent who stays at home to take care of the children and manage the household.

(38) housekeeper: someone who cleans rooms in a hotel, or someone a person hires to do the household chores in a private home.

LANGUAGE & CULTURE NOTES

1. **journalist/reporter:** someone who writes the news.

2. **lawyer:** someone who advises others on law and represents clients in court.

3. **machine operator:** someone who operates a machine in a factory.

4. **mail carrier/letter carrier:** someone who delivers mail to homes and businesses.

5. **manager:** someone in charge of the running of a business.

6. **manicurist:** someone who specializes in the care of fingernails and toenails.

7. **mechanic:** a person who fixes cars.

8. **medical assistant/physician assistant:** someone who helps doctors tend to patients.

9. **messenger/courier:** a person who delivers items, either by car or by bicycle.

10. **mover:** someone who moves people and businesses from one location to another.

11. **musician:** someone who plays an instrument well and performs in public.

12. **painter:** a term for someone who paints houses and for an artist who paints pictures.

13. **pharmacist:** someone who prepares and dispenses medicines and drugs.

14. **photographer:** someone who takes photographs.

15. **pilot:** someone who flies a plane.

16. **police officer:** a person who enforces the law and protects citizens and their property.

17. **postal worker:** someone who sorts, loads, and unloads mail for delivery.

18. **receptionist:** a person in an office who answers the telephone, greets people as they enter, and directs them to the person or place they have come for.

19. **repairperson:** a general term for someone who repairs items such as televisions, radios, and heating systems.

20. **salesperson:** a general term for a person who sells merchandise in a store.

21. **sanitation worker/trash collector:** a city employee who collects trash.

22. **secretary:** someone who makes appointments, organizes records, and takes care of correspondence in an office.

23. **security guard:** someone who guards a building.

24. **serviceman /** 25. **servicewoman:** a person who serves in the armed forces, whether army, navy, air force, or marines.

26. **stock clerk:** a person in a store who brings items from a storage room into the selling area and takes inventory of stock.

27. **store owner/shopkeeper:** someone who owns and manages a small store.

28. **supervisor:** someone who oversees the work of employees.

29. **tailor:** a person who designs and alters clothing, especially men's clothing.

31. **telemarketer:** someone who calls private homes and tries to sell products.

32. **translator/interpreter:** someone who speaks two languages fluently and translates so people from different nations understand each other.

33. **travel agent:** someone who plans trips and makes travel arrangements.

35. **veterinarian/vet:** a doctor who treats animals.

36. **waiter/server /** 37. **waitress/server:** someone who serves food in a restaurant.

38. **welder:** someone who melts and joins metal with a welding machine.

(1) **act:** This refers to both stage and screen acting.

(2) **assemble *components*:** to put together.

(3) **assist *patients*:** To *assist* is to help someone do something. Health aides assist patients in their feeding and bathing.

(14) **grow *vegetables*:** A synonym for *grow* is *raise* (e.g., *raise vegetables/raise crops*).

(16) **manage *a restaurant*:** This means to supervise a workplace. People can manage a restaurant (as on *Picture Dictionary* page 116), an office, a mechanic's garage, a music group, etc.

(18) **operate *equipment*:** This means the same as *use* when you refer to equipment or machinery.

(19) **paint:** This refers to what both house painters and artists do.

(20) **play the *piano*:** *Play* refers to both musical instruments (*play the piano/violin*) and sports (*play baseball/soccer*).

(21) **prepare *food*:** To *cook* is to make a dish from raw ingredients. To *prepare* includes more steps of food preparation. To *prepare food* can mean to wash, peel, or cut food, to heat up a dish that is already cooked, or to cook.

(28) **supervise *people*:** similar to *manage* (see word 16). To *supervise* usually means to oversee a few workers and to *manage* usually means to oversee the whole workplace.

(33) **type:** When someone refers to computers, it is equally common to say *to key in*.

(36) **write:** This refers to both journalists and authors.

LANGUAGE & CULTURE NOTES

(1) help wanted sign: Help wanted signs are in the actual workplace that is seeking to employ new workers.

(2) job notice/job announcement: Job notices are on bulletin boards in unemployment centers, career counseling centers, community centers, and in the staff room/break room of most companies.

(3) classified ad/want ad: Traditionally, these were only in the newspaper. Now they are also on Internet websites.

(4) full-time: This usually means 40 hours a week.

(5) part-time: This is any less than 40 hours a week.

(A) respond to an ad: The job ad explains how to make contact with the employer. This may be by phone, e-mail, or with a formal letter of interest.

(B) request information: Before someone applies for a job, he or she may want to know: Where is the company located? What is the job description? What are the hours? What is the pay? Are there benefits included?

(C) request an interview: For some jobs, it is appropriate for the job applicant to call for an interview. For other jobs, the applicant must first submit an application and if the company is interested, the company will then invite the applicant to come in for an interview.

(D) prepare a resume: A resume lists the applicant's work and educational history and provides contact information and references. Resumes are a required part of an application for a professional job.

(E) dress appropriately: What is appropriate varies according to the work environment. A businessperson should wear a business suit to an interview, while a teacher may wear a sports jacket.

(F) fill out an application (form): In retail businesses and other low-skilled positions, the applicant needs to fill out an application. Applications request information about educational and work history, as well as contact information and references.

(G) go to an interview: In the interview, the applicant should talk about his or her skills and qualifications (H) and about previous work experience (I).

(J) ask about the salary: Companies pay salaries to employees in professional positions. A salaried position specifies the job responsibilities but not the number of hours an employee works. It is possible and quite common for a salaried worker to work more than 40 hours a week. Companies pay a wage (hourly pay) to less skilled labor and part-time employees. In the United States there is a national minimum wage. Employees who work more than 40 hours a week are also guaranteed overtime, which is one and a half times the regular hourly rate.

(K) ask about the benefits: Benefits include health insurance, dental insurance, savings plans, retirement plans, paid sick leave, and paid vacation time.

(L) write a thank-you note: After an interview, it is customary for the applicant to send a brief note thanking the interviewers for their time and interest.

(M) get hired: A company hires (employs) a worker. In the United States there are several layers of paperwork that companies must complete after they hire someone. The I-9 form requires proof that the employee is legal resident or citizen. Employees who work with the public or with children also must get a Cory check to make sure they have no criminal background.

LANGUAGE & CULTURE NOTES

(A) reception area: a place where people wait for an appointment.

(B) conference room: a room that people use for meetings.

(C) mailroom: the area where office assistants (8) sort mail for distribution.

(D) work area: an open area where people work at desks, machines, or in cubicles.

(E) office: a work area where people with managerial and executive positions work.

(F) supply room: a place where offices store large amounts of supplies.

(G) storage room: a place to keep files and records that are no longer current.

(H) employee lounge: a place where employees relax on their breaks.

(1) coat rack: a piece of furniture with hooks that people hang their coats on.

(3) receptionist: the person who greets visitors and answers the telephone.

(4) conference table: A large table at which many people can sit to have a meeting.

(5) presentation board: an area for presenting reports that includes a screen for LCD computer projections.

(7) postage meter: a machine that stamps letters and packages with the correct postage and date.

(8) office assistant: a person who does a variety of tasks for the office.

(9) mailbox: Certain office employees have their own mailbox.

(10) cubicle: a small semi-private workspace with three or four short walls.

(11) swivel chair: an upholstered desk chair that rotates in different directions.

(12) typewriter: More and more, computers are replacing typewriters.

(13) adding machine: a device that bookkeepers use to do arithmetic operations.

(15) paper shredder: a device that tears paper into tiny unreadable pieces.

(16) paper cutter: a device that trims paper to any desired size.

(17) file clerk: an office worker who stores and retrieves files.

(20) computer workstation: a place where a person can sit at a computer and work.

(21) employer/boss: the head of an organization.

(22) administrative assistant: a person who assists someone in a managerial or executive position.

(23) office manager: the person in charge of the day-to-day operations of an office.

(24) supply cabinet: a place where offices keep supplies and stationery items.

(25) storage cabinet: a place where companies store larger supply items.

(26) vending machine: an automated machine that dispenses a variety of cold drinks and snacks.

(27) water cooler: contains cold bottled water.

(29) message board: a place where employers and employees can post messages and announcements.

(a) take a message: A receptionist takes a message for an employee who is out.

(b) give a presentation: Most presentations are now on Power Point software.

(e) file: to put files away in file cabinets.

(f) type a letter: Although computers have replaced typewriters in most workplaces, some companies want their employees to type letters on typewriters.

LANGUAGE & CULTURE NOTES

(4) **rotary card file:** a revolving file that is a reference for names, addresses, and telephone numbers.

(5) **desk pad:** a padded rectangular board that people lean on when they write.

(6) **appointment book:** a booklet in which someone writes down the times of appointments and/or meetings. In the United States, people conduct business by appointments that they schedule in advance. It's common to use an appointment book to keep track of these scheduled meetings.

(10) **desk calendar:** a calendar with a full sheet for each day, usually with lines on which you mark down appointments or reminders.

(11) **Post-It note pad:** a brand name for small pieces of paper that adhere by means of an adhesive strip on the back. The pads come in different colors and are convenient to use because they stick on and come off very easily. They are also called *stickies*.

(12) **organizer/personal planner:** a compact personal reference tool that may contain an appointment book, an address book, a calendar, a pad of paper, a small calculator, and pockets for pens, pencils, and personal papers.

(18) **legal pad:** 8-1/2 by 14-inch paper that is common in law offices, but people use in other offices as well.

(19) **file folder:** folders that have a tab on which you label the contents for easy identification and access in a file cabinet.

(20) **index card:** These come blank or with ruled lines. The most common size is 3 inches by 5 inches, although larger sizes are also available.

(22) **stationery/letterhead (paper):** Paper for correspondence that has the company contact information and logo on it.

(23) **mailer:** a padded envelope that is available in different sizes at stationery stores and at the post office.

(24) **mailing label:** a piece of paper with a sticky back that you can print on and then place on an envelope.

(26) **ink cartridge:** Black or colored ink for the computer printer.

(27) **rubber stamp:** Rubber stamps are available with many different messages on them—for example, *PAID IN FULL*, *RECEIVED*, or the current date.

(29) **glue stick:** solid glue in a tube.

(31) **rubber cement:** a fast-drying glue that you apply to paper with a brush.

(32) **correction fluid:** a liquid that you apply to block out typographical errors. People often refer to it as *white out*, which is actually a band name that has become the generic name for this type of fluid.

(33) **cellophane tape/clear tape:** a multipurpose lightweight tape. *Scotch* is actually a brand name that is so identified with this type of tape that *scotch tape* has become the generic name for cellophane tape.

(34) **packing tape/sealing tape:** a strong, extremely sticky tape that people commonly use when they want to seal a package.

LANGUAGE & CULTURE NOTES

Factory is a term that usually applies to large single- or multi-building complexes where manufacturing occurs.

Manufacturing may be done on an assembly-line basis, such as the one on *Picture Dictionary* page 121. Here a product moves along a conveyor belt, and each worker performs one assembly task.

Factories in the United States usually operate on *shifts*—the *day shift* from 8:00 A.M. to 4:00 P.M., the *night shift* from 4:00 P.M. to midnight, and the *graveyard shift* from midnight to 8:00 A.M. Some companies have *flex (flexible) hours*, whereby the worker selects the hours for his or her shift. Most shifts include a meal break and one or two short coffee breaks.

1 time clock / 2 time cards: When workers enter the factory at the beginning of their shift, they take their personal time card from the rack and insert it into the time clock to record the time. When they leave, they repeat the process.

3 locker room: a place for workers to keep their belongings and change in and out of any special work gear.

4 (assembly) line: a line of workers, machines, and equipment. Each worker performs one part of the assembly process.

6 work station: the work area of an individual worker.

7 line supervisor: someone who supervises a particular factory operation, department, or group of workers.

8 quality control supervisor: someone who inspects products during the manufacturing process.

10 conveyor belt: a mechanical moving apparatus that carries a product from one worker to the next for assembly.

11 warehouse: the storage area for manufactured merchandise.

12 packer: the worker who packs the product for shipment.

13 forklift: a small motor-driven vehicle that moves merchandise from one area to another.

14 freight elevator: a large elevator that transports merchandise from one floor to another.

15 union notice: Unions are formal organizations of workers whose elected officers represent them in contract negotiations with management.

16 suggestion box: Many factories take into consideration the views of their employees. Workers can write their opinions on management practices, decisions, and workplace issues and conditions and place their comments in the suggestion box.

17 shipping department: the department where the factory ships merchandise to stores.

19 hand truck/dolly: a cart on wheels that workers use to load and unload merchandise.

20 loading dock: the area where delivery trucks make deliveries and receive merchandise.

21 payroll office: the office that prepares and delivers paychecks.

22 personnel office: the office that hires new employees and handles other employee issues.

THE CONSTRUCTION SITE

LANGUAGE & CULTURE NOTES

Construction work is a general term for the building, renovating, remodeling, restoration, or demolition of all types of structures as well as for road or bridge work and repair.

(1) sledgehammer: a very large, heavy hammer.

(2) pickax: a tool with a double pointed head that breaks up concrete.

(4) wheelbarrow: a three-legged cart with a wheel in the front that workers use to move materials.

(5) jackhammer/pneumatic drill: a tool that operates by air pressure to break up concrete and asphalt.

(6) blueprints: the drawings or plans for the construction. They are on blue paper with white markings.

(8) tape measure: a flexible metal strip you use to make measurements.

(10) trowel: a tool that spreads or smoothes the mortar between bricks.

(11a) cement: a lime and clay mixture that hardens when dry. When cement mixes with gravel and sand, it produces concrete (19a).

(12) scaffolding: a structure of metal pipes and wooden planks that gives workers access to work areas above the ground.

(13) dump truck: a truck with a movable bed, an open box that raises and lowers in order to unload (dump) dirt.

(14) front-end loader: a piece of heavy machinery that scoops up dirt, carries it from one spot to another, and loads it in a dump truck.

(15) crane: a piece of equipment with an extendable arm and pulley that lifts and moves heavy objects. There are a variety of attatchments (buckets, hooks, and magnets) that the crane uses for different kinds of lifting jobs.

(16) cherry picker: a machine with a basket on the end of a moveable arm. The basket is large enough to hold one or two people.

(17) bulldozer: a piece of heavy machinery that pushes dirt from one spot to another.

(18) backhoe: a piece of heavy machinery with a movable jointed arm that draws a bucket toward the machine in order to dig holes.

(19) concrete mixer truck / (19a) concrete: a machine that combines cement powder with sand, gravel, and water and funnels the wet concrete to the worksite.

(20) pickup truck: a small truck with a shallow open bed that workers use to haul cargo. There is separate cab where the driver and passengers sit.

(21) trailer: a structure that typically serves as an office or rest area for the workers.

(22) drywall: large sheets of flat plaster board that construction workers use to build walls.

(23) wood/lumber: *Wood* is a general term for the material no matter how you use it (in a fire, in furniture, in a building). *Lumber* is the name for any kind of wood for building.

(24) plywood: an inexpensive grade of wood that consists of thin sheets of wood that are glued together.

(25) insulation: material that goes in the walls and ceilings of buildings so heat doesn't escape from the building.

(28) shingle: a flat strip of rubber, fiberglass, wood, or other material for construction of a roof.

(30) girder/beam: also called an *I-beam*.

LANGUAGE & CULTURE NOTES

(1) **hard hat/helmet:** to protect the head from falling objects. These hats can take on many different shapes according to the safety hazards of the work.

(2) **earplugs:** to protect the ears from loud noises.

(3) **goggles:** to protect the eyes from flying objects.

(4) **safety vest:** to protect the chest from sudden impact.

(5) **safety boots:** to protect the lower legs, ankles, and feet from impact.

(6) **toe guard:** to protect the feet from impact.

(7) **back support:** to support the back while doing strenuous lifting or long periods of standing.

(8) **safety earmuffs:** to protect the ears from loud noises, as well as keep them warm.

(9) **hairnet:** to keep hair from falling into sensitive materials, such as laboratory samples or prepared food.

(10) **mask:** to prevent contamination of germs from a person's breath.

(11) **latex gloves:** to protect hands from hazardous materials such as chemicals or blood.

(12) **respirator:** to protect the lungs while working with hazardous material (such as asbestos) or gases (such as smoke).

(13) **safety glasses:** to protect eyesight while under strain of bright light.

(14) **flammable:** quick to catch on fire or start a fire.

(15) **poisonous:** toxic if swallowed.

(16) **corrosive:** any material with acid as an ingredient. Acid can burn away at any material.

(17) **radioactive:** danger of radiation.

(20) **biohazard:** any biological substance that is hazardous, such as blood infected with HIV or salvia infected with TB.

(21) **electrical hazard:** danger of electrical shock or electrocution.

(23) **fire extinguisher:** U.S. law requires factories to have a certain number of fire extinguishers based on the size of the premises.

(24) **defibrillator:** medical equipment that shocks the heart into beating if it has stopped. People use it as a last resort to save someone's life.

In the United States, people travel between cities on a public train service called Amtrak, and on private bus and airline companies. Within urban areas, people travel on public trains, buses, and subway systems and in private taxis.

(A) bus: The name of bus lines or routes is typically a number, a color, or the final stop the bus makes.

(1) bus stop: the place where passengers wait for the bus.

(4) (bus) fare: the price of the bus ride.

(5) transfer: a piece of paper that allows the person to transfer from one bus line to another.

(7) bus station: also called a *bus terminal*.

(8) ticket counter: Here a ticket agent provides information on fares and schedules and sells tickets.

(B) train: Amtrak, a semi-public national train service, provides intercity and commuter passenger service.

(11) train station: A train station has public restrooms and may have restaurants, snack bars, vending machines, newspaper stands, and gift shops.

(12) ticket window: the place where passengers purchase tickets and get information on fares and schedules.

(14) information booth: the place with maps and information about routes and schedules.

(16) platform: the area where passengers wait for a train.

(18) conductor: collects and sometimes also sells tickets.

(C) subway: The name of the subway line is typically a number, a color, or the final stop the subway makes.

(19) subway station: A distinctive sign at street level indicates the location of a subway station.

(20) (subway) token: a coin you purchase at subway stations that substitutes for money.

(22) fare card: Passengers use this instead of a token or money on some public transportation systems.

(23) fare card machine: a device that automatically dispenses fare cards.

(D) taxi: Taxi service in the United States is through private companies.

(24) taxi stand: a designated parking area where taxis wait for passengers.

(25) taxi/cab/taxicab: Some taxis have a light on the roof that lights up if the cab is off duty, i.e., if the cab isn't accepting passengers.

(26) meter: the machine that indicates the amount of the *fare*, the cost of the cab ride.

(27) cab driver/taxi driver: Drivers must display a card that shows their photograph and identification number.

(E) ferry: a large boat that travels back and forth between two points.

LANGUAGE & CULTURE NOTES

1. **sedan:** a model car with either two or four doors and a lockable, enclosed trunk compartment for storage in the rear. It is the standard style for cars, and historically all other styles developed from this basic model.

2. **hatchback:** sedan in which there is no lockable, enclosed trunk compartment. The rear of the car is a door that lifts up, and there is extra open storage space behind the rear seat.

3. **convertible:** a car whose roof is a heavyweight canvas that is stretched over a frame that retracts.

4. **sports car:** a car with a very fast engine and aerodynamic design with race-car styling.

5. **hybrid:** a car that uses both electricity and gas for power.

6. **station wagon:** like a hatchback but longer, with an expanded storage area behind the rear seat. This is a popular vehicle for families.

7. **S.U.V. (sport utility vehicle):** A blend of a car and jeep (see word 8). S.U.V.'s have the all-terrain ability of a jeep but the passenger comfort of a car.

8. **jeep:** a vehicle that the military developed during World War II. It sits higher off the ground than a standard car and has large, rugged tires. Jeeps for non-military purposes have become increasingly popular in recent years. Jeeps have four-wheel drive or all-wheel drive for better steering control in mud and water. Jeeps are called *all terrain vehicles* because you can drive them on any kind of land.

9. **van:** a large vehicle with doors on the side and back. People use vans to carry small loads or equipment. Some vans can hold as many as ten passengers.

10. **minivan:** a small van that carries up to seven passengers.

11. **pickup truck:** a small truck with an open rear storage area.

12. **limousine:** an elongated car that can carry many passengers comfortably. They may have features such as a bar, a refrigerator, and a television set. Groups of people often rent limousines for special occasions such as weddings or parties. To drive a limousine you must have a special license. As a result, limousines always have hired drivers.

13. **tow truck:** a special truck that tows a disabled vehicle to a garage for repairs.

14. **R.V. (recreational vehicle)/camper:** a truck that carries a cabin for lodging. R.V.s are equipped with a kitchen, a bathroom, a dining area, and a sleeping area. They are very popular for vacation travel in the United States.

15. **moving van:** a truck that carries furniture. Many people in the United States rent a moving van for a day or two in order to move from house to house.

16. **truck:** a vehicle that transports goods with a driver's cabin and either an enclosed or an open area in the rear.

17. **tractor trailer/semi:** also called *an eighteen wheeler* for the number of wheels it uses. The trailer part is detachable.

18. **bicycle/bike:** As bike riding has become more popular, there are more specialized varieties of bikes, such as mountain bikes and racing bikes.

19. **motor scooter:** a lightweight vehicle that can carry two passengers but cannot travel over 50 miles per hour. Motor scooters are most appropriate for city transportation. The most popular brand is a *Vespa,* hence some people call all motor scooters *Vespas.*

20. **moped:** a motorized bicycle for only one rider.

21. **motorcycle:** a vehicle that can carry two passengers. In most states, there are laws that require motorcycle riders to wear helmets.

LANGUAGE & CULTURE NOTES

1 bumper: the part of the fender (see word 5) that can touch another car and not cause much damage.

2 headlight: These can be on two different settings—*high* or *bright* for country roads and *low* for busier roads.

5 fender: the part of the car that protrudes on the front and back.

12 roof rack: very common on station wagons as a way to carry extra loads.

13 sunroof: a movable section of roof that retracts in nice weather.

14 antenna: receives radio signals.

16 rear defroster: eliminates fogging (interior condensation) and exterior icing.

19 brake light: a light that goes on when the driver steps on the brakes.

20 backup light: a light that goes on when the car is in reverse gear.

21 license plate: Every state has a distinctive plate, with color combinations unique to that state.

22 tailpipe/exhaust pipe: This device carries into the atmosphere the vapors that remain after the engine burns gasoline.

23 muffler: the device that reduces the noise of the engine.

24 transmission: the system of gears that transmits the engine power to the wheels.

26 jack: a device that lifts car in order to change a flat tire.

27 spare tire: a replacement for a flat or blown tire.

28 lug wrench: a tool that you use to tighten and loosen car parts.

29 flare: a safety device that you light to warn oncoming vehicles of an accident or a car stopped on the side of the road.

30 jumper cables: cables you use to start a car with a *dead* battery.

31 spark plugs: use electricity to produce a spark that ignites the gasoline/air mixture in the engine.

32 air filter: the device that filters the air before it reaches the engine.

33 engine: generates power to turn the wheels and provide energy for the electrical system.

34 fuel injection system: the injection (under pressure) of fuel into the internal-combustion system.

35 radiator: Water circulates in a closed system. The engine heats it and the radiator cools it.

36 radiator hose: the hose that carries water from the radiator to the engine.

37 fan belt: a belt that moves the fan that draws cool air across the radiator and the engine.

38 alternator: the part of the electrical system that generates electricity and sends it to the battery.

39 dipstick: a long stick that measures the level of oil that lubricates the engine.

40 battery: the part of the electrical system that stores electricity.

41 air pump: a pump you use to fill tires with air.

42 gas pump: All pumps must show the octane level and the price per gallon of the gas.

43 nozzle: the metal device that regulates the flow of gas into the car.

44 gas cap: the lid to the gas tank.

45 gas: Gasoline may be unleaded or diesel.

47 coolant: a liquid that runs through the radiator to cool the engine down.

LANGUAGE & CULTURE NOTES

(49) **air bag:** a safety device that inflates in head-on collisions.

(50) **visor:** the flap that lowers to block the sun.

(52) **dashboard/instrument panel:** the area that houses the car's instruments and gauges.

(53) **temperature gauge:** the gauge that indicates the heat level of the water in the radiator that cools the engine.

(54) **gas gauge/fuel gauge:** the gauge that indicates the level of gas in the tank.

(55) **speedometer:** the gauge that indicates the speed the car is moving.

(56) **odometer:** the gauge that indicates the number of miles a car has been driven.

(57) **warning lights:** indicate if the oil or water level is low.

(59) **steering wheel:** Most cars come with power steering.

(60) **horn:** The horn alerts a pedestrian or another car of a dangerous situation.

(61) **ignition:** the slot where you insert the key to start the car.

(62) **vent:** a system of valves that allows fresh air to circulate in the car.

(63) **navigation system:** provides directions to the driver's destination.

(68) **defroster:** a fan that forces hot air against the windshield to rid the glass of interior condensation and exterior ice.

(69) **power outlet:** an outlet that supplies electrical energy off the engine.

(70) **glove compartment:** a place for storage.

(71) **emergency brake:** a safety device when parking on a hill.

(74) **automatic transmission:** a transmission system where the driver does not have to use a clutch (78) or stickshift (77).

(75) **gearshift:** the lever in an automatic transmission system that the driver moves into either *park, reverse, neutral.*

(76) **manual transmission:** the transmission system where the driver moves a stickshift (77) and at the same time steps on a clutch (78) in order to change the gears.

(81) **shoulder harness:** a strap that stretches across a person's shoulder and chest for protection in case of an accident.

(85) **seat belt:** Many states require the use of seat belts to protect individuals in case of an accident.

Because the United States relies heavily on cars for transportation, traffic jams are a fact of life in most cities during commuter rush hours, the time period when commuter travel is heaviest—typically from 7:00 to 9:00 A.M. and from 4:30 to 6:30 P.M. Public campaigns encourage the use of car pools—in which people share rides rather than driving individually. In fact, some highways have special lanes for carpool vehicles and buses during rush hour.

Parking is available at public metered spaces on the street and in public and private parking garages. Meter maids (see *Picture Dictionary* page 40, word 17) issue parking tickets if the time on the parking meter has expired. Double-parking, i.e., parking parallel to an already parked car, is illegal. Handicap parking spaces are only for cars with special handicap license plates. These parking spaces have signs or stencils of a wheelchair on the pavement.

(3) **tollbooth:** the place where people stop to pay tolls on toll roads.

(4) **route sign:** the sign that indicates the route number of the road.

(5) **highway:** typically a four-lane road in urban and suburban areas, and a two-lane road in rural areas.

(6) **road:** a general term that is interchangeable with *highway, interstate (highway),* and *street.*

(7) **divider/barrier:** a concrete block that separates lanes going in opposite directions.

(10) **entrance ramp/on ramp:** the access road to an interstate highway.

(11) **interstate (highway):** typically a three- to six-lane road with a normal speed limit of 55 miles per hour in most states.

(12) **median:** a grassy area thatseparates lanes on an interstate highway.

(13) **left lane:** A lane is the portion of the road marked by white lines for a single car to drive on.

(15) **right lane:** On multi-lane highways, this lane is for slow-moving vehicles and cars who are entering or exiting the roadway.

(16) **shoulder:** the gravel or dirt area that abuts a road. In emergencies it serves as a place to stop.

(17) **broken line:** a line that indicates that passing is permitted.

(18) **solid line:** a line that indicates that passing is not permitted.

(19) **speed limit sign:** the sign that indicates the speed limit—the maximum speed that is allowed in good travel conditions.

(20) **exit (ramp):** the exit road from an interstate highway.

(21) **exit sign:** Exit ramps on interstate highways are either numbered sequentially or by the mile number of the exit's location on the highway.

(22) **street:** the common term for roads in urban areas.

(24) **double yellow line:** Like a solid line (18), it indicates an area where passing is not permitted. It also indicates that turning is not possible.

(25) **crosswalk:** the area for pedestrians to cross a road, typically at corners of intersections.

(26) **intersection:** the place where two roads cross or meet.

(27) **traffic light/traffic signal:** a light over an intersection or on a post at the corner of an intersection. It regulates the flow of traffic.

(29) **block:** a term used in cities to describe the land bounded by four streets.

(4) around: A person can go around an area such as a block or a neighborhood.

(5) up / (6) down: In the scene, the people are walking up and down a hill. It is also common to say a person walks/goes/drives up or down a street even though there is no slope.

(7) across: A person can go across anything that has two sides—for example a street, a lake, a field, a highway, or a bridge.

(8) past: means to go alongside but not stop to stay.

(9) on / (10) off: A person gets on and off a train, a bus, a subway, a boat, or a plane. A person also gets off a highway (see *onto*, word 13).

(11) into / (12) out of: A person gets into and out of a car, a taxicab, or a truck.

(13) onto: A person gets onto and off a highway, a road, or a street.

(1) **stop:** a sign that indicates that the driver must come to a full stop before proceeding.

(4) **no U-turn:** This sign indicates to the driver that it is not legal to turn around.

(6) **do not enter:** This is usually on a one-way street facing against the direction of the traffic so that drivers will not enter a one-way street the wrong way by accident.

(8) **dead end/no outlet:** means that the road does not connect to any other roads.

(9) **pedestrian crossing:** means there is a crosswalk nearby and cars must yield to pedestrians in the crosswalk.

(10) **railroad crossing:** Railroad crossings always have an *X* sign, and may have additional warning devices such as flashing lights, a barrier gate, and/or a warning horn.

(11) **school crossing:** Speed limits are usually reduced in school areas. School crossing guards monitor children who are crossing the road near a school. Drivers are not allowed to pass a school bus with flashing lights. This indicates that the bus has stopped to let children on or off.

(13) **yield:** the sign that indicates that a driver who is entering a road must allow oncoming vehicles to proceed before they enter the road.

(14) **detour:** This sign indicates a new route because the current road is obstructed.

(17) **north /** (18) **south /** (19) **west /** (20) **east:** There are also intermediary directions of *northwest, northeast, southwest,* and *southeast.*

Road Test Instructions

When someone is applying for a driver's license, the applicant must take a written test as well as a road test. The road test covers the driver's ability to do #21–26.

---

(24) **Parallel park.** This means to park the car into a line of parked cars, not into a parking space in a parking lot with cars side by side.

(25) **Make a 3-point turn.** This means to make a sharp turn that requires the car to turn sharply, then reverse a bit, and then to finish the sharp turn.

LANGUAGE & CULTURE NOTES

(A) Check-In: the area where a traveler buys or presents a ticket, receives a boarding pass, and checks baggage.

(1) ticket: indicates the flight number, departure time, destination, and fee.

(2) ticket counter: the place where passengers check in for flights, make reservations, and purchase tickets.

(3) ticket agent: the person who works at the ticket counter.

(4) suitcase: an individual piece of baggage.

(5) arrival and departure monitor: This typically shows only one airline's arrivals and departures.

(B) Security: It is illegal to carry onto a plane a gun or any object that someone may use as a weapon.

(6) security checkpoint: the place where security agents check for weapons or other dangerous objects.

(7) metal detector: the electronic passageway that detects metal objects a passenger is wearing or carrying.

(9) X-ray machine: the machine that hand luggage goes through for inspection.

(10) carry-on bag: a smaller bag that fits under the seat in front of the passenger or above in the overhead bins.

(C) The Gate: the area where passengers board an airplane.

(11) check-in counter: the counter where ticketed passengers check in and receive a boarding pass.

(12) boarding pass: the pass that shows the flight number, departure time, gate number, and assigned seat number.

(D) Baggage Claim: where passengers pick up their baggage.

(15) baggage claim (area): the area where passengers retrieve their luggage.

(16) baggage carousel: the conveyor belt where passengers pick up their baggage.

(17) baggage: Also called *luggage*. This is a general term for one or more items that a passenger checks.

(18) baggage cart/luggage cart: a rack on wheels that passengers use to move baggage in the airport.

(19) luggage carrier: a rack on wheels on which it's possible to stack two small pieces of luggage.

(20) garment bag: a piece of luggage that many people use to transport suits or dresses.

(21) baggage claim check: a stub attached to a passenger's ticket that identifies the piece of luggage.

(E) Customs and Immigration: In international flights, passengers must pass through a document check and declare the contents of their baggage before they are allowed to enter the country of arrival.

(22) customs: the area where passengers present items they are bringing into the country. Passengers must declare (report) any merchandise on the customs declaration form (24) and present both the form and their luggage to a customs officer (23) for inspection.

(25) immigration: the area where passengers show their passport (27) and visa (28), to an immigration officer (26).

(27) passport: the identification booklet that a country issues to its citizens.

(28) visa: There are a variety of visas for different lengths of time and for different situations, such as *tourist, student,* or *work.*

LANGUAGE & CULTURE NOTES

(1) **cockpit:** the area where the pilot, co-pilot, and flight engineer sit.

(2) **pilot/captain:** Pilots receive training in special private and airline company flight schools.

(3) **co-pilot:** the assistant to the pilot in the operation of the airplane.

(5) **flight attendant:** a person who provides assistance to passengers and serves food and beverages.

(6) **overhead compartment:** the area where passengers store coats and carry-on bags.

(7) **aisle:** the narrow passageway for passengers and crew to move around.

(8) **window seat / (9) middle seat / (10) aisle seat:** Passengers can ask for their preference of seats when they buy their ticket or check in.

(11) **Fasten Seat Belt sign:** a sign that lights up during take-off and landing and when there is air turbulence.

(12) **No Smoking sign:** Smoking is not allowed on any flights.

(13) **call button:** the button passengers use to call a flight attendant for service.

(14) **oxygen mask:** The mask drops automatically if there is a change in air pressure inside the airplane.

(15) **emergency exit:** Before take-off, the flight attendants indicate the location of emergency exits.

(16) **tray (table):** the table that folds down for passenger use.

(17) **emergency instruction card:** Flight attendants encourage the passengers to look for further emergency response information on the emergency card in their seat pocket.

(18) **air sickness bag:** in the seat pocket in case a passenger suddenly feels sick.

(19) **life vest/life jacket:** required for all flights over water.

(20) **runway:** the long asphalt field that airplanes use to take off and land.

(21) **terminal (building):** Large airports have multiple buildings called terminals.

(22) **control tower:** the place where air traffic controllers work.

(23) **airplane/plane/jet:** These all refer to the same aircraft.

(A) **take off your shoes:** If a metal detector sounds as a passenger walks through, the security officer may ask the passenger to take off his or her shoes.

(B) **empty your pockets:** Passengers place the contents of their pockets into trays that go through the X-ray machine.

(C) **put your bag on the conveyor belt:** Passengers place their carry-on bags onto the conveyor belt that goes through the X-ray machine.

(D) **put your computer in a tray:** Passengers place their laptop computers in a tray that carries them through the X-ray machine.

(E) **walk through the metal detector:** If passengers set off the metal detector, a security officer may pass a metal detector wand over them or even pat them down (touch their bodies to check for bulges).

(F) **check in at the gate / (G) get your boarding pass:** If the passenger did not check in at curbside check-in or at the check-in counter, the passenger can check in at the gate to get a boarding pass.

(I) **stow your carry-on bag:** Passengers must put this small piece of luggage under the passenger's seat in front or in the overhead compartment.

(J) **find your seat:** The flight attendants can help passengers locate their seats.

(K) **fasten your seat belt:** All passengers and crew must wear a seat belt during take-off and landing.

LANGUAGE & CULTURE NOTES

(1) **doorman:** the hotel employee who greets hotel guests, opens the front door for them, and hails taxis.

(2) **valet parking:** A parking system by which the guest drives to the front door of the hotel and then a parking attendant drives the car to a parking lot area.

(3) **parking attendant:** the hotel employee who drives a guest's car to the parking lot and then later retrieves the car when the guest requests it.

(4) **bellhop:** the hotel employee who assists guests with their bags.

(5) **luggage cart:** a rack on wheels the bellhop uses to transport the luggage to the guest's room.

(6) **bell captain:** the hotel employee who manages and supervises all bellhop services.

(7) **lobby:** the large entry room of a hotel where there are chairs and couches for people to sit and wait for one another and a front desk for guests to check in.

(8) **front desk:** the place an arriving guest checks-in and checks-out.

(9) **desk clerk:** the hotel employee who works at the front desk. This person greets hotel guests, checks them in, answers their questions, and checks them out.

(10) **guest:** the customer who stays at a hotel.

(11) **concierge desk / (12) concierge:** A concierge is a hotel employee who gives hotel guests advice about restaurants, entertainment, and sightseeing in the area and can make arrangements/reservations for the guests. Guests can contact the concierge at the concierge desk.

(14) **meeting room:** Many hotels provide meeting rooms for business people to conduct business. Some hotels have enough meeting rooms to convene large conventions.

(15) **gift shop:** a small shop that sells small tourist items and other easily portable gifts for the hotel's guests.

(16) **pool:** Some hotels have indoor or outdoor pools available to their guests.

(17) **exercise room:** Most hotels in the United States provide a room where guests can exercise. Usually these rooms have just a few machines for weightlifting and bicycling. Occasionally hotels have health club facilities that are open to the paying public which guests may use while they stay at the hotel.

(19) **ice machine:** On every floor of a hotel, an ice machine is available to provide guests with free ice. Every hotel room provides an ice bucket and some glasses for drinks.

(22) **housekeeping cart:** where the housekeeper stores the housekeeping supplies (cleaning supplies, as well as towels and sheets).

(23) **housekeeper:** the hotel employee who cleans the guest rooms, makes the beds, and supplies fresh towels, soaps, and shampoos.

(24) **guest room:** also called a *hotel room*.

(25) **room service:** a limited menu is available for guests to eat in their room. Room service brings the food to the guests' rooms. There is always a room service fee. In addition, it is customary to add a tip for the person who brings the food to the room.

Crafts: activities that involve manual skill.

(A) sew: People sew by hand and on sewing machines. A man who sews for a career is a *tailor*, and a woman is a *seamstress*.

(1) sewing machine: Sewing machines come in a variety of styles. More expensive models offer fancy stitching and button-hole makers. Hand-operated sewing machines are not common in the United States.

(2) pin: temporarily holds fabric in place until it is sewn together.

(3) pin cushion: a soft cushion that holds pins and needles.

(4) (spool of) thread: Thread is the material and a spool (the round cylinder) is the package it comes in.

(5) (sewing) needle: The *Picture Dictionary* depicts a hand-sewing needle. Sewing machines use machine needles.

(6) thimble: Someone wears this on the middle finger to prevent pricks from needles while he or she is sewing by hand.

(7) safety pin: a pin with a covered clasp.

(B) knit: to link yarn in a series of stitches with a pair of needles.

(8) knitting needle: These are long thin sticks of either metal or wood.

(9) yarn: a thick thread of synthetic material or animal hair such as wool, angora, or mohair.

(C) crochet: to link thick cotton thread or yarn in a series of stitches with a crochet hook (10).

(D) paint: People paint in a variety of mediums, such as watercolor, pen and ink, charcoal, and oil paint.

(12) easel: This holds the framed canvas or paper the artist is working on.

(13) canvas: a thick cotton material stretched over a wooden frame.

(14) paint / (a) oil paint / (b) watercolor: There are many different kinds of paint (acrylic, tempera, etc.), but the two most common types are oil-based or watercolor.

(E) draw: Drawing includes cartoon drawing, sketching, and figure drawing. The most common materials for drawing are pencils, charcoal, and erasers.

(15) sketch book: a pad of medium weight paper for sketches (informal drawing).

(16) (set of) colored pencils: Some colored pencils can become watercolor paint when you dab their markings on paper with water.

(17) drawing pencil: Drawing pencils vary in the hardness of the lead.

(F) do embroidery: to stitch yarn or thread on fabric stretched on a wooden hand-held hoop.

(G) do needlepoint: to stitch yarn on a mesh canvas. The canvas may have a pattern (20) with different colors of yarn, or it may be plain, in which case the person creates a design with different stitches.

(H) do woodworking: to make things out of wood.

(21) woodworking kit: a woodworking project that comes in a box with all the necessary supplies to complete the work.

(I) do origami: originally a Japanese art form. To do origami, you fold paper in intricate ways to make miniature forms of animals and other objects.

(J) make pottery: Pottery is clay (23) that someone shapes by hand or on a potter's wheel (24) and then dries.

LANGUAGE & CULTURE NOTES

Hobbies: activities that people do in their leisure or spare time, purely for enjoyment.

(K) **collect stamps:** A stamp collector uses a magnifying glass (26) to see the details of the stamp better.

(L) **collect coins:** The collector can arrange and store the coin collection (28) in a coin catalog (27).

(M) **build models:** Models are small replicas of objects, most commonly airplanes, trains, and cars.

(N) **go bird-watching:** Bird watchers often keep records of the place, date, and time of bird sightings.

(O) **play cards:** Card playing is very popular in the United States, particularly the games of bridge, poker, and gin rummy.

(P) **play board games:** Board games are very popular with children, families, and adults.

(35) **chess:** a game that two people play on a board with rows of alternating black and white squares. Playing pieces have different names and shapes, and move in different ways.

(36) **checkers:** a game that two people play on a board with rows of alternating red and black squares.

(37) **backgammon:** a game that two people play on a board that has twenty-four

spaces with fifteen discs per person. The object of backgammon is to move the discs from their starting positions to the home base and then off the board.

(38) **Monopoly:** a board game in which each space is the name of a property, such as Park Place or Indiana Avenue. Each player has a playing piece and receives a quantity of play money.

(39) **Scrabble:** a board game with pieces called tiles that have a letter of the alphabet and a numeric point value.

(Q) **go online/browse the Web/"surf" the net:** Many people go online for hours and browse the Web or "surf" the Internet. In both these activities, the person is exploring different websites on the Internet.

(40) **web browser:** a software program you use to search and view various kinds of Internet resources such as information on a website.

(41) **web address/URL:** the address of a site on the Internet.

(R) **photography:** With a digital camera, the photographer can enhance and arrange the pictures on a computer. With a traditional camera (42), the photographer develops the film.

(S) **astronomy:** a popular hobby for those interested in stars and planets.

LANGUAGE & CULTURE NOTES

1. **museum:** There are many different types of museums that are dedicated to the collection and study of many different subjects—for example: fine arts, science, natural history, computers, and transportation.

2. **art gallery:** a small privately owned shop that exhibits art.

3. **concert:** a performance by professional musicians. A concert can be of any type of music—classical, rock, country, etc.

4. **play:** a theater production. Actors and actresses *perform* in a play.

5. **amusement park:** a permanently installed park that has rides and food; compare to carnival (19) and fair (20).

6. **historic site:** a place where something historically significant happened. The historic site depicted on *Picture Dictionary* page 136 is The Alamo, an 18th-century mission in San Antonio, Texas.

7. **national park:** In the United States, there are two systems that take care of conservation land—States Parks and National Parks. State parks are the responsibility of local states and tend to be smaller. The national parks are large tracks of unique or impressive land forms.

8. **craft fair:** an event where many artists and craft hobbyists convene to show and sell their work to the public.

9. **yard sale:** also called a *garage sale*. When a family or group of people decide to sell things they no longer want, they have a yard sale, which they advertise in a newspaper or on local bulletin boards.

10. **swap meet/flea market:** A swap meet is when a group of people agree to swap a particular kind of product—for example, children's clothes, books, or garden plants. A flea market is an organized event where people who collect antiques, collectibles, or used items rent a table to sell their selection to the public.

11. **park:** any tract of public land that a city, town, or state maintains for the enjoyment of the public.

12. **beach:** a sandy area where people sunbathe and swim in a pond, lake, or ocean.

13. **mountains:** In the plural form, mountains refers to a group of mountains and not a singular peak.

14. **aquarium:** a museum with tanks or pools filled with water for live fish and underwater animals.

15. **botanical gardens:** a garden open to the public.

16. **planetarium:** a domed half hemisphere ceiling on which a light projects the positions of the stars and planets.

17. **zoo:** any park which has live animals for public exhibition or viewing.

18. **movies:** This means a place as well as the thing people watch. As a place, the article *the* always precedes it—for example: We go to *the movies* every Saturday night.

19. **carnival:** a small entourage of sideshows and rides and games that travels from town to town.

20. **fair:** a large event with rides, games, and sideshows, as well as extensive exhibits of farmer's produce and livestock.

Parks are grassy areas or green spaces for relaxation and recreation. Parks may have playgrounds, picnic areas, and playing fields for organized sports such as soccer, volleyball, tennis, and baseball.

1 bicycle path/bike path/bikeway: a road for bikes so that bikers don't endanger others who are walking. Some cities and towns have bike paths that are not just limited to parks but that actually run through the area.

2 duck pond: a pond where ducks or swans live. Many people feed breadcrumbs to the ducks. Occasionally a duck pond may also have paddle boats, which people can rent to paddle around the pond.

3 picnic area / 5 grill / 6 picnic table: Many parks have a picnic area set aside for people to eat. They usually have picnic tables and a grill.

4 trash can: a receptacle for discarded food and paper. People who do not use trash cans are said to *litter* and are called *litterbugs*. *Do Not Litter* signs are common in park areas.

7 water fountain / 12 fountain: A water fountain is for people to drink from. A fountain is for people to look at.

8 jogging path: a trail for walkers or runners (joggers).

10 tennis court: Many parks provide tennis courts with nets. Players bring their own racquets and balls. Tennis courts are asphalt or clay.

11 ballfield: also called a *baseball field*.

13 bike rack: a place to park and lock a bicycle.

14 merry-go-round/carousel: a traditional ride for small children that spins slowly around. Children sit on moving horses or in small booths. Many merry-go-rounds require admission.

15 skateboard ramp: a paved area for skateboarders.

16 playground: an area for children to play. In cities, playgrounds aren't always just in parks. They can be in any space, even between two tall buildings.

17 climbing wall: a wall with small ledges on which children use only the tips of their fingers and toes to climb.

18 swings: Each swing is one seat. The whole piece of equipment is called a *swing set*. Many playgrounds have swings with a belt for toddlers and large swings with a belt for older children with disabilities.

19 climber: a metal structure on which young children climb up and down.

20 slide: The child goes up the ladder and down the slide.

22 sandbox: an enclosed area with sand (23) for young children to play in. Children usually bring buckets and shovels and other toys in order to play with the sand.

THE BEACH

LANGUAGE & CULTURE NOTES

Going to the beach is a popular summer recreational activity for those who live near a lake or an ocean. Some beaches have boardwalks (wooden sidewalks), shops, and restaurants along the length of the beach. For example, Coney Island is a famous beach near New York City with a boardwalk and amusement park.

Water pollution is a growing concern at many beaches. Swimming is sometimes banned due to high bacterial content in the water. Beach erosion due to the force of the tides, the wind, or storms is a problem at some locations. In order to stop erosion, many beaches have wind-barrier fences and special breakwaters—stone or concrete barriers that go from the beach out into the water.

(1) **lifeguard:** a person who has successfully passed a Red Cross training program to save swimmers who are in danger.

(2) **lifeguard stand:** a seat at the top of a ladder to give the lifeguard a good view of the water.

(3) **life preserver:** a floating device you throw to a swimmer in danger.

(4) **snack bar/refreshment stand:** Snack bars at the beach typically sell fast foods and snacks such as hot dogs, french fries, soda, and ice cream.

(5) **vendor:** a person who walks around the beach or sets up a stand to sell drinks, snack foods, and items such as sunglasses, suntan lotion, and beach toys.

(7) **wave:** Swimming in areas where the waves are high may be dangerous because of the undertow (the underwater current moving away from the beach).

(8) **surfer:** someone who rides the waves on a surfboard (18).

(10) **beach chair:** a collapsible chair usually that people often take to the beach to sit on.

(11) **beach umbrella:** a large portable umbrella that beach-goers use to protect themselves from harsh sunlight.

(12) **sand castle:** Some beaches have organized sand castle competitions, with prizes for the best creations.

(13) **boogie board:** a small wide board you use to ride waves and play in the surf.

(14) **sunbather:** Health professionals warn about the dangers of too much sunbathing and recommend that people use sunscreen (23).

(15) **sunglasses:** glasses that shade the eyes in strong sunlight.

(16) **(beach) towel:** a large colorful towel with a tight weave to take to the beach.

(17) **beach ball:** an inflatable ball that floats on water and blows easily in the wind.

(18) **surfboard:** a longer narrower board you use to ride waves. See surfer (8).

(19) **seashell/shell:** Collecting shells is a popular activity for children and adults.

(20) **rock:** Rock (non-count noun) is the material of rocks and cliffs. A rock (count noun) means a piece of rock.

(21) **cooler:** an insulated box that keeps foods and beverages cool.

(22) **sun hat:** a hat with a wide brim that protects the face and neck from the sun.

(23) **sunscreen/sunblock/suntan lotion:** a general term for a lotion that may either enhance or inhibit suntanning. A sunscreen screens the sun's ultraviolet rays that cause burning.

(24) **(beach) blanket:** a regular cotton blanket that people use at the beach and at picnics.

(25) **shovel /** (26) **pail:** You use these to play with sand, collect seashells (19) and build sand castles (12).

Camping, hiking, mountain climbing, and picnicking are popular recreational activities in the United States for families and groups of friends. Rock climbing (also called *technical climbing*) and rigorous mountain climbing are not as common because they require specialized training, extraordinary strength, and equipment.

(A) camping: a general term for living outdoors overnight. It refers to both tent camping and camping with a camping trailer.

(1) tent: Tents come in a variety of shapes, sizes and materials for different climatic conditions.

(2) sleeping bag: Sleeping bags come in a variety of sizes and materials for different climatic conditions. They come in different grades according to the lowest temperature at which a camper can be comfortable in the bag.

(3) tent stakes: metal or wooden pegs that secure a tent to the ground.

(4) lantern: a portable lamp that uses batteries, gas, or propane.

(5) hatchet: a small short-handled ax.

(6) camping stove: a portable cooking unit that uses gas or propane.

(7) Swiss army knife: a folded knife which also has other useful tools such as a screwdriver, tweezers, a cork screw, and a can opener.

(8) insect repellent: a smelly lotion that mosquitoes and black flies do not like.

(9) matches: Campers usually carry their matches in a water repellent box so that rain doesn't ruin them.

(B) hiking: This can refer to a very long walk over relatively level terrain or to a more strenuous climb up a mountain trail.

(10) backpack: a bag you use to carry and store camping and personal gear or equipment.

(11) canteen: a traditional water bottle with a long strap so it's easy to carry.

(12) compass: a device that indicates direction.

(13) trail map: There are thousands of miles of designated and marked trails throughout the US. Maps of these trails are available at state and national parks.

(14) GPS device: a Global Positioning System receiver that calculates your absolute geographic position.

(15) hiking boots: special thick-soled insulated boots that may be high-sided for ankle support.

(C) rock climbing/technical climbing: This refers to climbing steep vertical rock faces of mountains. Rock climbers should use harnesses (16) and ropes (17) and always climb with a friend for safety.

(D) mountain biking: This refers to riding a bike on rugged mountain trails (not asphalt paths).

(18) mountain bike: a rugged bike with thick tires that can handle the heavy jostling and bumping involved in mountain biking.

(19) (bike) helmet: a hard hat that protects a biker's head in case of accident.

(E) picnic: Common picnic food includes sandwiches, chips, cold drinks, hamburgers, hot dogs, cold or barbecued chicken, and salads.

(21) thermos: an insulated container for hot or cold food and beverages.

(22) picnic basket: Some baskets come with plates, serving utensils, and eating utensils.

INDIVIDUAL SPORTS AND RECREATION

LANGUAGE & CULTURE NOTES

There are generally two ways to form the word for a person who does a sport:

Add *-er* to the sport's verb: jogger, runner.

Add *player* to the name of the sport: tennis player, racquetball player.

With verb sports names, *go* is used: go jogging, go running.

With noun sports names, *play* is used: play tennis, play squash.

With some noun sports names, *do* is used: do martial, do gymnastics.

(**A**) **jogging:** running at a slow pace on a track or on the street.

(**1**) **jogging suit:** Many people find jogging suits so comfortable that they wear them as everyday casual clothing.

(**B**) **running:** a faster pace than jogging.

(**3**) **running shorts:** small light shorts.

(**C**) **walking:** People who walk for exercise generally walk at a rapid pace.

(**D**) **inline skating/rollerblading:** a popular sport among children and adults in parks and streets.

(**6**) **inline skates/rollerblades:** It's common to call inline skates by a popular brand name—Roller Blades.

(**E**) **cycling/biking:** Many children ride their bicycles to school. Some adults ride bicycles to work, but more go bicycle riding for pleasure during their free time.

(**8**) **bicycle/bike:** A man's bicycle has a horizontal bar from the seat to the handlebars, and a woman's bike doesn't.

(**9**) **(bicycle/bike) helmet:** People wear helmets while they bicycle to prevent head injuries in case of a fall.

(**F**) **skateboarding:** People do skateboarding on the street or on special ramps and chutes in public parks.

(**G**) **bowling:** similar to Canadian *five pins*, European *nine pins*, and Italian *bocce*. The object is to throw the ball so that it

rolls down an alley and knocks over the wooden club pins.

(**13**) **bowling shoes:** special leather shoes that don't damage the wood lanes they play on.

(**H**) **horseback riding:** There are two types of horseback riding—English and western. Western riding is based on the life of the American cowboy. Western saddle competitions are called rodeos, with events based on the skills cowboys use in their work. English riding is based on European riding. It takes place in a ring or on special bridle paths.

(**14**) **saddle:** The English saddle is flat, padded, and smaller than the western saddle. The western saddle has a rounded seat, is unpadded, and has a horn or pommel that cowboys used to rope cows. The saddle on *Picture Dictionary* page 140 is an English one.

(**15**) **reins:** the lines the rider holds to guide the horse.

(**16**) **stirrups:** where the rider places his or her boots to stay secure.

(**I**) **tennis:** People play tennis in an indoor or outdoor tennis court. The object is to hit the ball across a net to the opponent's side of the court in such a way that the opponent cannot return it.

(**19**) **tennis shorts:** Traditionally tennis players wear white.

LANGUAGE & CULTURE NOTES

(J) **badminton:** a game you play on a court with light long-handled rackets (20) that you use to volley a birdie/shuttlecock (21) over the net.

(K) **racquetball:** People play racquetball in a four-walled indoor court.

(L) **table tennis/ping pong:** similar to tennis, but you play it on a table.

(M) **golf:** The object of the game is to hit the golf ball (30) with a golf club (29) from a spot called the tee, down the stretch of lawn called the fairway, into a hole marked with a flag on a small area called the green.

(29) **golf clubs:** There are three kinds of golf clubs—*woods, irons,* and *putters.*

(N) **Frisbee:** a hard plastic disc that one person throws and a second person catches.

(O) **billiards/pool:** The object of the game is to knock the billiard balls (34) into small pockets on the sides of the pool table with a pool stick (33).

(P) **martial arts:** fighting sports such as Judo or Karate.

(35) **black belt:** The color of the martial art belt symbolizes the skill level: white for beginners; brown, green, and purple for intermediates; and black for experts.

(Q) **gymnastics:** a favorite activity for teenagers and young adults.

(36) **horse:** the gymnast leaps onto this from a springboard and then performs flips and jumps.

(37) **parallel bars:** two bars on which male gymnasts pull their own weight to flip and balance.

(38) **mat:** a large soft mat on which gymnasts perform their floor routines.

(39) **balance beam:** a narrow beam on which the gymnast moves, turns, leaps, and does cartwheels and flips.

(40) **trampoline:** a training apparatus, not used in gymnastic competitions.

(R) **weightlifting:** Some people lift free weights simply to strengthen their bodies. Others train in order to compete in weightlifting competitions.

(S) **archery:** The center of the target is the *bull's eye.*

(T) **box:** The boxer hits the opponent above the waist in order to gain a knockout (when the person is knocked down and remains lying on the floor until the count of 10).

(U) **wrestle:** The wrestler uses a variety of maneuvers (called *holds*) to throw and immobilize (*pin*) the opponent to the mat (48).

(V) **work out:** doing body conditioning exercises with a variety of exercise equipment.

(49) **treadmill:** a stationary machine with a moving belt.

(50) **rowing machine:** a stationary machine with a moving seat and bar.

(51) **exercise bike:** a stationary bicycle for exercising.

(52) **universal/exercise equipment:** an apparatus that exercises and strengthens various parts of the body with weights.

LANGUAGE & CULTURE NOTES

Team sports are very important in the United States. They're popular as a school activity and at an amateur or professional level. In schools, children may begin to play team sports at age seven and often go to sports camps in the summer. American parents often become involved in their children's sports. It's common for them to drive carpools to games and daily practices to serve as volunteer coaches.

At the professional level, baseball, football, basketball, and hockey are the most popular team sports. Teams are associated with the cities where they are located and have special names, such as the Chicago Bulls or the Boston Red Sox. Sports fans usually follow a favorite team. Many buy season tickets if their city has a team and listen to radio or television coverage of away games. Most fans read sports magazines and the sports section of newspapers, which not only cover sporting events but also the personal lives of the players.

At sporting events, it is typical for everyone to sing the national anthem before the game begins. Hot dogs, popcorn, peanuts, ice cream, beer, and soft drinks are popular snacks people buy at food stands or from vendors who walk around selling them.

A) baseball: Teams play baseball outside on a large grassy area called a baseball field or ballfield (2) which has a dirt path in the shape of a diamond that the players run around after they hit a hard leather-covered ball with a bat.

B) softball: a game like baseball, but the softball field is smaller than the baseball field, the ball is larger and is soft leather, and the pitching is *underhand* rather than *overhand*.

C) football: American football should not be confused with European football, which is called soccer [H] in the United States. The football field is a large, grassy or turf (synthetic grass) rectangle with lines that divide the length into segments of ten yards.

D) lacrosse: Two teams of ten players each play lacrosse on a grassy rectangular field with a small rubber ball and a stick with a net at one end.

E) (ice) hockey: Two opposing teams play ice hockey on an ice rink with a hard rubber disk (puck) and flat sticks that curve at the base to form a hitting surface (hockey sticks).

F) basketball: Teams play basketball indoors on a rectangular hardwood court or outdoors on a concrete court. The basketball is a large inflated rubber ball.

G) volleyball: Teams play volleyball in a gymnasium on a rectangular hardwood court or outdoors on soil or sand. Players hit a large leather-covered ball over a net that is suspended across the court.

H) soccer: American *soccer* is the same as European *football*. Two teams of eleven players each play it on a rectangular grass field with a black-and-white leather-covered ball. A player may not touch the ball with his or her hands, but kicks the ball down the field into the opponent's goal.

TEAM SPORTS EQUIPMENT

LANGUAGE & CULTURE NOTES

Sports equipment is usually available in special sporting goods stores, in sporting departments of discount department stores, through catalogs, and online over the Internet.

(1) **baseball:** a small, hard leather-covered ball.

(2) **bat:** a tapered wooden stick with a knob at the base.

(3) **batting helmet:** a helmet for protection during batting.

(4) **(baseball) uniform:** Each team has its own color and team emblem for its outfit or uniform.

(5) **catcher's mask:** The catcher wears a mask, as well as a thickly padded chest protector and shinguards (27) as protection from the force of the pitched ball.

(6) **(baseball) glove:** special gloves baseball players and fielders wear with a web between the thumb and fingers to help them catch the ball.

(7) **catcher's mitt:** a special round-shaped mitt that has extra padding to protect the catcher from the force of the pitched ball.

(8) **softball:** a larger and softer version of a baseball.

(10) **football:** an oval-shaped, inflated leather-covered ball. Laces across one seam help the players grip the ball. Rubber or plastic footballs are common in recreational football.

(11) **football helmet:** a helmet that all players wear throughout the game. Helmets use the team's colors and logo and display the player's number.

(12) **shoulder pads:** Players wear these to protect the upper body and neck from injury.

(13) **lacrosse ball:** a rubber ball, smaller than a baseball.

(14) **face guard:** Lacrosse players wear these to protect the head and face.

(15) **lacrosse stick:** a wooden stick with a net basket on top for throwing and catching the ball.

(16) **hockey puck:** a hard rubber disk.

(18) **hockey mask:** a special mask for the goalie, the person who protects the goal.

(19) **hockey glove:** a glove that all players except the goalie wear. The glove is padded to protect the hand and arm.

(20) **hockey skates:** These have a single blade with a smooth curved tip. They are different from ice skates for figure skating (page 144, word 9), which have a series of jagged points at the tip.

(21) **basketball:** a large inflated rubber ball with a pebbly surface to improve the grip.

(22) **backboard:** The backboard is suspended above the court on a metal pole and holds the hoop (23). Outdoor backboards are usually wooden. Indoor backboards are often Plexiglas so that the spectators' view is not obstructed.

(23) **basketball hoop:** a round metal circle that has an open-ended net. The name derives from the fact that the target was originally a basket.

(24) **volleyball:** a large, inflated leather-covered ball, slightly smaller than a basketball.

(26) **soccer ball:** a large, inflated leather-covered ball with a pattern of black hexagons. It is slightly smaller than a basketball.

(27) **shinguards:** the shin is the front part of the leg between the knee and the ankle.

A **(downhill) skiing:** Downhill skiing is a popular sport in cold hilly and mountainous areas. A ski lift carries the skier the top of a ski run, which the skier then skis down.

Skiing takes place in public and private ski areas. Private ski areas are called ski resorts and are more expensive than public ski areas.

1 **skis:** Skis originally were wood, but now they are metal and synthetic materials that are laminated together.

2 **ski boots:** insulated molded plastic boots that go above the ankle and open and close with a series of clasps.

3 **bindings:** these are metal and attach the ski boot to the ski.

4 **(ski) poles:** Skiers use these aluminum poles to help them balance.

B **cross-country skiing:** Cross-country skiing takes place on ski trails in the open country or in wooded areas on flat or hilly terrain. It is a popular sport because of the simplicity of the equipment and the beauty of the setting.

5 **cross-country skis:** These are lighter and thinner than downhill skis. The skier applies different kinds of waxes to the bottom surface for different kinds of snow and temperature conditions.

C **(ice) skating:** Recreational ice skating takes place on ice rinks and on frozen ponds and lakes. Some communities flood public tennis courts to make winter ice skating rinks.

6 **(ice) skates / 7** **blade:** Ice skates have a laced boot with a metal blade (7) that attaches to the bottom from the toe to the heel. Young children may wear skates with two blades for added stability.

8 **skate guard:** rubber covers for the ice skate blades.

D **figure skating:** a popular sport both recreationally and in competitions. Competitive figure skating involves a series of complicated jumps and turns, with points for the performance of required elements in a figure skating routine.

9 **figure skates:** These have a series of jagged teeth at the tip of the blade that helps the skater make jumps and turns.

E **snowboarding:** The snowboarder places both feet into bindings on a snowboard (10) and then snowboards down a slope.

F **sledding:** a popular activity for children and families.

11 **sled:** The sled on *Picture Dictionary* page 144 is a traditional sled with a wood board on metal runners. There are also plastic sleds that don't have metal runners.

12 **sledding dish/saucer:** a round plastic form that easily slides down hills.

G **bobsledding:** Bobsledding requires a special track. The riders lean into the turns and banked walls of the track in order to increase their speed.

13 **bobsled:** A bobsled holds two to four people in a sitting position with their legs stretched out around the person in front of them.

H **snowmobiling:** Snowmobiling takes place on trails in open country or woods.

14 **snowmobile:** a small gas-motored vehicle with a set of skis in the front of a revolving tread in the rear. There is space for one or two riders.

WATER SPORTS AND RECREATION

LANGUAGE & CULTURE NOTES

A **sailing:** People sail on rivers, lakes, and oceans.

1 **sailboat:** A sailboat is either wood, fiberglass, or aluminum.

2 **life jacket/life vest:** a floatation device people use if a boat sinks or if someone has fallen overboard.

B **canoeing:** People canoe on rivers and lakes.

3 **canoe:** A canoe may be aluminum, fiberglass, or wood.

4 **paddles:** long wooden or aluminum poles with narrow flat heads that you pull through the water.

C **rowing:** People row on rivers and lakes.

5 **rowboat:** a wooden or aluminum flat-bottomed boat that people use for recreational rowing and fishing.

6 **oars:** long wooden or aluminum poles with wide flat heads that you pull through the water.

D **kayaking:** People usually kayak on rivers that have sections of fast-flowing water called rapids or white water.

7 **kayak:** similar to a shell people use in competitive rowing, but the top is enclosed so water doesn't fill the inside.

8 **paddles:** These have two heads at either end of the paddle that kayakers dip alternately into the water.

E **(white-water) rafting:** White water refers to sections of a river where fast-flowing water creates foamy bubbles on the surface.

9 **raft:** an inflated rubber boat.

10 **life jacket/life vest:** a safety flotation device people wear in case of accidents.

F **swimming:** People swim in pools and in oceans, lakes, and rivers.

11 **swimsuit/bathing suit:** A man's bathing suit is also called swimming trunks. A woman's bathing suit may be one-piece or two-piece.)

12 **goggles:** People wear these so they can see underwater.

13 **bathing cap:** This keeps the hair dry while someone is swimming.

G **snorkeling:** Snorkeling is particularly popular at oceans with warm water and a rocky shore where fish gather.

15 **snorkel:** a mouthpiece and tube that allows the snorkler to breathe while his or her head is under the water.

16 **fins:** special rubber devices that snorklers wear on their feet to help propel them through the water.

H **scuba diving:** Scuba is an acronym for *self-contained underwater breathing apparatus.*

17 **wet suit:** the rubber outfit that a scuba diver or snorkler wears for protection.

18 **(air) tank:** the apparatus that allows a diver to breathe underwater.

I **surfing:** People surf along ocean resorts where there are waves.

J **windsurfing:** People windsurf on lakes and oceans.

21 **sailboard:** like a surfboard with a sail.

K **waterskiing:** People usually waterski on lakes.

23 **water skis:** People waterski either on a pair of skis or on a single ski, one foot behind the other (slalom).

24 **towrope:** the rope attached to the ski boat that tows the waterskier.

L **fishing:** People fish in rivers, lakes, and oceans (deep-sea fishing).

29 **bait:** The kind of bait people use depends on the kind of fishing they're doing.

LANGUAGE & CULTURE NOTES

1 hit: The action depicted is a baseball player who is hitting the ball with a bat. Other sport hitting actions take place when a boxer hits his or her opponent, and when a golfer or tennis player hits the ball.

2 pitch: the action of a baseball pitcher throwing the ball to the batter.

3 throw: The action depicted is a baseball player who is throwing a baseball to another player.

4 catch: The action depicted is a baseball player who is receiving a ball that another player threw.

5 pass: to throw an object, usually a ball, from one player to another.

6 kick: to hit with the foot. Football and soccer are two sports where kicking takes place.

7 serve: to begin play with a tennis ball, racquetball, volleyball, or ping pong ball.

8 bounce: to hit an object (usually a ball) against a surface and have the object come back.

9 dribble: In basketball (depicted), a player dribbles when he or she runs and bounces the ball with each step.

10 shoot: In basketball (depicted), to shoot is to throw the ball toward the basket.

11 stretch: to extend your muscles. This is a good warm-up and cool-down activity after strenuous exercise.

12 bend: The person depicted is bending from his waist.

14 run: Running in place is common when you exercise indoors. You use the body movements of running, but do it in one place without moving forward.

15 hop: to make small jumps with one foot.

16 skip: to go forward by a series of moves—a hop on one foot and then a long stride and hop with the other foot, followed by a long stride and hop with the first foot.

17 jump: to lift both feet off the ground and go up in the air.

18 reach: to stretch your body as much as possible in one direction.

19 swing: to move your body from side to side.

20 lift: to raise something up.

23 shoot: In archery (depicted), to shoot is to launch the arrow from the bow.

24 push-up: The action begins when you lie down and face the floor with your arms bent and hands resting near the chest. You then extend your arms and raise your upper body off the floor.

25 sit-up: The action begins when you lie down on your back with your legs extended or bent. You then raise your body to a sitting position.

26 deep knee bend: In this activity, you completely bend your knees and then straighten them again.

27 jumping jack: The action begins when you stand with your legs together, and rest your arms at your sides. You then jump in place, spread your legs when you land, and raise your arms over your head. You then jump back to the starting position.

28 somersault: When you do this exercise, you bend into a ball with your head touching the floor and then you roll over.

29 cartwheel: In this activity, you turn your entire body in a circle.

30 handstand: In this activity, you balance on your hands.

LANGUAGE & CULTURE NOTES

Theater, concerts, opera, and ballet are more typically found in large urban areas and at universities. Movie theaters that show several movies simultaneously are often found in suburban areas near shopping malls.

Newspaper entertainment sections and their corresponding websites list current and upcoming performances, current movie schedules, reviews, and informational articles on performers and issues related to entertainment.

(A) play: a theatrical work. Most plays are in three acts.

(1) theater: The word *theater* refers to the specific building where performances take place. ("We're standing in front of the theater.") The term *theater* as entertainment refers to the presentation of plays (see *Picture Dictionary* page 148, words 13–16). People say, "I like theater, meaning "I like to see plays."

Broadway is the most famous theater area in the United States. It is a group of theaters in New York City where famous actors and actresses perform in plays and musicals.

(2) actor / (3) actress: the traditional terms for male and female stage and movie performers. In an effort to be non-sexist, some female performers refer to themselves as actors instead of actresses. See (15) and (16).

(B) concert: a musical performance.

(4) concert hall: a large theater where concerts take place.

(5) orchestra: an orchestra that plays primarily classical music.

(6) musician: a person who plays a musical instrument.

(7) conductor: the person who leads a symphony.

(8) band: a group of musicians who play any kind of music together, aside from classical music.

(C) opera: a play set to music in which performers sing and act their lines.

(9) opera singer: a term that refers to both male and female singers. There are four voice tones in opera: soprano (high range), contralto (mid-high range), counter tenor (mid-range), and tenor (low range).

(D) ballet: a classical form of dance. It also refers to a ballet company's performance.

(10) ballet dancer: refers to a male or female ballet performer.

(11) ballerina: a female ballet performer.

(E) music club: also called a night club. A music club is a small place where musicians play to small audiences.

(12) singer: a person who sings any kid of music, except for opera, professionally.

(F) movies: The term movie is used for the film itself. ("I saw a wonderful movie last night.") It also refers to the type of entertainment. ("I enjoy movies.")

(13) (movie) theater: the place that shows movies.

(14) (movie) screen: A projector projects the movie on the screen.

(G) comedy club: the place where audiences see comedians perform.

(17) comedian: a stage performer who entertains people by telling funny jokes and stories.

(A) music: There are popular music stations on the radio, with disc jockeys who play a wide variety of music. There are also classical radio stations.

(1) classical music: Technically speaking, classical refers to a specific period in Western music history, from 1750 to 1825. In its general usage, classical music refers to music of these periods that large symphony orchestras, small ensembles of instruments, and individuals play.

(2) popular music: a general term that refers to music that popular singers perform that is not specifically one of the other types (3)–(12).

(3) country music: originally rural music of the southern United States. Ballads about love and lost love are common themes in country music.

(4) rock music: Rock music has a strong, pulsating beat. Musicians play electric and electronic equipment along with a lead singer and one or more back-up singers.

(5) folk music: music of the people. It has its roots in the native countries of America's immigrants. Typically unwritten, these songs changed as they passed from generation to generation. Many folk songs are work chants, songs of social protest, as well as songs purely for fun and enjoyment.

(6) rap music: the repetition of rhymed text in a rhythmic, chanting style to a musical background.

(7) gospel music: religious music originally from African-American churches. It is primarily vocal music, with either a sad, mournful tone or a happy, upbeat tone.

(8) jazz: a type of music with instrumental improvisations. It developed in the late 1800's from the blues that African-American musicians typically played. Most consider New Orleans as the birthplace of jazz.

(9) blues: To be blue means to be sad. The blues typically has a sad, mournful tone and is similar to gospel music, but with a secular rather than religious theme.

(10) bluegrass: country music of Kentucky and surrounding Appalachian mountain states.

(11) hip hop: a music style that developed out of rapping (6), which includes rapping and break dancing.

(12) reggae: Originally from Jamaica and the Caribbean Islands, it has a smooth melodic sound.

(B) plays: the performance of a story, with actors and actresses portraying and speaking the dialog of the story's characters.

(13) drama: a general term for all plays or theatrical productions. It also refers specifically to plays with a serious theme.

(14) comedy: a play with a humorous or light, non-serious theme.

(15) tragedy: a drama in which a character comes to a disastrous end.

(16) musical (comedy): a theatrical production in which dialog and musical numbers are combined.

(C) movies/films: A system of ratings indicates the amount of violence and/or adult content of film. G is for general audiences, PG stands for parental guidance suggested, PG-13 states that an adult must accompany children under 13, R means that an adult must accompany young people under 17, and X is only for people over 18.

(19) western: a film that depicts western U.S. life in the 1800s and features cowboys on horses, usually in conflict with each other and with Indians.

(20) mystery: a movie that depicts a murder and the investigation of that murder.

LANGUAGE & CULTURE NOTES

(22) **cartoon:** also called an animated film, usually intended for younger audiences.

(23) **documentary:** a non-fiction film which investigates a person or historic fact through interviews with real people.

(24) **action movie/adventure movie:** This type of movie is usually suspenseful, with a great deal of action (running, chasing, and things exploding).

(25) **war movie:** This type of movie sometimes glamorizes war, and other times shows its horror.

(26) **horror movie:** This type of movie usually depicts some awful monster or creature.

(27) **science fiction movie:** This type of movie usually takes place in outerspace or has as its villains creatures who come to Earth from outerspace.

(28) **foreign film:** any non-U.S. film.

(D) **TV programs:** There are three types of television channels in the United States. First are the commercial networks: CBS, NBC, ABC, and Fox. These networks broadcast programs that company sponsors pay for. Commercials for their products come before, during, and after the program.

Second is PBS (the Public Broadcasting System), which relies on government and company grants and public donations. There are no commercials on PBS.

Third are the cable television channels. Viewers pay to have a cable attached to their TV that relays 100 or more different channels—some devoted to particular areas such as sports, news, music, movies, shopping, or educational programming.

(29) **drama:** See (13). Dramas usually have a serious theme. Some are single dramatic presentations. Others are ongoing TV programs that use the same setting and

cast of main characters who face a new problem in each weekly program.

(30) **(situation) comedy/sitcom:** a weekly comedy program with a continuing cast of characters.

(31) **talk show:** features a host or hostess who interviews celebrity guests.

(32) **game show/quiz show:** There are a number of different game shows, all of which involve a host and contestants who play the game for prizes.

(33) **reality show:** A show that chronicles what happens to a group of people as they undergo a strenuous experience.

(34) **soap opera:** an ongoing story about the sentimental problems of a group of people. The name originally came from radio shows whose sponsors were usually companies that advertised soap products.

(35) **cartoon:** an animated film with human and/or animal characters.

(36) **children's program:** This may be an animated cartoon or a program that incorporates educational material.

(37) **news program:** In the United States, television stations usually broadcast a news program in the morning, at noon, in the early evening, and late in the evening.

(38) **sports program:** Commercial networks broadcast major sporting events of popular American sports such as football, baseball, basketball, and hockey. There are also cable TV sports channels that provide coverage of a wide variety of sports.

(39) **nature program:** a study of the habitat and behavior of a certain kind of animal.

(40) **shopping program:** a program that feature various items to buy. Viewers can call in and buy with a credit card the item on the TV screen.

MUSICAL INSTRUMENTS

LANGUAGE & CULTURE NOTES

Strings: The inclusion of stringed instruments you play with a bow (the violin, viola, cello, and bass) distinguishes an orchestra from a band.

(1) **violin:** an instrument you play with long, connected, smooth sweeps of the bow.

(2) **viola:** an instrument larger than a violin that you play with a bow.

(3) **cello:** an instrument larger than a viola that you play with a bow.

(4) **bass:** an instrument larger than a cello that you play with a bow.

(5) **(acoustic) guitar:** an instrument you pluck or strum.

(6) **electric guitar:** Electric instruments allow sounds to be transmitted as electrical signals that can be amplified.

(7) **banjo:** an instrument you pluck or strum, often used in country music.

(8) **harp:** The largest of the stringed instruments.

Woodwinds: Once exclusively wood, these are now often metal. Woodwind instruments, with the exception of a recorder, are part of both orchestras and bands.

(9) **piccolo:** a small flute pitched an octave higher than the ordinary flute.

(10) **flute:** a high-pitched woodwind instrument.

(11) **clarinet:** a woodwind instrument with a single reed mouthpiece.

(12) **oboe:** a woodwind instrument with a double reed mouthpiece.

(13) **recorder:** U.S. elementary schools often teach the recorder as an introduction to woodwind instruments.

(14) **saxophone:** a woodwind instrument with a single reed.

(15) **bassoon:** a double-reed woodwind instrument with a range two octaves lower than that of the oboe.

Brass: Brass instruments are a part of orchestras and bands.

(16) **trumpet:** The trumpet is a brass musical instrument with a brilliant tone that you play by means of valves.

(17) **trombone:** a brass instrument in which you slide the tubing, not the valves (as in the trumpet) to makes notes.

(18) **French horn:** a brass instrument that consists of a spiral tube that uses valves to control the pitch.

(19) **tuba:** a low pitched brass instrument that uses valves to control the pitch.

Percussion: Drums produce sound when you hit them with a drumstick or your hands.

(20) **drums /** (a) **cymbals:** The illustration on *Picture Dictionary* page 150 shows a drum set for a single percussionist to play. It includes a bass drum (that you hit with a foot pedal), a snare drum (that you hit with drumsticks), and cymbals (that you hit with drumsticks).

(21) **tambourine:** a small round drum with cymbals in its rim.

(22) **xylophone:** This is a percussion instrument with wooden bars that are tuned to produce a chromatic scale.

Keyboard Instruments: In keyboard instruments, the strings are inside a case and vibrate when you strike the key that is attached to each string.

(23) **piano:** Pianos come in grand, upright, and spinet styles.

(24) **electric keyboard:** This instrument can nearly imitate the sound of a piano, as well as produce electronic sounds for electronic music.

(25) **organ:** It's common to hear the organ in churches and at professional sporting events.

(26) **accordion:** has a keyboard on one side and single note and chord buttons on the others.

(27) **harmonica:** To produce sound, you draw in and blow out air.

THE FARM AND FARM ANIMALS

LANGUAGE & CULTURE NOTES

1. **farmhouse:** the home where the farmer's family lives.

2. **farmer:** the person who operates a farm.

3. **(vegetable) garden:** This is the term for vegetables that people raise for home consumption.

4. **scarecrow:** a figure that scares crows away from a crop.

5. **hay:** a variety of grass that farmers grow and feed to animals.

6. **hired hand:** a person who helps out in the general operation and maintenance of a farm.

7. **barn:** the place where farmers keep animals, farm machines, and implements.

8. **stable:** a barn used exclusively for horses.

10. **barnyard:** the area that surrounds the barn, usually with a fence enclosure.

11. **turkey:** It's typical to serve turkey during the Thanksgiving holiday.

12. **goat:** The male goat is often called a billy goat.

13. **lamb:** a young sheep. Farmers raise lamb primarily for their meat.

14. **rooster:** a male chicken. The rooster is well-known for its crowing at dawn, *cock-a-doodle-doo.*

15. **pig pen:** the enclosed area on a farm for pigs.

16. **pig:** also called a hog. Farmers raise pigs commercially for their meat (pork).

17. **chicken coop:** a wooden or wire-mesh house for chickens.

18. **chicken:** Birds (chickens, turkeys, and ducks) that farmers raise for market are called poultry.

19. **hen house:** a wooden house that has nesting boxes for hens.

20. **hen:** a female chicken that farmers raise to lay eggs.

21. **crop:** a planting of any vegetable or grain, such as wheat, corn, rye, or barley.

22. **irrigation system:** a system of viaducts or sprinklers that serves to disperse and regulate water for crops.

23. **tractor:** a multi-use farm machine that pulls wagons and different farm implements, such as cultivators and planters.

24. **field:** a large plot of land that may or may not be cultivated.

25. **pasture:** a field without crops for grass-feeding of cows and horses.

26. **cow:** a cow that farmers raise for milk production, as opposed to cattle that farmers raise for their meat.

27. **sheep:** The singular and plural from of this noun is the same. The meat from a sheep is called mutton.

28. **orchard:** a garden of fruit trees (29) such as apple, pear, or cherry.

30. **farm worker:** a person who specializes in farm work, usually to help in the harvesting of crops.

31. **alfalfa:** a crop rich in protein and minerals that farmers grow to feed cattle.

32. **corn:** There are different varieties for human or animal consumption. Much corn in the United States is genetically engineered to resist bacteria and insects better.

33. **cotton:** You spin the long hairy fibers of this plant to make cotton fabric.

34. **rice:** a grass crop that yields rice grains for food.

35. **soybeans:** also called soy. Farmers grow this crop, native to Asia, for food and feeding animals.

36. **wheat:** You grind the seeds of this grassy plant to make flour.

(1–33) Animals 1–33 are common to North America.

(1) **moose / (a) antler:** A moose is a large animal in the deer family with enormous flattened antlers (bony growths) in the male. Moose are called elk in Europe.

(2) **polar bear:** These live only in the Northern Hemisphere.

(3) **deer:** A female deer is a doe. A male deer is a buck or a stag.

(4) **wolf-wolves:** These often appear as villains in fairy tales and fables.

(5) **(black) bear / (a) claw:** The American black bear is smaller and less ferocious than the grizzly bear (7).

(6) **mountain lion:** also called a puma. Mountain lions are solitary creatures that live in caves in the mountains.

(7) **(grizzly) bear:** The grizzly gets its name from the silver tips of its fur.

(8) **buffalo/bison:** It was common to hunt buffalo for their shaggy fur coats in the nineteenth century.

(9) **coyote:** a wolf-like wildog that lives a group (pack).

(10) **fox:** well-known for its ability to steal chickens and not get caught.

(11) **skunk:** gives off a strong odor in order to frighten away possible aggressors.

(12) **porcupine / (a) quill:** a member of the rodent family that has sharp feather-like protrusions called quills.

(13) **rabbit:** also called a bunny. Rabbits are symbols of spring and of fertility. Many people carry a rabbit's foot for good luck.

(14) **beaver:** Beavers build dams across a stream or lake in order to construct a lodge, which they make from the logs of trees.

(15) **raccoon:** sometimes called bandits because of the mask-marking on their faces.

(16) **possum/opossum:** a nocturnal tree-living animal with a large tail that can grab onto things.

(18) **pony:** not a baby horse, but a small version of a horse.

(19) **donkey:** a member of the horse family, distinguished by its smaller size and long ears. The donkey is the symbol of the Democratic Party in the United States.

(20) **armadillo:** has a protective covering of bony plates.

(21) **bat:** the only flying mammal. Most Western cultures consider bats as bad omens, while Asian cultures associate bats with good luck, happiness, and long life.

(22) **worm:** Worms may be both beneficial and detrimental parasites.

(23) **slug:** People typically consider the slug a garden pest.

(24–28) Animals 24–28 are common to Central and South America.

(24) **monkey:** Scientists commonly use monkeys in scientific research.

(25) **anteater:** Anteaters have a long head with a long, tubular mouth and long tongue, but no teeth.

(26) **llama:** People commonly use llamas to carry heavy loads.

(27) **jaguar / (a) spots:** the third largest cat after tigers (51) and lions (55).

(28–33) Animals 28–33 are common rodents.

(28) **mouse-mice:** People often consider mice as pests and associate them with places that are not very clean. On the other hand, scientists widely use mice in scientific research.

(29) **rat:** People typically consider rats as pests and associate them with sewers. Like mice, scientists commonly use them in scientific research.

(30) **chipmunk:** a ground squirrel.

LANGUAGE & CULTURE NOTES

(31) **squirrel:** The two most common types of squirrels are red squirrels and gray squirrels.

(32) **gopher:** a small rodent that lives in the ground and has large cheek pouches that can be stuffed.

(33) **prairie dog:** any of several ground-dwelling rodents of North American prairies that live in large complex burrows.

(34–43) Animals 34–43 are common pets in the United States.

(34) **cat /** (a) **whiskers:** A cat's whiskers help it judge if it can pass through a narrow space.

(35) **kitten:** a baby cat.

(36) **dog:** A dog of mixed breeding is called a mongrel or a mutt. Working dogs include guide dogs for the blind and deaf, police dogs, and herding dogs.

(37) **puppy:** a baby dog.

(38) **hamster /** (39) **gerbil /** (40) **guinea pig:** These are popular pets for children.

(41) **goldfish:** a small golden or orange-red freshwater fish of Eurasia that people use as pond or aquarium fishes.

(42) **canary:** The canary is well-known for its song.

(43) **parakeet:** also called a budgie. Parakeets are native to tropical climates.

(44–51) Animals 44–51 are common to Asia.

(44) **antelope:** any of a graceful deer-like animal with long legs and horns.

(45) **baboon:** a member of the ape family.

(46) **rhinoceros /** (a) **horn:** an endangered species because hunters commonly poach for its horn.

(47) **panda:** Native to China, the panda is not a true bear, but a member of the raccoon family.

(48) **orangutan:** a member of the ape family.

(49) **panther:** a leopard (60) with black fur.

(50) **gibbon:** a member of the ape family.

(51) **tiger /** (a) **paw:** Tigers have massive paws that help them attack and kill their prey.

(52–61) Animals 52–61 are common to Africa.

(52) **camel /** (a) **hump:** The camel may have one or two humps (fatty tissue growths).

(53) **elephant /** (a) **tusk /** (b) **trunk:** There are two kinds of elephants—African (the larger type) and Asian (the smaller type). Elephants use their trunks as we use our hands. The elephant is the symbol of the Republican Party in the United States.

(54) **hyena:** a scavenger with a bark that sounds like laughing.

(55) **lion /** (a) **mane:** The female lion is called a lioness.

(56) **giraffe:** a long-necked African animal.

(57) **zebra:** This relative of a horse is distinguished by its black stripes.

(58) **chimpanzee:** a member of the ape family. The *chimp* is noted for its intelligence.

(59) **hippopotamus:** The *hippo* is endangered because of poaching for its ivory teeth.

(60) **leopard:** a large cat that lives in African and Asian forests that usually has a golden coat with black spots.

(61) **gorilla:** a member of the ape family.

(62) **kangaroo /** (a) **pouch:** A kangaroo carries its young in a pouch after birth. Kangaroos have a unique hopping method of moving.

(63) **koala (bear):** Not a true bear, the koala is a marsupial that is native to Australia.

(64) **platypus:** The platypus lays eggs, but is a mammal because it feeds its young with milk.

Birds are warm-blooded animals with feathers and wings that hatch their young from eggs. A bird's beak, wings, feathers, and feet vary and reflect adaptations to the habitat—e.g., the small beak of seed-eaters and the webbed feet of water fowl.

Fowl or *poultry* are the terms for a group of wild or domesticated birds that serve as food, such as ducks, chickens, geese, and turkeys.

Each state in the United States has a *state bird*, one that is typical of that state. The national bird of the United States is the bald eagle (10).

(1) **robin:** Robins are found in cities, in suburbs, and in wooded areas throughout the United States.

(2) **blue jay:** Blue jays have a particularly loud cry. They are well-known for their greed and aggressive behavior.

(3) **cardinal:** The cardinal is distinguished by the bright red plumage of the male and its crested head.

(4) **crow:** Crows are scavengers. They make a distinctive *cawing* noise.

(5) **seagull:** found typically near oceans, lakes, and rivers. Seagulls are scavengers and often fly around garbage dumps.

(6) **woodpecker:** well-known for the drumming sound it makes when it pecks on trees for insects.

(7) **pigeon:** well-known for its distinctive *cooing* sound. Many people feed the pigeons in urban parks.

(8) **owl:** a nocturnal bird with a distinctive *hooting* voice.

(9) **hawk:** well-known for their soaring style of flying and as hunters.

(10) **eagle:** the national bird of the United States.

(10a) **claw:** also called a *talon.* This type of foot is typical of birds that perch on branches.

(11) **swan:** Swans are famous for their beauty and grace.

(12) **hummingbird:** well-known for its small size and long needle-like beak that it uses to suck nectar.

(13) **duck:** Ducks are popular game birds for hunters.

(14) **sparrow:** very common throughout North America.

(15) **goose-geese:** Geese may be domesticated or wild. They are well-known for their *honking* noise and their migratory *V* flying pattern.

(16) **penguin:** found only in the southern half of the world and most typically in Antarctica. Penguins are flightless birds.

(17) **flamingo:** typically found in the state of Florida.

(18) **crane:** Cranes are wading birds.

(19) **stork:** Adults often tell young children that the stork brings all new babies.

(20) **pelican:** The pelican is distinguished by an expandable pouch below its beak.

(21) **peacock:** Male peacocks have a colorful tail called a *train.* To be *proud as a peacock* is a common expression.

(22) **parrot:** Parrots are popular pets in the United States because they can learn things.

(23) **ostrich:** The ostrich is the largest of all birds. It doesn't fly.

BIRDS AND INSECTS
(continued)

LANGUAGE & CULTURE NOTES

Insects, also called *bugs,* are typically small six-legged animals, often with wings and antennae, and a body in three parts.

Americans usually put screens on their homes to keep insects out. Americans also fumigate or spray their homes with poisons called pesticides. When people work outside, they often use cream and spray bug repellents. People who are severely allergic to bug bites carry antidote kits.

The use of pesticides to kill insects on farm crops is controversial. Many people who feel that the poisons could have secondary effects on humans protest against their use. Fruits and vegetables that are free of chemical pesticides and/or fertilizers are referred to as *organically grown.*

(24) **fly:** Flies are pests because they gather around food waste and garbage dumps, not because they bite humans.

(25) **ladybug:** also called a *ladybird.*

(26) **firefly/lightning bug:** Young children like to catch fireflies in jars to watch them light up.

(27) **moth /** (29) **butterfly:** Moths and butterflies have similar features, but the moth is smaller, less brightly colored, and has different antenna than the butterfly. (See word 29 below.)

(28) **caterpillar /** (a) **cocoon:** the larval form of moths and butterflies, which hatch from the eggs. The *cocoon* is the shell or house that a caterpillar creates and lives in during the metamorphosis from a *pupa* into a moth or butterfly. A pupa is a caterpillar that has stopped growing and is in a transitional state to becoming a moth or butterfly.

(30) **tick:** commonly bites humans as well as animals such as dogs and deer. In the United States, the deer tick is the carrier of Lyme disease, which has afflicted many people especially in the Northeast.

(31) **mosquito:** Mosquitoes commonly bite people, which causes an itchy swelling. They also transmit diseases such as yellow fever and malaria through their bites.

(33) **spider /** (a) **web:** The spider spins a filament trap, a *web,* to catch its food. A spider's web in a building is called a cobweb. Two of the most feared spiders are the *black widow* and the *tarantula.*

(34) **praying mantis:** It gets its name because it appears to hold its front legs in a position of prayer.

(36) **bee /** (a) **beehive:** valuable for their role in the pollination of flowers and for their ability to make honey. Bees live together in a bee hive.

(37) **grasshopper:** also called a *katydid* or *locust.* Farmers consider grasshoppers to be pests, since they can cause considerable crop damage.

(38) **beetle:** any insect with biting mouthparts and hard shell front wings shaped to cover soft rear wings.

(39) **scorpion:** People fear scorpions because of their poisonous sting.

(40) **centipede:** an insect with a flat body of 15 to 173 segments each with a pair of legs. Centipede means *one hundred feet.*

(41) **cricket:** makes a distinctive sound that is most apparent at night in late summer.

LC154a

LANGUAGE & CULTURE NOTES

(1–10) **Fish:** cold-blooded animals that live in water, breathe with gills, and move by means of fins.

(1) **trout:** primarily a fresh-water fish that lives in brooks and lakes.

(1a) **fin:** The fins of a fish are comparable to the arms and legs of a person. Fish use fins for balance and direction.

(1b) **gill:** the breathing organ of a fish.

(1c) **scales:** the small thin, bony overlapping plates that protect a fish.

(2) **flounder:** a flatfish that lives on the bottom of the ocean.

(3) **tuna:** a large, sleek, predatory fish that swims the oceans of the world. Tuna is a very popular food fish around the world.

(4) **swordfish:** one of the largest of the ocean fish. It is well-known for its long *bill* and spectacular jumping.

(5) **bass:** typically a fresh-water fish that lives near the surface in ponds and lakes.

(6) **shark:** probably the best-known of all fish because of its reputation as a *man-eater* and because of its threatening appearance.

(7) **eel:** typically a bottom dweller that lives in both fresh-water lakes and salt water.

(8) **cod:** a large fish that often lives close to the sea floor in cold waters.

(9) **ray/sting ray:** any of a variety of broad flat fish that has a long poisonous serrated spine at the end of its tail.

(10) **sea horse:** an unusual fish with bony, protective plates that cover its body.

(11–25) **Sea Animals**

(11) **whale:** The whale is the largest of all mammals.

(12) **dolphin:** a mammal that many sailors consider good luck. It is an extremely intelligent animal.

(13) **porpoise:** related to and often confused with the dolphin. The dolphin has sharp teeth, jumps out of the water often, and lives in large groups. The porpoise is more solitary, is shyer of human contact, has flat teeth, and rarely jumps out of the water.

(14) **jellyfish:** Some varieties are poisonous, and beaches may be closed because of their presence.

(15) **octopus:** The octopus has eight tentacles (a). The plural of octopus is *octopi*.

(16) **seal:** A baby seal is called a pup. Seals live off the northern eastern and western coasts of the United States.

(17) **sea lion:** Seals and sea lions are often confused. The sea lion moves more easily on land and has a small ear flap unlike the seal that has just a hole.

(18) **otter:** The otter is well-known for its playful antics.

(19) **walrus:** The walrus has tusks (a) made of ivory.

(20) **crab:** There are hard-shelled and soft-shelled varieties.

(21) **squid:** The squid has ten tentacles.

(22) **snail:** The snail has a hard external shell. It lives on both land and in water.

(23) **starfish:** The appendages of the starfish are called *arms*. If an arm is lost, a new arm regenerates.

(24) **sea urchin:** The sea urchin has a soft body enclosed in thin spiny shells.

(25) **sea anemone:** resembles a flower, but has rings of tentacles.

(26–31) These animals are reptiles—cold-blooded animals that lack legs or have short, stubby legs. They have dry, scaly skins and bear live young or eggs.

LANGUAGE & CULTURE NOTES

(26) tortoise / (27) turtle: The term *turtle* is often used interchangeably with *tortoise*. Turtles live both on land and in the water. Tortoises live just on land.

(26a) shell: the protective outer covering of a turtle and tortoise.

(28) alligator / (29) crocodile: The nose of the alligator is shorter and broader than that of the crocodile.

(30) lizard: The lizard typically lives in hot, dry climates or in tropical rain forests.

(31) iguana: a type of lizard found in North and South America.

(32–35) These animals are amphibians—cold-blooded animals whose young live in water and breathe with gills but as adults develop lungs and live on land.

(32) frog / (35) toad: A toad is kind of frog that often has bumpier skin and shorter hind legs that they use for walking rather than hopping.

(33) newt / (34) salamander: Salamanders live in water, on land, or in trees. Newts tend to live on land during the warm months of summer.

(36–39) These animals are snakes.

(36) snake: also called a *serpent*. All snakes are reptiles. Some cultures and religions, such as Hinduism, consider snakes to be sacred. Others regard snakes as symbols of evil.

(37) rattlesnake: a poisonous snake that typically lives in the deserts and woods of western North America.

(38) boa constrictor: a non-poisonous snake that kills by wrapping itself around the victim's body and squeezing.

(39) cobra: a poisonous snake native to India that opens its hood when it is threatened.

The vocabulary of this lesson is organized as follows:

[1]–[10] parts of a tree   [30]–[33] kinds of vines

[11]–[22] kinds of trees   [34]–[39] parts of a flower

[23]–[29] kinds of bushes and plants   [40]–[59] kinds of flowers

(1) tree: Trees grow on tree farms and at nurseries.

(2) leaf-leaves: Broad-leaf trees may lose their leaves in autumn (deciduous) or keep them year around (evergreen).

(3) twig: a small branch from which leaves grow.

(4) branch: a division of the trunk or a limb of a tree that further divides into twigs.

(5) limb: a division of the trunk of the tree that further divides into branches.

(6) trunk: the woody stem of a tree.

(7) bark: the protective outer layer of the tree.

(8) root: draws water and minerals from the earth and anchors the tree in the ground.

(9) needle: the leaf of a coniferous tree.

(10) pine cone: the reproductive unit that produces and contains the seeds of coniferous plants.

(11) dogwood: Its beautiful pink or white flowers are a sign that springtime has come.

(12) holly: a broad-leaved evergreen whose red berries are beautiful, but poisonous.

(13) magnolia: well-known for its fragrant pure, white flowers.

(14) elm: Dutch elm disease has destroyed a large number of elm trees.

(15) cherry: important both as a fruit tree and ornamental tree.

(16) palm: a tree native to tropical or desert areas.

(17) birch: The ancient Egyptians used the bark of the birch tree as paper.

(18) maple: a shade and ornamental tree famous for its sap, which people cook into a syrup.

(19) oak: a shade tree whose wood is common in furniture and building structures.

(20) pine: a tree commonly associated with Christmas. People use its boughs and cones decoratively.

(21) redwood: a tree native to California that may grow to 300 feet (91 meters).

(22) (weeping) willow: a tree native to China that is usually found near water.

(23) bush / (26) shrub: a low woody perennial plant that usually has several branches that do not grow as tall as trees.

(24) holly: the shrub form of the holly tree.

(25) berries: simple, pulpy fruit developed from a plant or bush.

(27) fern: a green plant whose leaves are called *fronds*.

(28) plant: In a general sense, a plant is any member of the plant kingdom. Specifically, a plant has a non-woody stem that can support the plant in an upright position to a limited height.

(29) cactus-cacti: Cacti have spiny thorns instead of leaves.

(30) vine: a plant with a non-woody stem.

(31) poison ivy: a plant with clusters of three leaves that excrete an oil which causes a painful rash in most people.

LANGUAGE & CULTURE NOTES

(32) **poison sumac:** Like poison ivy, poison sumac excretes an oil which causes a painful rash in most people.

(33) **poison oak:** a shrub with clusters of three leaves that excrete an oil which causes a painful rash in most people.

(34) **flower:** the reproductive unit of broad-leaf plants.

(35) **petal:** the outer covering of a flower that protects the inner reproductive organs.

(36) **stem:** the structure that carries nutrients throughout the plant.

(37) **bud:** an immature flower.

(38) **thorn:** a sharply pointed protrusion of the stem that serves to protect the plant.

(39) **bulb:** refers to both underground buds and the flowers that grow from them.

(40) **chrysanthemum:** a flower associated with autumn.

(41) **daffodil:** People consider the daffodil one of the early signs of spring.

(42) **daisy:** In American folk culture, it is common to use a daisy to predict love by repeating a chant as you pick the petals: "He loves me, he loves me not," or "She loves me, she loves me not."

(43) **marigold:** an annual flower with a strong scent that deters rabbits from gardens.

(44) **carnation:** a flower with long-lasting bloom and a variety of colors.

(45) **gardenia:** Gardenias are very common in corsages for special occasions.

(46) **lily:** In western cultures, the white lily is a symbol of purity and everlasting life. In Christian religions, it is associated with

Easter. In eastern cultures, it symbolizes fertility. The lotus, or water lily, is sacred in Buddhism and Hinduism.

(47) **iris:** A plant with tuberous roots, the iris blooms soon after daffodils and tulips.

(48) **pansy:** often a part of ornamental borders around homes.

(49) **petunia:** frequently a part of ornamental borders in shady areas around homes.

(50) **orchid:** Many people build special greenhouses and raise orchids as a hobby. Orchids are very common in corsages.

(51) **rose:** Many people raise roses as a hobby, and there are organized clubs and shows. In the US, people often give roses for Valentine's Day and wedding anniversaries.

(52) **sunflower:** Sunflower seeds are a popular American snack.

(53) **crocus:** a bulb that is the first to bloom in the spring.

(54) **tulip:** originally from the Netherlands. The tulip is a sign of spring.

(55) **geranium:** a popular potted plant.

(56) **violet:** a popular house plant in the US.

(57) **poinsettia:** a tropical plant that is a popular indoor plant during the Christmas season.

(58) **jasmine:** Jasmine is a medicinal herb and an ingredient in teas.

(59) **hibiscus:** Hibiscus grows as both trees and shrubs and can tolerate dry and wet conditions.

ENERGY, CONSERVATION, AND THE ENVIRONMENT

LANGUAGE & CULTURE NOTES

> Words 1–8 represent major energy resources. The burning of fossil fuels—oil, natural gas, and coal—meets most current energy needs. Three concerns exist regarding the reliance on fossil fuels for energy. First, they are limited resources; second, their burning releases harmful contaminants; and third their burning contributes to global warming (18).

(1) oil/petroleum: provides energy for heating and transportation as well as chemicals that factories use in the manufacturing of a variety of products. The nickname for oil is *black gold.*

(2) (natural) gas: found in underground pockets that can be tapped. This allows the gas to be piped out and burned as a source of energy.

(3) coal: obtained by strip-mining or by deep shaft mining. Strip-mining is highly destructive to the land surface, and shaft mining is very dangerous for the miners.

(4) nuclear energy: energy from molecular action, nuclear fusion, or nuclear fission that involves uranium.

(5) solar energy: energy from the sun's rays that light-sensitive cells called solar panels capture. There are experimental cars that run on solar energy. Also, some homeowners use solar panels to heat their homes.

(6) hydroelectric power: energy that results from the force of running water.

(7) wind: Wind energy is generated by the use of windmills.

(8) geothermal energy: the heat energy available in the rocks, hot water, and steam in the earth's subsurface. Geothermal generation uses steam from geothermal sources to run turbines and generate electricity.

(9–12) These are means of conservation to protect the earth's resources and environment.

(9) recycle: Most U.S. cities and town now provide recycling services so that residents can return newspapers, glass jars and bottles, and metal cans to be recycled.

(10) save energy/conserve energy: There are many ways to conserve energy. For example, people can switch off lights, use efficient light bulbs, use energy efficient appliances, use appliances to their capacity (by washing full loads of laundry), and insulate heat and hot water pipes.

(11) save water/conserve water: There are many ways to conserve water. For example, you can turn faucets off frequently, take short showers, create outdoor yards and gardens that do not need a great deal of water, fix leaks in faucet and toilets, and use *low-flow* shower heads and toilets.

(12) carpool: In a carpool, people who commute to a common area share the work and cost of driving by riding with each other. In the United States, carpools are also common among families with children who move from activity to activity. Some communities dedicate highway lanes for the exclusive use of cars with more than one person to promote carpooling.

ENERGY, CONSERVATION, AND THE ENVIRONMENT
(continued)

LANGUAGE & CULTURE NOTES

> Words 13–18 are important environmental issues. Conservation of the earth's environment and resources is a major world concern. In addition to the examples in the vocabulary list, there is concern about global warming, which results from the destruction of oxygen-generating forests. This destruction depletes the ozone layer of the atmosphere and there allows higher levels of the sun's harmful ultraviolet rays to reach the earth.

(13) air pollution: *Smog* is a general term for air pollution. Contaminants are typically emissions from manufacturing plants or from cars. They harm both plant and animal life. Air pollution is related to the greenhouse effect, in which pollutants are trapped in the atmosphere.

(14) water pollution: Pollution is a concern in all bodies of water (lakes, ponds, rivers, and oceans). Polluting substances may be the by-products of manufacturing, leakage of raw materials like chemicals or oil, and/or animal waste.

(15) hazardous waste/toxic waste: any harmful by-product of a process such as radiation (17) and poisonous chemicals. Toxic wastes that factories and manufacturing plants improperly dispose of threaten underground water supplies that plants and animals use.

(16) acid rain: results from air pollution and occurs when rain falls with contaminating chemicals in smog. Acid rain threatens plant growth and development.

(17) radiation: a particular type of toxic waste—the rays of heat and/or light that are emitted during the molecular changes that create nuclear energy (4). Nuclear accidents such as Chernobyl in Russia and Three Mile Island in the United States are dangerous because of possible radiation leaks.

(18) global warming: an increase in the average temperature of the earth's atmosphere sufficient to cause climatic change. Most scientists believe that a rise in carbon dioxide levels from automobiles, power plants, and other emissions leads to global warming.

(1) **earthquake:** a shaking of the earth as a result of a sudden movement of rock beneath the Earth's surface. An earthquake occurs on a fault, which is a thin layer of crushed rock between two blocks of rock. A fault can range in length from a few centimeters to thousands of miles. The *San Andreas Fault* in California is 650 miles long and ten miles deep in places. Stresses in the Earth's outer layer push the sides of the fault together. Stress builds up and the rocks slip suddenly. This releases energy in waves that travel through the rock to cause the shaking that we feel during an earthquake. The National Earthquake Information Center locates about 12,000 to 14,000 earthquakes annually. That's about 35 a day.

(2) **hurricane:** the name for a tropical cyclone with sustained winds of 74 miles per hour or greater in the North Atlantic Ocean, Caribbean Sea, Gulf of Mexico, and in the eastern North Pacific Ocean. This same tropical cyclone is known as a typhoon (3) in the western Pacific and a cyclone in the Indian Ocean.

(3) **typhoon:** the name for a tropical cyclone with sustained winds of 74 miles per hour or greater in the western North Pacific Ocean. This same tropical cyclone is called a hurricane (2) in the eastern North Pacific and North Atlantic Ocean, and a cyclone in the Indian Ocean.

(4) **blizzard:** a winter storm with low temperatures, winds of 35 mile per hour or greater, and blowing snow that reduces visibility to 1/4 mile for more than 3 hours.

(5) **tornado:** the most destructive of all storms. A tornado is a violently rotating column of air that touches the ground. Tornadoes usually develop from severe thunderstorms and can produce winds

of 100 to 300 mph. Tornadoes can occur anywhere in the world given the right conditions, but are most frequent in the flat plains of the United States.

(6) **flood:** when bodies of water overflow onto dry land.

(7) **tsunami:** an ocean wave that results from an underwater earthquake or landslide, or volcanic eruption. It may travel unnoticed across the ocean for thousands of miles from its point of origin. It builds up to great heights in shallow water. It is also called a seismic sea wave, and incorrectly, a tidal wave.

(8) **drought:** an extended period of abnormally dry weather that causes problems such as crop damage and water supply shortages in the area. Droughts can occur in almost all climates.

(9) **forest fire:** an unplanned fire that is out of control in a wooded area. Sometimes forest managers will burn tracts of forest to maintain a natural balance in the forest, but forest fires are not planned fires.

(10) **wildfire:** an unplanned fire that is out of control. Contrast wild fire with a planned fire that burns within prepared lines under planned conditions.

(11) **landslide:** a mass of loose rocks or earth that slides down a slope or hillside.

(12) **mudslide:** a landslide (11) of mud that results from massive rains.

(13) **avalanche:** a slide of large amounts of snow and ice down a mountain. When enough snow accumulates on a steep mountain slope a small movement or loud noise can provoke an avalanche.

(14) **volcanic eruption:** the sudden violent explosion of steam and volcanic material from a live volcano.

LANGUAGE & CULTURE NOTES

1 driver's license: Each state in the United States issues its own driver's licenses so requirements for the license vary. Some states permit people as young as sixteen to have a license. Others wait until teenagers are eighteen.

2 social security card: The social security program is a national program of old-age pension payments that the U.S. government manages. Anyone who earns money must report these earnings to the government. The employer deducts a portion and pays it to the government. Each person receives a social security number at birth and will receive social security payments at age 62 for women and age 65 for men. The social security number frequently serves as an identification number in other situations, for example in bank transactions and credit reports.

3 student I.D. card: Most high schools, colleges, and universities provide student identification cards to their students to ensure security. Students must present these cards when they enter school buildings and request school services. These cards also give students access to special student discount rates.

4 employee I.D. badge: To ensure security, many companies require their workers to wear badges that identify who they are.

5 permanent resident card: also called a *green card* due to its original color many years ago. The permanent resident card allows residents to live and work in the United States indefinitely. After five years, the permanent resident can apply for citizenship via naturalization.

6 passport: an internationally recognized document that identifies the holder's nationality, name, birth date, and other personal information. Only a nation's citizens can hold the national passport. As a foreign traveler enters a country, he or she presents the passport at the immigration checkpoint. If the passport is not valid or it does not carry the required visa (see word 7), the country of entry will usually deport the traveler back to his or her home country.

7 visa: a permit to visit, live, or work in a foreign country. Some countries have visa agreements which automatically allow their citizens to visit each other's countries for up to six months as tourists. When countries do not share this agreement, the traveler must first apply for a visa and wait for it to be granted before he or she can travel in the foreign country. Some countries have no state-to-state relations, so it's difficult to acquire a visa to travel between such countries.

8 work permit: Unlike a permanent resident card, it's necessary to renew a work permit at frequent intervals. Foreign temporary residents must acquire a work permit to work legally in the United States.

9 proof of residence: When residents apply for local permits, the government agencies may request some proof of residence, which usually means a recent utility bill with the applicant's name and address.

10 birth certificate: a document that identifies the place and time of a child's birth and the names of the child's parents. In the United States, each state manages the documentation of its residents' births. The birth certificate is the principal form of personal identification upon which a person acquires all other identity cards (including a social security card).

The government of the United States has three parts. These parts are called the three branches of government—the legislative branch, the executive branch, and the judicial branch.

The legislative branch:

The legislative branch of the government is called the Congress. It makes the laws of the United States. The Congress has two parts: the senate and the house of representatives. Both houses of Congress work in the Capitol Building.

Senators work in the senate. There are one hundred senators. There are two senators from each state. A senator's term is six years.

Representatives work in the house of representatives. A representative is also called a congressperson (or congressman or congresswoman). There are 435 representatives. There are different numbers of representatives from different states. States with many people have more representatives. States with fewer people have fewer representatives. A representative's term is two years.

The executive branch:

The president of the United States is the head of the executive branch of the government. The executive branch enforces the laws of the United States. The president is the chief executive. The president is also Commander-in-Chief of the armed forces. The President signs bills into law. The president appoints members of the Cabinet. The Cabinet advises the president.

The president lives and works in the White House. The president's term is four years. The president can serve two terms. The vice-president works with the president. The American people elect the president and the vice-president at the same time. If the president dies, the vice-president becomes the new president.

A person must meet certain requirements to become president. The president must be a natural-born citizen of the United States. The president must be age 35 or older. The president must live in the United States for at least 14 years before becoming president.

The judicial branch:

The Supreme Court and other federal courts are the judicial branch of the government. The judicial branch explains the laws of the United States. The Supreme Court is the highest court in the country.

There are nine judges in the Supreme Court. They are called Supreme Court justices. They serve for life. The American people don't elect the Supreme Court justices. The president appoints them and the senate approves them. The head of the Supreme Court is the chief justice of the United States.

THE CONSTITUTION AND THE BILL OF RIGHTS

LANGUAGE & CULTURE NOTES

The Constitution:

The Constitution is the highest law in the United States. It is the supreme law of the land. Representatives from the original thirteen states wrote the Constitution in Philadelphia in 1787.

The Constitution established the form of government in the United States. It established the three branches of government—legislative, executive, and judicial. It described the powers of the national government and the powers of the state governments.

The Preamble to the Constitution:

The introduction to the Constitution is called the Preamble. It begins with three very famous words: We the People. The three words describe the power of the people in the government of the United States. The people give power to the government. The government serves the people.

*We the People of the United States,
in order to form a more perfect Union,
establish justice, ensure domestic tranquility,
provide for the common defense,
promote the general welfare,
and secure the blessing of liberty to
ourselves and our posterity,
do ordain and establish this Constitution for
the United States of America.*

The Bill of Rights:

The people of the United States can change the Constitution. These changes are called amendments. There are 27 amendments to the Constitution.

The first ten amendments are called the Bill of Rights. These ten amendments were added to the Constitution in 1791. The Bill of Rights gives rights and freedoms to all people in the United States.

The 1st Amendment guarantees freedom of speech, freedom of the press, freedom of religion, and freedom of assembly. Other amendments in the Bill of Rights guarantee the rights of people who are accused of crimes. They have the right to go to court, have a lawyer, and have a fair and quick trial. The Bill of Rights also protects people in their homes. The police need a special document from the courts before they can go into a person's home.

Other Amendments to the Constitution:

Other amendments to the Constitution are very important. The 13th Amendment ended slavery. The 14th Amendment made all Blacks citizens of the United States. The 15th Amendment gave African-Americans the right to vote.

The 16th Amendment established income taxes. The 19th Amendment gave women the right to vote. The 26th Amendment gave citizens eighteen years old and older the right to vote. Eighteen is now the minimum voting age in the United States.

LANGUAGE & CULTURE NOTES

The 1600s:

People from England first came to America in the 1600s. These people were called colonists. The original thirteen states were called colonies.

The first colony was in Jamestown, Virginia. Colonists from England came to Jamestown in 1607. They grew tobacco and traded with England.

In 1620 other colonists came to Plymouth, Massachusetts. These colonists were called Pilgrims. They came to America because they wanted religious freedom. They sailed to America on a ship named the *Mayflower*.

The 1700s:

The American colonists didn't want England to control the colonies. They didn't like English taxes, they didn't like English laws, and they didn't have any representatives in England. The colonists wanted to be independent.

The Revolutionary War began in 1775. In 1776 the colonists met at Independence Hall in Philadelphia. They decided to declare their independence. Thomas Jefferson wrote the Declaration of Independence. Representatives of all thirteen colonies signed it on July 4, 1776. The colonies won the Revolutionary War in 1783. They were free and independent states.

In 1787 representatives from the states met in Philadelphia and wrote the Constitution. In 1789 George Washington became the first president of the United States. He is known as "the father of our country." In 1791 the Bill of Rights was added to the Constitution.

The 1800s:

There was a war between the states in the North and the states in the South from 1861 to 1865. This was called the Civil War. The Northern states were also called the Union. The Southern states were also called the Confederacy. One main cause of the Civil War was slavery. Slaves were African people who were forced to come to the United States. They didn't have any rights or freedoms. Their owners bought and sold them like property.

The Southern states said they needed slaves to work on the farms. The Northern states wanted to end the system of slavery.

Another main cause of the Civil War was economics. The North had many new factories. The South had many big farms called plantations. The North and the South disagreed about taxes. These taxes helped Northern factories grow, but they made Southern farm products more expensive overseas.

Abraham Lincoln was president during the Civil War. He was the leader of the Northern states during the war. In 1863 he signed the Emancipation Proclamation. This document freed the slaves. In 1865, five days after the war ended, President Lincoln was assassinated.

The Industrial Revolution began in the 1790s and continued through the 1800s. During this time Americans invented the telephone, the typewriter, the phonograph, and the lightbulb. Railroads went across the country from the East coast to the West coast. Many factories opened, and people came from farms and immigrants came from other countries to work in the factories.

The 1900s:

World War I began in 1914. England, France, and Russia fought against Germany and Austria-Hungary. The United States entered World War I in 1917 and helped England, France, and Russia win the war. The war ended in 1918.

From 1929 to 1939 there was a Great Depression. The American economy collapsed. Factories closed, workers lost their jobs or their salaries were cut, many banks closed, and many people lost all their money in the stock market.

World War II began in 1939. The United States, England, Russia, and other countries (the Allied nations) fought against Germany, Italy, and Japan. The United States entered the war in 1941 when the Japanese bombed Pearl Harbor in Hawaii. The Allied nations won the war in 1945.

LANGUAGE & CULTURE NOTES

After World War II, the United States and the Soviet Union became major world powers. The two countries had very different political systems: the American system is democratic, and the Soviet system was communist. The United States and the Soviet Union did not fight each other directly. They competed with each other politically and economically. This was called the Cold War. The United States fought Communist forces in two wars. From 1950 to 1953, the United States fought in the Korean War. From 1964 to 1973, it fought in the Vietnam War. In 1991 the United States fought against Iraq in the Persian Gulf War, also called Operation Desert Storm.

During the 1950s and 1960s, the civil rights movement worked to end discrimination against Blacks in the United States. It worked for equal rights for all Americans. The Reverend Martin Luther King, Jr. was the most famous leader of the civil rights movement. In 1963 he led hundreds of thousands of people in a demonstration to support new civil rights laws. It was called the March on Washington. In 1968 Martin Luther King, Jr. was shot and killed. The United States remembers him in a national holiday on the third Monday in January every year.

September 11, 2001:

On the morning of September 11, 2001, terrorists hijacked four airplanes from Boston, New Jersey, and the Washington, D.C. area. They crashed two planes into the twin towers of the World Trade Center in New York City. Both towers of the World Trade Center collapsed. One plane crashed into the Pentagon—the headquarters of the U.S. armed forces, in Arlington, Virginia. One plane crashed in Pennsylvania. Thousands of people died in the buildings and on the airplanes. People from more than eighty different countries died in the attacks. Most of the victims were Americans.

The U.S. government asked other nations to join in a fight against terrorism around the world. President George W. Bush ordered air attacks against Afghanistan and then sent troops there to fight against the terrorist organization responsible for the attacks on the United States.

HOLIDAYS

LANGUAGE & CULTURE NOTES

(1) **New Year's Day:** January 1. On this national holiday, the custom is to visit with friends and family and eat a large meal together. Many people make New Year's resolutions on January 1 to start good new habits and leave behind bad old habits.

(2) **Martin Luther King, Jr. Day:** falls on the Monday closest to Martin Luther King's birthday (January 15). Martin Luther King, Jr. (1929–1968) was an extraordinary leader in the civil rights movement.

(3) **Valentine's Day:** February 14. On this holiday, children exchange valentine cards with one another in school, and romantic partners send one another red roses, chocolates, and love poetry. The traditional colors of this day are red, pink, and white.

(4) **Memorial Day:** falls on the last Monday of May. This national holiday is a day of remembrance for military personnel who died in the service of their country.

(5) **Independence Day:** July 4th. This national holiday commemorates the day the colonists declared independence from England in 1776. Towns and cities celebrate this day with parades and firework displays at night. The traditional colors of this holiday are the colors of the United States flag—red, white, and blue.

(6) **Halloween:** October 31. On this holiday, children dress up in costumes and knock on their neighbors' doors and say "Trick or treat!" In the old days, if their neighbors gave them treats (candy or sweets), they would smile and leave, but if the neighbors didn't give the children candy, the children would play tricks on them. Nowadays, most children do not play tricks on their neighbors.

(7) **Veterans Day:** November 11. This national holiday commemorates the people who served honorably in the military—in wartime or peacetime.

(8) **Thanksgiving:** falls on the fourth Thursday of November. This national holiday commemorates the legendary meal the Pilgrims and Native Americans shared after they survived their first full year in the new colony. The traditional food for this holiday is turkey, potatoes, sweet potatoes, and squash.

(9) **Christmas:** December 25. This national holiday is a Christian holiday that celebrates the birth of Jesus. Christians bring a pine tree inside their home and decorate it as a symbol of everlasting life. People put gifts, especially for children, under the tree.

(10) **Ramadan:** Ramadan is the ninth month of the Muslim calendar. It is a time of worship and contemplation. For the whole month, Muslims do not eat or drink during the daylight hours. At the end of the day their fast is broken with prayer and a meal called the *iftar*.

(11) **Kwanzaa:** December 26 to January 1. Kwanzaa is an African American and Pan-African cultural holiday which celebrates family, community, and culture. It started in 1966 in an African American effort to connect to African cultural identity and provide a focal point for the gathering of African peoples.

(12) **Hanukkah:** This is a Jewish festival which commemorates the victory of the Maccabees (led by Judah) over the Syrians in a revolt that took place around 165 BC. The most important Hanukkah ritual is the candle lighting in a special candleholder called a *menorah*. Each night, one more candle is added.

(A) **be arrested:** When a police officer arrests a person, the officer puts on handcuffs and reads the person the Miranda rights (see word 4).

(B) **be booked at the police station:** The officer takes the arrested person to the police station where the station officer files the arrested person's personal information. The identification includes fingerprints (5) and a mug shot/police photo (6).

(C) **hire a lawyer/hire an attorney:** The arrested person has a right to a lawyer/attorney (7) during the police interrogation. The person may hire a personal lawyer or accept one that the court appoints. *Attorney* and *lawyer* both refer to the legal counsel a person hires.

(D) **appear in court:** Before a court trial, there is a hearing to determine whether a trial is necessary. The suspect must appear in court for the hearing and possible subsequent trial. If the suspect is held in custody at the local jail, the police will bring the suspect to court that day. For less serious crimes, the suspect may be free on bail (after he or she pays a deposit) and lives at home until the court hearing and possible trial.

(E) **stand trial:** When a suspect is accused of a crime, he or she stands trial and appears in court during the trial. The suspect is the defendant (9) and the accuser is the prosecutor.

(F) **be acquitted:** When the jury or judge delivers a not-guilty verdict, the defendant is acquitted of the crime.

(G) **be convicted:** When the jury or judge delivers a guilty verdict, the defendant is convicted of the crime. The defendant is now called a *convict*.

(H) **be sentenced:** The convict is sentenced to punishment which usually is years in prison, but can occasionally be community service. One of the most severe sentences possible is "sentenced for life with no parole" which mean the convicted must spend the rest of his or her life in prison and never get a chance to leave on good behavior.

(I) **go to jail/prison:** Jails are local places of confinement where suspects stay while on trial or where accused criminals serve short terms. Prisons are large compounds outside of cities and towns where convicts serve long terms.

(J) **be released:** After completion of the prison term, and maybe getting time off for good behavior, the prisoner is released. Most released prisoners have to be in touch with their parole officers for the first period after they leave jail.

(1) **suspect:** the person accused of the crime. In most legal systems around the world, the suspect is innocent until proven guilty in a trial.

(2) **police officer:** also known informally as a *cop* (constable on patrol).

(3) **handcuffs:** metal bracelets that keep the suspect's hands behind the back. *Handcuff* is also a verb, for example: The police officer *handcuffed* the suspect.

(4) **Miranda rights:** These are the legal rights the suspect has. The police officer says them during the arrest. "You have the right to remain silent. If you give up the right to remain silent, anything you say can and will be used against you in a court of law. You have the right to an attorney. If you desire an attorney and cannot afford one, an attorney will be obtained for you before police questioning."

(8) **judge:** the public official authorized to decide questions bought before a court of justice. A judge has a degree in law.

(10) **bail:** The money deposit the suspect pays to be temporarily released from custody until the trial. If the defendant *jumps bail* and leaves town, the police keep that money deposit and pursue the defendant.

THE LEGAL SYSTEM
(continued)

LANGUAGE & CULTURE NOTES

11 courtroom: the place where a trial takes place.

12 prosecuting attorney: the attorney who tries to prove the defendant is guilty. Sometimes the prosecuting attorney represents the state and sometimes represents a person or a group of people.

13 witness: a person that the defense or prosecution calls to testify who saw the crime or has some information about the crime.

14 court reporter: the person who records everything people said in the trial.

15 defense attorney: the attorney who tries to prove the defendant is not guilty.

16 evidence: information or material that proves something. A gun is piece of evidence in a murder trial.

17 bailiff: a court attendant who keeps order in the courtroom and has custody of the jury.

18 jury: a body of citizens assembled to judge the truth according to the evidence presented in a trial. The courts randomly select citizens to serve their *jury duty*. It is a required civic duty and is not easily avoided. Jurors receive some financial compensation for the time they spend during the trial.

19 verdict / 20 innocent/not guilty / 21 guilty / 22 sentence / 23 fine: The verdict is the decision by the jury or judge as to the guilt of the defendant. If the verdict is innocent, the defendant is released (J). If the verdict is guilty, the defendant receives a fine or a sentence (H).

24 prison guard: security personnel who works inside a prison.

25 convict/prisoner/inmate: the person who is convicted is called a convict. A person who serves a term in prison is a prisoner, inmate, or convict. When a person has finished the sentence and is released from prison, the person is called an ex-convict.

LANGUAGE & CULTURE NOTES

Citizens' Rights and Responsibilities:

The most important right U.S. citizens have is the right to vote. Citizens can vote for federal, state, and local officials. Every four years, in November, citizens can vote for the president and vice-president of the United States.

Citizens also have responsibilities. They should vote, obey the laws, pay taxes, serve on a jury, and be active in their communities. Citizens should know what is happening in their city, in their state, and in the nation. They should follow the news on TV, on the radio, or in the newspaper.

The Path to Citizenship:

The process of becoming a United States citizen is called the naturalization process. For current information about applying for citizenship, you can go to the government's website at http://uscis.gov. Applicants must learn about U.S. government and history and take a citizenship test. They have an interview with an officer of the Bureau of Citizenship and Immigration Services. (This was previously called the INS—Immigration and Naturalization Service.) After the application is approved, new citizens attend a naturalization ceremony and recite the Oath of Allegiance to the United States.

(Chorus)
What's your name?
Where do you live?
What's your address?
I'd like to say, "Hello. How do you do?"
Oh-oh-oh-oh!
I'd like to introduce myself to you.

If I want to talk to you on the telephone,
what number should I call?
I could ask the operator for "Information, please!"
But I don't know your name at all!

Chorus (2x)

Let's take a walk on over to my house
and meet my family.
I live in this apartment with
my father and mother,
my sister and brother,
my niece and nephew . . .
There are more, let me tell you!
My uncle and aunt.
I know you think we can't all fit,
but we're a close family, you see.

What's your name? (What's your name?)
Where do you live? (Where do you live?)
What's your address?
I'd like to say, "Hello. How do you do?"
Oh-oh-oh-oh!
I'd like to introduce myself to you.
I'd like to say, "Hello. How do you do?"

I'd like to introduce myself to you.

What's your _ _ _ _ ?
Where do you _ _ _ _ ?
What's your _ _ _ _ _ _ _ ?
I'd like to say, " _ _ _ _ _ . How do you do?"
Oh-oh-oh-oh!
I'd like to introduce myself to _ _ _ .

> If I want to talk to you on the _ _ _ _ _ _ _ _ _ ,
> what _ _ _ _ _ _ should I call?
> I could ask the _ _ _ _ _ _ _ _ for "Information, please!"
> But I don't know your _ _ _ _ at all!

What's _ _ _ _ name?
Where do _ _ _ live?
What's your _ _ _ _ _ _ _ ?
I'd like to say, "Hello. _ _ _ do you do?"
Oh-oh-oh-oh!
I'd like to _ _ _ _ _ _ _ _ myself to you.

> Let's take a walk on over to my _ _ _ _ _
> and meet my _ _ _ _ _ _ .
> I live in this _ _ _ _ _ _ _ _ with
> my father and _ _ _ _ _ _ ,
> my sister and _ _ _ _ _ _ _ ,
> my niece and _ _ _ _ _ _ . . .
> There are more, let me tell you!
> My uncle and _ _ _ _ .
> I know you think we can't all fit,
> but we're a close _ _ _ _ _ _ , you see.

What's your _ _ _ _ ?
_ _ _ _ _ do you live?
What's your _ _ _ _ _ _ _ ?
I'd like to say, "Hello. How _ _ you do?"
Oh-oh-oh-oh!
I'd like to _ _ _ _ _ _ _ _ myself to you.
I'd like to say, "Hello. How do you do?"

I'd like to introduce myself to _ _ _ .

It's another day . . . woh – woh . . . another day!
It's time to work! No time for play!
It's another day!

"Good morning! It's time to get up!"
The sun shines in my eyes.
It's time to brush my teeth, wash my face,
stack the breakfast dishes high!

What clothes should I be wearing?
That's when I turn on the radio.
I listen to what the weatherman says,
and it's off to work I go!

It's another day . . . woh – woh . . . another day!
It's time to work! No time for play!
It's another day!

Another day . . . woh – woh . . . another day!
When one day ends, one begins again.
It's another day!

After work I pick up dinner
at the local grocery store.
Then I go home to my family.
They greet me at the door.

We all sit down for dinner.
Then we read or watch TV.
We take our baths and say goodnight,
all sleeping peacefully.

It's another day . . . woh – woh . . . another day!
It's time to work! No time for play!
It's another day!

Another day . . . woh – woh . . . another day!
When one day ends, one begins again.
It's another day!
Another day!

It's another day . . . woh – woh . . . another _ _ _ !
It's time to work! No time for _ _ _ _ !
It's another day!

"Good morning! It's time to _ _ _ _ _!"
The _ _ _ shines in my eyes.
It's time to brush my _ _ _ _ _ , wash my _ _ _ _ ,
stack the _ _ _ _ _ _ _ _ dishes high!

What _ _ _ _ _ _ _ should I be wearing?
That's when I turn on the _ _ _ _ _ .
I _ _ _ _ _ _ to what the weatherman says,
and it's off to _ _ _ _ I go!

It's another day . . . woh – woh . . . another _ _ _ !
It's time to _ _ _ _ ! No time for play!
It's another day!

Another day . . . woh – woh . . . another _ _ _ !
When one day ends, one _ _ _ _ _ _ again.
It's another day!

After work I pick up _ _ _ _ _ _
at the local grocery _ _ _ _ _ .
Then I go _ _ _ _ to my family.
They greet me at the _ _ _ _ .

We all sit down for _ _ _ _ _ _ .
Then we _ _ _ _ or watch TV.
We take our _ _ _ _ _ and say goodnight,
all _ _ _ _ _ _ _ _ peacefully.

It's another day . . . woh – woh . . . _ _ _ _ _ _ _ day!
It's _ _ _ _ to work! No time for _ _ _ _ !
It's another day!

Another day . . . woh – woh . . . another day!
When one day _ _ _ _ , one begins again.
It's another _ _ _ !
Another day!

Any day, any week,
any month, any year,
I'm gonna wait right here
to be with you.

In the spring, in the summer,
in the winter, or the fall.
Just call. I'm waiting here
to be with you.

I'm gonna wait from
January, February,
March, April, May,
June and July,
August, September,
October and November,
and all of December.
I'm gonna wait . . .

It's one o'clock, a quarter after.
It's half past one, a quarter to two.
And I'm gonna wait right here
to be with you.

Any day, any week,
any month, any year,
I'm gonna wait right here
to be with you.

Yes, I'm gonna wait right here
to be with you.

Any day, any _ _ _ _ ,
any month, any _ _ _ _ ,
I'm gonna wait right here
to be with _ _ _ .

In the spring, in the _ _ _ _ _ _ ,
in the winter, or the _ _ _ _ .
Just call. I'm waiting here
to _ _ with you.

I'm gonna wait from
January, _ _ _ _ _ _ _ _ ,
March, _ _ _ _ _ , May,
June and _ _ _ _ ,
August, _ _ _ _ _ _ _ _ _ ,
October and _ _ _ _ _ _ _ _ ,
and all of _ _ _ _ _ _ _ _ .
I'm gonna wait . . .

It's _ _ _ o'clock, a quarter after.
It's half past one, a quarter to _ _ _ .
And I'm gonna wait right _ _ _ _
to be with _ _ _ .

Any _ _ _ , any week,
any _ _ _ _ _ , any year,
I'm gonna _ _ _ _ right here
to be _ _ _ _ you.

Yes, I'm gonna wait right _ _ _ _
to be with _ _ _ .

In my house, in my house
there's a living room with a fireplace.
There's a cozy couch next to a tall bookcase
in my house, in my house.

In my house, in my house
there's a dining room where everybody eats.
There's a table with a flower centerpiece
in my house, in my house.

    It's so nice to come home,
    wherever home may be.
    A place that feels safe and warm
    for you and me, and a family.

In my house, in my house
there's a kitchen with an oven and a sink,
a refrigerator full of things to eat and drink
in my house, in my house.

In my house, in my house
there's a baby's room we call the nursery.
There's a bathroom with a mirror above the vanity
in my house, in my house.

    It's so nice to come home,
    wherever home may be.
    A place that feels safe and warm
    for you and me, and a family.

In my house, in my house
there's a bedroom with a giant king-size bed
with two fluffy pillows and a quilted spread
in my house, in my house.

Oh! In my house, in my house!
Oh! In my house, in my house!

In my house, in my _ _ _ _ _
there's a _ _ _ _ _ _ _ _ _ _ with a fireplace.
There's a cozy _ _ _ _ _ next to a tall bookcase
in my house, in my house.

In _ _ house, in _ _ house
there's a _ _ _ _ _ _ _ _ _ _ where everybody eats.
There's a _ _ _ _ _ with a flower centerpiece
in my house, in my house.

It's so nice to come _ _ _ _ ,
wherever home may be.
A place that feels safe and warm
For _ _ _ and _ _ , and a family.

In my house, in my house
there's a _ _ _ _ _ _ _ with an oven and a _ _ _ _ ,
a _ _ _ _ _ _ _ _ _ _ _ _ full of things to eat and drink
in my house, in my house.

In my house, in my house
there's a baby's room we call the _ _ _ _ _ _ _ .
There's a _ _ _ _ _ _ _ _ with a mirror above the vanity
in my house, in my house.

It's so _ _ _ _ to come home,
wherever _ _ _ _ may be.
A place that feels safe and warm
for you and me, and a _ _ _ _ _ _ .

In my house, in my house
there's a _ _ _ _ _ _ _ with a giant king-size bed
with two fluffy _ _ _ _ _ _ _ and a quilted spread
in my house, in my house.

Oh! In my house, in my house!
Oh! In my house, in my house!

I love the city,
the sounds and the lights,
the hustle and bustle from morning til night.
So many people and places to see!
It's where I want to be!
The city life is for me!

    Hotels and motels
    and skyscrapers tall!
    Wonderful restaurants
    and big shopping malls!
    Museums and theaters!
    There's so much to do!
    Every day's an adventure that's new!

I love the city,
the sounds and the lights,
the hustle and bustle from morning til night.
So many people and places to see!
It's where I want to be!
The city life is for me!

    Taxis and buses
    move people around.
    There's even a subway
    that runs underground.
    There's a park, and a zoo,
    a library, too!
    It's a place to make dreams come true!

Oh! I love the city,
the sounds and the lights,
the hustle and bustle from morning til night.
So many people and places to see!
It's where I want to be!
The city life is for me!

I love the city,
the sounds and the lights.
The city life is for me!

I love the _ _ _ _ ,
the sounds and the _ _ _ _ _ _ ,
the hustle and bustle from morning til _ _ _ _ _ .
So many people and _ _ _ _ _ _ to see!
It's where I want to be!
The _ _ _ _ life is for me!

Hotels and _ _ _ _ _ _
and skyscrapers tall!
Wonderful _ _ _ _ _ _ _ _ _ _
and big _ _ _ _ _ _ _ _ _ _ _ _ _ !
Museums and _ _ _ _ _ _ _ _ !
There's so much to do!
Every day's an adventure that's new!

I _ _ _ _ the city,
the _ _ _ _ _ _ and the lights,
the hustle and bustle from _ _ _ _ _ _ _ til night.
So many _ _ _ _ _ _ and places to see!
It's where I want to be!
The city life is for _ _ !

Taxis and _ _ _ _ _
move people around.
There's even a _ _ _ _ _ _
that runs underground.
There's a _ _ _ _ , and a zoo,
a _ _ _ _ _ _ _ , too!
It's a place to make dreams come true!

Oh! I love the _ _ _ _ ,
the sounds _ _ _ the lights,
the hustle and bustle from morning til _ _ _ _ _ .
So many people and places to _ _ _ !
It's where I want to _ _ !
The _ _ _ _ life is for me!

(Chorus)
We're opposites, opposites. We're like night and day.
We're completely different in everything we do and say.
We're opposites, opposites. But we get along.
We laugh about our differences when we sing our "Opposites" song.

My hair is curly.
My hair is straight.
I'm always early.
I'm always late.
My car is new.
My car is old.
I'm always hot.
I'm always cold.

My apartment's big.
My apartment's small.
My brother's short.
My brother's tall.
I'm very messy.
I'm very neat.
I have big hands.
I have big feet.

Chorus

I live in a place that's very new.
I live in a place that's very old.
I like the weather when it's hot.
I like the weather when it's cold.
My favorite season is the spring.
My favorite season is the fall.
When I was young I was very short.
When I was young I was very tall.

I take a shower every morning.
I take a bath every night.
When I dress up I like to wear black.
When I dress up I like to wear white.
When you say "No," I say "Yes."
When you say "Yes," I say "No."
When you drive your car, you drive too fast.
When you drive your car, you drive too slow.

Chorus

We're opposites, opposites. We're like night and _ _ _ .
We're completely different in everything we do and _ _ _ .
We're opposites, opposites. But we get along.
We laugh about our differences when we sing our "Opposites" song.

My hair is curly.
My hair is _ _ _ _ _ _ _ _ .
I'm always early.
I'm always _ _ _ _ .
My car is new.
My car is _ _ _ .
I'm always hot.
I'm always _ _ _ _ .

My apartment's big.
My apartment's _ _ _ _ _ .
My brother's short.
My brother's _ _ _ _ .
I'm very messy.
I'm very _ _ _ _ .
I have big hands.
I have big _ _ _ _ .

I live in a place that's very new.
I live in a place that's very _ _ _ .
I like the weather when it's hot.
I like the weather when it's _ _ _ _ .
My favorite season is the spring.
My favorite season is the _ _ _ _ .
When I was young I was very short.
When I was young I was very _ _ _ _ .

I take a shower every morning.
I take a bath every _ _ _ _ _ _ .
When I dress up I like to wear black.
When I dress up I like to wear _ _ _ _ _ .
When you say "No," I say "Yes."
When you say "Yes," I say " _ _ ."
When you drive your car, you drive too fast.
When you drive your car, you drive too _ _ _ _ .

(Chorus)
Her name is Supermarket Sally.
She works the checkout line,
ringing up the groceries
every day til nine.
She takes my discount coupons.
I save money every time.
Her name is Supermarket Sally.
She's a friend of mine.

I see her every Monday.
That's the day I shop.
My list is always very long.
My cart's filled to the top.

Sally sees me coming.
She stops and waves hello,
standing at her register.
That's where I always go – o – o!

Chorus

She weighs each fruit and vegetable
on her supermarket scale.
She enters in the price per pound.
She knows just what's on sale.

She knows where every item is
by section and by aisle.
So if you have a question,
just look for Sally's smile!

Chorus

Her name is Supermarket Sally.
She works the checkout line.
Supermarket Sally!
She's a friend of mine!

Her _ _ _ _ is Supermarket Sally.
She works the _ _ _ _ _ _ _ _ line,
ringing up the _ _ _ _ _ _ _ _ _
every day til nine.
She takes my discount _ _ _ _ _ _ _ .
I save _ _ _ _ _ every time.
Her name is Supermarket Sally.
She's a friend of mine.

I see her every Monday.
That's the day I _ _ _ _ .
My _ _ _ _ is always very long.
My cart's filled to the top.

Sally sees me coming.
She stops and waves _ _ _ _ _ ,
standing at her _ _ _ _ _ _ _ _ .
That's where I always go – o – o!

Her name is _ _ _ _ _ _ _ _ _ _ _ Sally.
She works the checkout _ _ _ _ ,
ringing up the _ _ _ _ _ _ _ _
every _ _ _ til nine.
She takes my _ _ _ _ _ _ _ _ coupons .
I _ _ _ _ money every time.
Her name is Supermarket Sally.
She's a friend of mine.

She weighs each _ _ _ _ _ and vegetable
on her supermarket _ _ _ _ _ .
She enters in the price per _ _ _ _ _ .
She knows just what's on _ _ _ _ .

She knows where every item is
by _ _ _ _ _ _ _ and by _ _ _ _ _ .
So if you have a question,
just look for Sally's smile!

(Chorus)
Fashion! Fashion!
It's in the way we look
and the clothes we wear!
Fashion! Oh, fashion!
It's in our style of dress
and the way we comb our hair!
It's fashion! Fashion!

A three-piece suit!
A jacket and tie!
Let's add a hat!
Let's accessorize!
Shoes and sneakers!
There's so much to buy!
A sweatshirt, a leotard!
It's time to exercise!

Chorus

A polo shirt!
An evening gown!
Go casual or formal
for a night on the town!
Dressing up
or dressing down!
An outfit for the way you feel,
for walking around!

Chorus (2x)

It's fashion! Fashion!
It's fashion! Fashion!
It's fashion! Fashion!
It's fashion!

Fashion! Fashion!
It's in the way we look
and the _ _ _ _ _ _ _ we wear!
Fashion! Oh, fashion!
It's in our style of dress
and the way we _ _ _ _ our hair!
It's fashion! Fashion!

A three-piece _ _ _ _!
A jacket and _ _ _!
Let's add a _ _ _!
Let's accessorize!
Shoes and _ _ _ _ _ _ _ _!
There's so much to buy!
A _ _ _ _ _ _ _ _ _ _, a leotard!
It's time to exercise!

Fashion! Fashion!
It's in the way we _ _ _ _
and the clothes we _ _ _ _!
Fashion! Oh, fashion!
It's in our style of dress
and the way we comb our _ _ _ _!
It's fashion! Fashion!

A polo _ _ _ _ _!
An evening _ _ _ _!
Go casual or formal
for a night on the _ _ _ _!
Dressing up
or _ _ _ _ _ _ _ _ down!
An outfit for the way you feel,
for walking around!

Let's go to Wilson's Department Store.

Let's take a look at the store directory.
Let's plan our shopping trip today.
The 1st floor has men's and women's clothing
with discounts and sale prices every day.

The 2nd floor has toys and children's clothing,
housewares, furniture, and lots of TVs.
I think we're getting close to the perfume counter.
It smells very nice, but it makes me sneeze!

We'll ride the escalator up!
We'll take the elevator down, down, down!

>   *(Chorus)*
>   Let's go to Wilson's Department Store.
>   They have wonderful products on every floor.
>   They have everything we need and so much more
>   at Wilson's Department Store.
>   Wilson's Department Store.

The 3rd floor is full of household appliances:
washers and dryers, and microwaves, too.
If you're buying presents for friends or family,
the gift wrap counter will wrap them for you.

Return or exchange things at customer service.
It's on the 4th floor. You'll need your receipt.
The ladies' and men's rooms are next to the snack bar.
I'm getting hungry. Let's get something to eat!

We'll ride the escalator up!
We'll take the elevator down, down, down!

>   *Chorus*

There's a store where they will always greet you
with "May I help you" and "It's nice to meet you."
We all know there's just one place to go . . . oh . . . oh . . .

>   *Chorus*

Let's go to Wilson's Department Store.

Let's take a look at the store directory.
Let's plan our _ _ _ _ _ _ _ _ trip today.
The 1st floor has men's and _ _ _ _ _ ' _ clothing
with discounts and sale prices every day.

The 2nd _ _ _ _ _ has toys and children's clothing,
housewares, furniture, and lots of TVs.
I think we're getting close to the perfume _ _ _ _ _ _ _ .
It smells very nice, but it makes me _ _ _ _ _ _ !

We'll ride the escalator up!
We'll take the elevator _ _ _ _ , _ _ _ _ , _ _ _ _ !

Let's go to Wilson's Department Store.
They have wonderful products on every _ _ _ _ _ .
They have everything we need and so much _ _ _ _
at Wilson's Department Store.
Wilson's Department _ _ _ _ _ .

The 3rd floor is full of household appliances:
washers and _ _ _ _ _ _ , and microwaves, too.
If you're buying presents for friends or family,
the _ _ _ _ _ _ _ _ counter will wrap them for you.

Return or exchange things at customer _ _ _ _ _ _ _ .
It's on the 4th floor. You'll need your _ _ _ _ _ _ _ .
The ladies' and men's _ _ _ _ _ are next to the snack bar.
I'm getting hungry. Let's get something to _ _ _ !

We'll ride the escalator _ _ !
We'll take the _ _ _ _ _ _ _ _ down, down, down!

There's a store where they will always greet you
with "May I _ _ _ _ you" and "It's nice to _ _ _ _ you."
We all know there's just one place to go . . . oh . . . oh . . .

It's the first day of the month.
All my household bills are due:
the gas, electric, and telephone bills,
the rent for the landlord, too.
I can write a check
or I can pay online.
One thing I've learned about paying
   bills
is to always pay on time.

   (Chorus)
   I've got bills to pay. (Bills to pay.)
   I've got bills to pay. (Bills to pay.)
   I've got so many bills to pay.
   They come in the mail every day.
   I've got bills, bills, bills to pay.
   I've got bills, bills, bills to pay.

I go to the A.T.M.
when I need to get some cash.
I insert my card and enter my PIN,
and the money comes out fast.
Every week I deposit my paycheck
and withdraw just a small amount.
I try to save as much as I can
so there's money in my account.
'Cause . . .

   Chorus

I need to buy a car
to drive to work from home.
So I went to the bank and filled out
an application for a loan.
The bank officer called this morning.
She said, "Buy used, not new.
Your credit card balance is very high.
A big car payment's not for you."

   'Cause you've got bills to pay. (Bills to
     pay.)
   You've got bills to pay.
     (Bills to pay.)
   I've got so many bills to pay.
   They come in the mail every day.
   I've got bills, bills, bills to pay.
   I've got so many bills to pay.
   I wish they would go away!
   I've got bills, bills, bills to pay.

(Oh, no! I forgot to pay my electric bill
  again!)

It's the first day of the month.
All my household bills are _ _ _ :
the gas, electric, and _ _ _ _ _ _ _ _
　　bills,
the _ _ _ _ for the landlord, too.
I can write a _ _ _ _ _
or I can _ _ _ online.
One thing I've learned about paying
　　bills
is to always pay _ _ _ _ _ _ .

　　I've got bills to pay. (Bills to pay.)
　　I've got bills to pay. (Bills to pay.)
　　I've got so many bills to pay.
　　They come in the _ _ _ _ every
　　　　day.
　　I've got bills, bills, bills to pay.
　　I've got bills, bills, bills to pay.

I go to the A.T.M.
when I need to get some _ _ _ _ .
I insert my _ _ _ _ and enter
　　my _ _ _ ,
and the _ _ _ _ _ comes out fast.
Every week I _ _ _ _ _ _ _ my
　　paycheck
and withdraw just a small amount.
I try to save as much as I can
so there's money in my _ _ _ _ _ _ _ .
'Cause I've got . . .

I need to buy a car
to drive to _ _ _ _ from home.
So I went to the _ _ _ _ and filled out
an application for a _ _ _ _ .
The bank officer called this morning.
She said, "Buy used, not new.
Your credit card _ _ _ _ _ _ _ is very high.
A big car payment's not for you."

　　'Cause you've got _ _ _ _ _ to pay.
　　　　(Bills to pay.)
　　You've got bills to _ _ _ . (Bills to pay.)
　　I've got so many bills to pay.
　　They come in the _ _ _ _ every day.
　　I've got bills, bills, bills to pay.
　　I've got so many bills to pay.
　　I wish they would go _ _ _ _ !
　　I've got bills, bills, bills to pay.

(Oh, no! I forgot to _ _ _ my electric
　　_ _ _ _ again!)

(Okay, everybody! Are you ready?
Here we go!
One! Two! Three! Four!)

Let's warm up, bend and stretch!
Let your hands reach for the sky!
Now pick up the pace and run in place!
Feel your heartbeat start to rise!

Working up a sweat, step by step!
Get ready! Get set!

Everybody, power up! Energize!
Everybody, power up . . . up . . . up!
It's time to exercise!
Everybody, power up! Energize!
Everybody, power up . . . up . . . up!
It's fun to exercise!
Everybody, power up!

(Here we go!
One! Two! Three! Four!)

Sit-ups, push-ups, deep knee bends!
Down to the floor, then up again!
Let's bounce the basketball around!
Catch it! Kick it! Throw it to a friend!

Working up a sweat, step by step!
Get ready! Get set!

Everybody, power up! Energize!
Everybody, power up . . . up . . . up!
It's time to exercise!
Everybody, power up! Energize!
Everybody, power up . . . up . . . up!
It's fun to exercise!

Everybody, power up!
Power up!

(Okay, everybody! Are you ready?
Here we go!
One! _ _ _! Three! _ _ _ _!)

Let's warm up, _ _ _ _ and stretch!
Let your hands _ _ _ _ _ for the sky!
Now pick up the pace and _ _ _ in place!
Feel your heartbeat start to rise!

Working up a sweat, step by _ _ _ _!
Get ready! Get set!

    Everybody, power up! Energize!
    Everybody, power up . . . up . . . up!
    It's time to _ _ _ _ _ _ _ _!
    Everybody, power up! Energize!
    Everybody, power up . . . up . . . up!
    It's _ _ _ to exercise!
    Everybody, power up!

(Here we go!
_ _ _! Two! _ _ _ _ _! Four!)

Sit-ups, _ _ _ _ - _ _ _, deep knee bends!
_ _ _ _ to the floor, then _ _ again!
Let's _ _ _ _ _ _ the basketball around!
_ _ _ _ _ it! _ _ _ _ it! _ _ _ _ _ it to a friend!

Working up a sweat, step by step!
Get ready! Get set!

    Everybody, power _ _! Energize!
    Everybody, power up . . . up . . . up!
    It's _ _ _ _ to exercise!
    Everybody, power up! Energize!
    Everybody, power up . . . up . . . up!
    It's fun to _ _ _ _ _ _ _ _!

    Everybody, power up!
    Power up!

(Chorus)
What are you doing after school?
What are you doing after school?
Tell me, what are you doing after school?
What are you doing after school?

Every day I hear the announcements
for teams and clubs that are looking for students.
There's an extracurricular activity
that's right for you and right for me.
There's a high school paper and a yearbook to write.
There's a dance in the lunchroom next Friday night.
I'd like to try out for our high school play,
but I can't 'cause I work four hours a day.

Chorus

In the gym some kids are playing basketball.
On the field the team is playing football.
There's a book club, a chess club, a track, and a pool.
We've got a student council that governs our school.
Every day I have to do my homework.
Twice a week I do some volunteer work.
Your grades are important on your college application,
but they're also looking for your school participation.

Chorus (2x)

What are you doing after _ _ _ _ _ _ ?
What are you _ _ _ _ _ after school?
Tell me, what are you doing _ _ _ _ _ school?
_ _ _ _ are you doing after school?

Every day I hear the announcements
for _ _ _ _ _ and _ _ _ _ _ that are looking for students.
There's an extracurricular _ _ _ _ _ _ _ _ _
that's right for you and right for me.
There's a high school _ _ _ _ _ and a _ _ _ _ _ _ _ _ _ to write.
There's a dance in the _ _ _ _ _ _ _ _ _ next Friday night.
I'd like to try out for our high school _ _ _ _ ,
but I can't 'cause I _ _ _ _ four hours a day.

In the _ _ _ some kids are _ _ _ _ _ _ _ basketball.
On the _ _ _ _ _ the team is playing football.
There's a _ _ _ _ club, a _ _ _ _ _ club, a _ _ _ _ _ _ , and a _ _ _ _ .
We've got a _ _ _ _ _ _ _ council that governs our school.
Every day I have to do my _ _ _ _ _ _ _ _ .
Twice a week I do some volunteer _ _ _ _ .
Your grades are important on your _ _ _ _ _ _ _ application,
but they're also looking for your _ _ _ _ _ _ participation.

What are you doing after _ _ _ _ _ _ ?
What are _ _ _ doing after school?
Tell me, what _ _ _ you doing after school?
_ _ _ _ are you doing after school?

(Chorus)
Working! Working!
Everybody's working!
Working! Working!
Working for a living!
Working! Working!
One thing in life is true!
Everybody's got a job to do!
Working!

A baker, a barber,
a chef who likes to cook.
A doctor, a lawyer,
an author writing books.
An actor, a waitress,
a scientist, a clerk.
So many occupations!
So many types of work!

Chorus

A teacher, a pilot
flying airplanes.
A farmer, a driver,
a conductor on a train.
An artist, a plumber,
an opera star who sings.
So many occupations!
Everybody does something!

Chorus

Working! Working!
Everybody's _ _ _ _ _ _ _ !
Working! Working!
Working for a living!
Working! Working!
One thing in _ _ _ _ is true!
Everybody's got a _ _ _ to do!
Working!

A baker, a _ _ _ _ _ _ ,
a _ _ _ _ who likes to cook.
A _ _ _ _ _ _ , a lawyer,
an _ _ _ _ _ _ writing books.
An actor, a _ _ _ _ _ _ _ _ ,
a scientist, a _ _ _ _ _ _ .
So many occupations!
So many types of _ _ _ _ !

Working! Working!
_ _ _ _ _ _ _ _ _ ' _ working!
Working! Working!
Working _ _ _ a living!
Working! Working!
One thing in _ _ _ _ is true!
Everybody's got a _ _ _ to do!
Working!

A teacher, a _ _ _ _ _
_ _ _ _ _ _ airplanes.
A farmer, a _ _ _ _ _ _ ,
a _ _ _ _ _ _ _ _ _ on a train.
An artist, a _ _ _ _ _ _ _ ,
an opera star who _ _ _ _ _ .
So many _ _ _ _ _ _ _ _ _ _ !
Everybody does something!

(Chorus)
It's a great big world, a great big world!
Oceans, continents . . . a great big world!
It's a great big world, a great big world!
So many places in this great big world!

You can drive from North America
all the way to South America.
Take a boat east to Africa.
Then go south to Antarctica.

You can sail the Atlantic.
You can take a trip to Europe.
Go to the Middle East and Asia.
Sail the Pacific to Australia.

Chorus (2x)

Tell me, "What's your native language?
And what country are you from?"
We live together in this great big world.
It's a home to everyone!

Chorus (2x)

It's a great big _ _ _ _ _, a great big _ _ _ _ _!
Oceans, _ _ _ _ _ _ _ _ _ _ . . . a great big world!
It's a great big world, a great big world!
So many _ _ _ _ _ _ in this great big world!

    You can drive from _ _ _ _ _ _ _ _ _ _ _ _
    all the way to _ _ _ _ _ _ _ _ _ _ _ _ .
    Take a boat east to _ _ _ _ _ _ .
    Then go _ _ _ _ _ to Antarctica.

    You can sail the _ _ _ _ _ _ _ _ .
    You can take a trip to _ _ _ _ _ _ .
    Go to the Middle East and _ _ _ _ .
    Sail the Pacific to _ _ _ _ _ _ _ _ .

It's a great _ _ _ world , a _ _ _ _ _ big world!
_ _ _ _ _ _ , continents . . . a great big world!
It's a great big world, a great big _ _ _ _ _!
So many _ _ _ _ _ _ in this great big world!

    Tell me, "What's your native _ _ _ _ _ _ _ _ ?
    And what _ _ _ _ _ _ _ are you from?"
    We live together in this great big _ _ _ _ _ .
    It's a _ _ _ _ to everyone!

(Chorus)
We're going to the beach!
We're going to the beach!
We're going to the beach!
Having fun in the sun in the summertime! (2x)

Grab your bathing suit, your surfboard, and beach chair!
Let's go where we can smell the ocean air!
Rub on suntan lotion right away
so we can stay and play at the beach all day!

Chorus (2x)

We'll buy hot dogs at the refreshment stand,
spread our blankets and picnic on the sand.
When it gets too hot, we'll go for a swim.
We'll have a race to see who'll be the first one in.

We're going to the beach!
We're going to the beach!
We're going to the beach!
Having fun in the sun in the summertime!

We're going to the beach!
We're going to the beach!
We're going to the beach!
Having fun in the sun in the summertime!
Having fun in the sun in the summertime!
Having fun in the sun in the summertime!

We're going to the _ _ _ _ _!
We're _ _ _ _ _ to the beach!
_ _ ' _ _ going to the beach!
Having fun in the _ _ _ in the summertime!

   Grab your _ _ _ _ _ _ _ _ _ _ _ _, your surfboard, and beach _ _ _ _ _!
   Let's go where we can smell the _ _ _ _ _ air!
   Rub on _ _ _ _ _ _ _ _ _ _ _ _ right away
   so we can stay and _ _ _ _ at the beach all day!

We're going _ _ the beach!
We're going to _ _ _ beach!
We're _ _ _ _ _ to the beach!
Having fun in the sun in the _ _ _ _ _ _ _ _ _!

   We'll buy hot dogs at the refreshment _ _ _ _ _,
   spread our _ _ _ _ _ _ _ _ and picnic on the _ _ _ _.
   When it gets too hot, we'll go for a _ _ _ _.
   We'll have a race to see who'll be the first one in.

We're going to the _ _ _ _ _!
_ _ ' _ _ going to the beach!
We're going to the beach!
Having _ _ _ in the _ _ _ in the summertime!

Word by word, word by word.
We bring the world a little closer together.
Word by word, word by word.
On our way we discover
how we're all sisters and brothers,
learning about each other
word by word.

When you look at the earth from up in space
you see the world's a much smaller place
and there aren't any far-off distant lands.
We're a world of languages under one sun.
Everybody's a neighbor to everyone,
sharing hopes and dreams all people understand.

Word by word, word by word.
We bring the world a little closer together.
Word by word, word by word.
On our way we discover
how we're all sisters and brothers,
learning about each other
word by word.

On our way we discover
how we're all sisters and brothers,
learning about each other
word by word.

Word by word, word by word.
We bring the _ _ _ _ _ a little closer together.
Word by word, word by word.
On our way we discover
how we're all _ _ _ _ _ _ _ and brothers,
learning about each other
word by word.

When you look at the _ _ _ _ _ from up in space
you see the world's a much smaller place
and there aren't any far-off distant _ _ _ _ _ _ .
We're a world of languages under one _ _ _ .
Everybody's a _ _ _ _ _ _ _ _ to everyone,
sharing hopes and dreams all _ _ _ _ _ _ understand.

Word by word, word by word.
We bring the world a little closer _ _ _ _ _ _ _ _ .
Word by word, word by word.
On our _ _ _ we discover
how we're all sisters and _ _ _ _ _ _ _ _ ,
_ _ _ _ _ _ _ _ about each other
word by word.

(Chorus)
I've come to make a better life.
This is my new home.
I'm so glad to be here.
I've come to make a better life.
And I hope one day
we can find a way
for everyone to live together.

I feel like a stranger here
in this new culture and new language.
Does anybody understand me?
Do they know the way I feel inside?
I miss my family and the friends I left behind.
I think about them all the time.

Chorus

I'm called an immigrant.
Some people think I don't belong here.
But many generations past
have shared the dream I have:
To live in freedom and with dignity
in this land of peace and liberty.

Chorus

I can't wait until the morning when
I take the oath to be a citizen.
Until that day there is so much to be done.
I guess my journey's just begun.

Chorus

I've come to make a better _ _ _ _ .
This is my new _ _ _ _ .
I'm so glad to be here.
I've come to make a _ _ _ _ _ _ life.
And I hope one _ _ _
we can find a way
for everyone to _ _ _ _ together.

I feel like a stranger here
in this new culture and new _ _ _ _ _ _ _ _ .
Does anybody _ _ _ _ _ _ _ _ _ me?
Do they know the way I _ _ _ _ inside?
I miss my _ _ _ _ _ _ and the friends I left behind.
I _ _ _ _ _ about them all the time.

I'm called an immigrant.
Some people think I _ _ _ ' _ belong here.
But many generations past
have shared the dream I have:
To live in _ _ _ _ _ _ _ and with dignity
in this land of peace and _ _ _ _ _ _ _ .

I can't wait until the morning when
I take the _ _ _ _ to be a _ _ _ _ _ _ _ .
Until that day there is so much to be done.
I guess my journey's just begun.

I've come to make a better _ _ _ _ .
This is my _ _ _ home.
I'm so glad to be here.
I've come to make a _ _ _ _ _ _ life.
And I _ _ _ _ one day
we can find a way
for everyone to live _ _ _ _ _ _ _ _ .